Faithful Witness

FAITHFUL WITNESS

*Foundations of Theology
for Today's Church*

Edited by Leo J. O'Donovan
and T. Howland Sanks

GEOFFREY
CHAPMAN

Geoffrey Chapman, an imprint of
Cassell Publishers Limited
Artillery House
Artillery Row
London
SW1P 1RT

First published in 1989

ISBN 0-225-66593 X

Printed and bound in the United States of America.

In honor of Avery Dulles, S.J.

Contents

Preface

The parents of this volume were gratitude and need. Our gratitude is to Avery Dulles, colleague, teacher, and friend, whom we have wanted to honor on the occasion of his seventieth birthday. Many of the contributors were his students, but all of us have been inspired and greatly influenced by him. Father Dulles began his teaching career just prior to the Second Vatican Council, at a time when theology was undergoing a laborious renewal. By his rigorous intellectual honesty, his fresh and critically inquiring approach, his consistently ecumenical respect for all viewpoints, and his wry and sometimes whimsical wit, he opened new worlds of intellectual possibility for us. These same qualities have characterized his multiple contributions to ecclesiology, foundational theology, and ecumenism. His acute awareness of the pluralistic and historically conditioned character of all theology has led him to develop theological typologies and to evaluate them critically. In thus forging and refining his own method of symbolic realism, he has contributed inestimably to the understanding that faith seeks.

In recognition of Father Dulles's great service, we decided not simply to contribute unrelated examples of work in progress but to offer instead a coherent set of essays in an area where he has himself been so active and where the need for constructive theology continues. In fact, many of our students have expressed the need for some treatment of basic questions that are presupposed or implied in their study of Scripture, Christian doctrine, or moral theology, as well as in their reading of church history and individual theologians. In Roman Catholic seminaries and graduate schools of theology before the Second Vatican Council, many of these questions—in particular, the possibility of a divine revelation, the risen Christ as its witness, and the church as its teacher—were discussed in an introductory tract most commonly known as "fundamental theology." The tract or discipline known by that name was conceived and developed in the largely ahistorical and extrinsecist categories of neoscholastic thought. It related to the rest of the theological curriculum in terms of the neoscholastic conception of theology and its method. And it could predictably be seen to be in need of serious reconsideration.

More recently, as the Christian churches and their theologians have paid increasing attention to the historical situation of their faith and to the cultural diversity in which it is proclaimed, we realize better how much the questions and concerns of fundamental theological reflection were shaped by the circum-

ix

stances of the church. When the various forms of positive theology first emerged in the sixteenth and seventeenth centuries, its authors reflected the influence of Renaissance humanism in their study of the sources of doctrine. Then in response to deist and rationalist critiques of revealed religion, theology in the eighteenth century sought to defend the truth of Christian revelation with the very type of historical and rational demonstrations employed by its opponents. In the course of the nineteenth century, whether in response to German idealism or through the neoscholastic revival of Thomism, treatises in fundamental theology were marked by the apologetical purpose of defending Christian revelation against its critics. They were equally concerned with providing a method of inquiry that could secure a solid foundation for the rest of theology itself. Early in this century some Catholic authors explored a method of immanence as a means of relating the truths of Christianity to the historical development of the human spirit. But neoscholasticism retained its hegemony, even while showing significant variations, for example, in the Roman and German schools. Meanwhile, mainstream Protestant neo-orthodoxy was resolutely rejecting the very conception of apologetics.

As Catholic authors in the years before Vatican II began to dialogue more seriously with modernity and as Protestant authors came to reconsider the grounding of their systematic theologies, a new and fruitful period opened in the history of this area of theological reflection. Concern about such grounding had previously been considered a peculiarly Roman Catholic concern, but during this period Lutheran and Reformed theologians argued that such issues were part of a venerable heritage in the churches of the Reformation. While some Protestant and Catholic writers still hold the very notion of apologetics in suspicion, many now recognize an operative distinction between the polemical marshalling of evidence to press for conversion, on the one hand, and a reasoned reflection on the credibility of the gospel as an offer of meaning and purpose for human life, on the other. Some authors continue to question the notion of fundamental theology as a separate theological discipline with distinctive principles and methods, but widespread agreement has emerged on the need to clarify certain themes and positions which any profession of faith and theological study of it imply. If it may also be argued that an overview of Christian doctrine and theology serves as the best introduction to a program of theological studies, even then foundational issues remain to be addressed, whether at the beginning or the end of the course of studies.

In contemporary discussions, Christian thinkers are being influenced by philosophical arguments against foundationalism, arguments that reject the view that human reason can establish permanant, irrefutable justification for its basic beliefs. The critique of foundationalism has reminded theologians not only of the historically and culturally conditioned character of all our knowledge but also of the ancient and radical, yet so easily forgotten truth that faith is ultimately a gift. If a community's most fundamental faith is given by grace rather than by reason, then even the most disciplined reflection on its roots, structure, and implications must resemble a way of discipleship as much as a free scientific inquiry.

Nevertheless, the faith of the Christian people is given and proclaimed not simply for their own sake but for the world's. It is a gift that cannot be accepted without being shared. It mirrors the open fecundity of the God who is its source. And fidelity to the reasonable, indeed far more than reasonable, character of the Giver requires fidelity to the reasonable character of the faith that is given. Theology must assume responsibility for making the truth claims of the Christian community understandable and available for all men and women of goodwill. With the same radicalness it is called to understand aright how God is seeking to set the world right.

Thus, every truth of Christianity—God's eternal life, the paschal mystery of Jesus, the church and life in the Spirit, Christian hope and commitment to justice—reimagines the world of human action and at the same time raises questions about the soundness and sense of the symbols it uses. As human knowledge has become self-critical in the modern period, it has learned a double vision, turning always to see what it really thinks and also whether its thought is justified. For theology, this means asking what the community believes and whether such belief is sustainable in today's world, what the call of discipleship entails and whether it is reasonable to follow that call.

Realizing how thoroughly historical Christian faith is, and how equally historical all reflection on it must be, some major Catholic theologians in recent years have proposed a closely interrelated treatment of questions dealing with content and those concerned with credibility. It does seem possible to present the scope of the church's faith in such a way that the method of the presentation and the warrants for it would be considered concomitantly. Still, given the importance of the issues to be considered, the range of opinions about them, and the variety of methods proposed to treat them adequately, other authors, albeit with varying nomenclature, have insisted on the need for a fundamental or foundational theology as a distinct moment in the theological enterprise. It may be studied as an introductory grounding for the various positions proposed in a full doctrinal theology or as a retrospective reflection on certain common themes implied there. It may address in an initial way the question of God and the identity of Christ; but today it will almost certainly consider, in one way or another, how a revelation of God is understood to occur, what the conditions and dynamics of faith are, how Scripture remains normative for the church and what other forms of authority there are, how Christianity understands itself in relation to the other great world religions as well as to movements of unbelief, and, finally, what methods it depends on. And most, if not all, of those who deal with such questions will also emphasize their social implications, whether for the First World in search of a just and meaningful use of its affluence or for the Third World in expectation of a liberation from idolatrous oppression.

Without pretending to resolve the range of methodological questions currently raised about theological foundations, the present volume addresses traditional topics and then some recently urgent ones as well. Monika Hellwig first offers a survey of concerns that were recognized as foundational at different times in the history of Christianity. Joseph Komonchak discusses the fundamental ecclesial and cultural tasks that every theology must assume if it is genuinely to offer a defense of the church's hope. Leo O'Donovan asks how the word of God can be said to communicate a true and saving future for humanity. Brian McDermott explores the process of faith in the God of Jesus Christ.

In chapter 5, linking the essays which precede and follow, Justin Kelly reflects on the symbolic structure of both God's revelation in Christ and the human response to it in faith. Peter Schineller's chapter analyzes the formation and characteristics of Scripture as the record of revelation. Next, T. Howland Sanks studies the origin of the community called church and the role of theology and authoritative norms in it. Examining the relations between systematic theology and the exegesis of Scripture, Pheme Perkins argues for a hermeneutic foundation for both exegesis and theology, shows the relevance of such an approach for theology and praxis, and draws lessons for ecumenism from the unity and pluralism of the biblical canon.

The four final essays address issues that are particularly acute for faith in the late twentieth century. In chapter 9 John Langan traces the development of historical thinking and modern historical consciousness and analyzes the challenges posed for theology by different types of historical consciousness. Thomas O'Meara's essay asks how we can recognize grace beyond the bounds of formal Christianity and yet still affirm the central role in religion and history that the Bible claims for Christ. After reviewing Vatican II's teaching on the relation between faith and ethics, David Hollenbach assesses the various contributions and shows their relevance to two specific moral issues, Christian participation in warfare and sexual equality; he himself argues for a hermeneutic of critical correlation among the various sources of moral understanding and wisdom. In the concluding chapter, Roger Haight discusses the importance of method in theology, analyzes some of the problems that underlie major areas of fundamental theology, and suggests several perennial tensions with which every theological method must deal.

Since each of these topics merits far more extensive treatment than any single chapter permits, recommendations for further reading have been made in each case. The recommended titles are briefly described, so that readers may chose among them according to interest and background, whether they are approaching the questions early in their theological studies or later, at a time of review and integration. In either case we hope the book may be useful in structuring a critical and constructive course on the scope and justification of theological thinking today. While no one view of theological foundations can or should be offered by a dozen different authors, all can welcome our readers to a journey of understanding that each of us has found as rewarding as it was required.

On that journey we are all fortunate to have the company of someone who has been not only a model theologian for us but also, in the expression of the Apocalypse, a "faithful witness." It is thus with great respect, deep gratitude, and lasting affection that we present this volume in honor of Avery Dulles.

Leo J. O'Donovan   T. Howland Sanks

O N E | Foundations for Theology: A Historical Sketch

Monika K. Hellwig

Fundamental theology is concerned with what exactly theologians are doing and why. Just as the believer's leap of faith, going beyond reason, must be based on reasonable grounds of credibility, so the theologian's discussion of the content of revelation must have a reasonable foundation. It is necessary to show some basis for claiming that there is such a reality as revelation, that there are criteria for discerning its event and its content, and that the methods used in a particular theology are valid ways of interpreting the content.

Fundamental or foundational theology as a formally organized academic discipline is a modern phenomenon, but in an informal sense it has existed as long as people have had to give an account of their religious faith and to justify their explanations. Often enough this has taken the form of a defense against unbelievers, outsiders, or adversaries. Yet careful perusal of such apologetics, or speeches for the defense, shows that there is always something more at stake. Those who hold the position must know that they are justified in holding it. In the long run this turns out to be the critical concern of all fundamental theology. We find an example of this in Acts 2:14–36 and 3:12–26. Here Peter's sermons to fellow Jews, justifying faith in Jesus as the revelation of God, are summarized for Christians of later generations to establish a foundation for the Christian interpretation of revelation from assumptions already accepted on the basis of their antiquity and endorsement by Israel. A similar example is found in Acts 17:22–31. There Paul's Areopagus speech to pagans is preserved for Christians, to show how the Christian claim to know the revelation of God may be justified in a pagan context.

The Traditional Issues of Fundamental Theology

The issues for Christian fundamental theology have not always been exactly the same. The starting point and foundations for theology depended in part on the historical period, the culture, the religious and philosophical context, and the questions that preoccupied people as a result of these circumstances. In each situation theologians have had to give preliminary reflection to what appeared

1

currently as most problematic or most controversial in the underlying assumptions on which their theological positions would be built.

In one context the principal foundational question might be the very possibility of knowing whether there is a God who creates purposefully. In another context it might be the possibility of divine revelation and human discernment of it. But there have also been contexts in which the pressing foundational question concerned the claim that Jesus of Nazareth embodied that revelation, or the claim of the church to be the authentic interpreter of the revelation he embodied. Some historical examples of this will be helpful as an indication of the contextual demands that shape the task of foundational theology.

Justin Martyr, living and writing in Rome about the middle of the second Christian century, proposed to teach the "Christian philosophy" and to defend it against arguments used in ridicule and persecution. Answering the particular arguments then brought against Christians, Justin shows that the Christian faith leads people to live good and law-abiding lives. This in itself, he maintains, constitutes grounds for the assumption that this faith is sound. He also argues that Christianity is based on the fulfillment of ancient Hebrew prophecies that shows that this apparently new faith is not some passing whim but has the authority of antiquity behind it—something much prized in that time and culture. Taking a third line of approach, Justin tries to ground the Christian claim of revelation philosophically by equating Jesus with the *logos* ("word" or "reason"), commonly understood as divinity immanent in the cosmos, a kind of universal soul active in the world.[1] In all of this Justin is grounding his Christian understanding of divine action in the world in assumptions, attitudes, and ideas that are seen as reasonable, perhaps even as self-evident, in the culture in which he lives.

Later in the same century the challenge of heterodox groups of Christians was more keenly felt than that of outsiders. Accordingly, the issues shifted a little and the arguments took a different focus. Irenaeus of Lyons gave his attention to grounding contemporary theology in the tradition openly handed down by the bishops as leaders of the churches. For him the foundational issue was not to demonstrate reasons for believing in the one God, nor to establish grounds for believing that the one God is revealed in Jesus Christ, but to determine the reliable channels through which the revelation of the one God in Jesus Christ might be correctly apprehended and interpreted.[2] This established a pattern that many Christian writers followed in subsequent centuries, locating the issues for fundamental theology mainly by referring to variant interpretations within the Christian tradition. Noteworthy exceptions to this include Origen of Alexandria. Living at a center of vigorous scholarly activity and exchange at the beginning of the third century, he was deeply involved in various foundational questions posed for Christian converts by the philosophical traditions stemming from pagan antiquity.[3]

The greatest fundamental theologian of Christian antiquity was Saint Augustine of Hippo, who wrote from North Africa in the early fifth century.

Among his many contributions is his anticipating (by well over a thousand years) a more introspective way of dealing with foundational questions concerning religious faith and its formulation in creedal propositions. For instance, in the famous autobiographical text known as the *Confessions*, Augustine describes and analyzes his own experience of coming to faith. He considers the grounds a human person can have for recognizing the call of the transcendent God and for making the response of faith within a particular religious tradition and community. In the *City of God* Augustine also shows how the interpretation of history is both a foundation for and a consequence of a particular religious and theological stance.

A great cultural hiatus occurred in the churches of the Latin-speaking West from the sixth century onward as their center of gravity moved northward into the barbarian regions. Forced mass conversions of whole populations were not uncommon, instruction was minimal, and conditions were rough, difficult, and often violent. The scholarship that continued in the monasteries concentrated of necessity on the conservation of the tradition. By the end of the eleventh century, however, we meet another Christian thinker who struggled with foundational questions in arguments that must still be taken into account today. Anselm of Bec and Canterbury enjoyed the luxury of dealing with such questions from a starting point within the faith, not in response to attacks from without. An Italian nobleman by birth, first monk and then abbot of the monastery of Bec in France, and later Archbishop of Canterbury, he lived in the atmosphere of Christendom, surrounded by the acceptance and practice of the faith on all sides. Yet he returned to the most basic question of all, namely, how we can really know that there is a God.

Although Anselm employed a literary device in which he projected "a fool" who denied the existence of God, and used this "fool" as a counterfoil for the arguments proposed in favor of God, Anselm's starting point is that of a believer. His whole argument is grounded in the process of thinking and the logic of definition.[4] He is satisfied when he shows that belief in God yields a completely coherent understanding of reality. Indeed, Anselm coined that excellent definition of theology: *fides quaerens intellectum*, faith in search of understanding. Moreover, the existence of God was not the only foundational question for Anselm. He was also concerned with establishing the very possibility of a theology that recognizes a triune God, and even with showing the reasonableness of such a notion of God. Similarly, he set out to show that a theology of redemption through the suffering and death of Jesus, the incarnate God, was not absurd on a priori grounds, but on the contrary rationally wholly coherent.[5] Clearly these are issues that might well be foundational for earnest believers of Anselm's time and milieu.

In the thirteenth century, however, Thomas Aquinas met a rather different kind of challenge to the foundations on which Christian theology rests. Aristotle, known in the earlier Middle Ages mainly for his logic, was far more widely translated and read by the beginning of the thirteenth century, largely due to the labors of Arab scholars who had treasured his works and who reintroduced them to the schools of Christian Europe. This gave rise to a twofold challenge. On the one hand, "extreme Aristotelians" such as Siger of Brabant thought that philosophy explained everything, providing an ultimate knowledge and wisdom that rendered theology unnecessary. On the other hand, many theologians of the time, who came to be known as the Augustinians (not to be confused with the religious order of that name) clung to Platonic philosophy as the traditional and normative medium for Christian theological reflection.

Thomas Aquinas therefore met two important foundational issues that were characteristic for his time. The first of these was the task of showing that theology, drawing on revelation, was an authentic intellectual discipline yielding true understanding. Thomas therefore began his magnificent Summa of theology with a careful exposition of the nature of the theological project, then still known as "sacred doctrine," to show the validity of theological argument.[6] Faced with the challenge of the extreme Aristotelians, he knew he had to show that there were characteristic data and methods that were appropriate to theology and which constituted it a separate discipline and a valid pursuit of understanding. Meanwhile, Thomas met the other challenge, which questioned the appropriateness of Aristotelian philosophy as a medium for theological reflection. His most effective answer to that challenge was demonstrating how theology based on Aristotelian categories and methods was done.

In the centuries that followed, new challenges threatening to undermine the project of theology came from the movement of thought known as nominalism and the consequent questions about the church as mediating the truth of revelation. William of Ockham and other nominalists of the fourteenth century suggested that the theology of the time had made entities out of abstractions and dealt with ideas as though they were independently existing realities. This gave rise to very urgent foundational issues that have preoccupied theologians in various forms since that time. But immediately they had implications of a practical kind for the way people thought about the church, especially as an authoritative channel of the truth of revelation. On the more theoretical side some of the problems had been anticipated by Duns Scotus at the very beginning of the century. He and his followers responded to the foundational questions by attempting to validate theology by defining the limits of human knowledge and human reason concerning the power and freedom of God that was far more modest than the estimate of the human faculties that had been operative in the two preceding centuries.

In any case, both the theoretical and the practical ecclesiological challenges that had been raised had consequences reaching into the Protestant Reformation of the sixteenth century and beyond. Through the writing of Marsilius of Padua, a contemporary of Scotus and Ockham, and through the later preaching and writing of John Wycliffe and Jan Hus, the foundational discussions moved to searching questions about the relationship between truth and authority, particularly the relationship between the magisterial claims of the church hierarchy and the truth of God's self-revelation in Jesus Christ as contained in Scripture. Thus the sixteenth century called for a new approach to establishing the foundations for Christian theology. This was true both for the Reformers and for those who remained with Rome. At this stage of Western history it was not a question of justifying the theological project of Christians against unbelievers, as it once had been and would be again. Nor was it then a question of defending the validity of theology against the claims of philosophy to be all-sufficient, as it had been in the thirteenth century and would be again in modern times. Nor yet was it primarily a question of providing arguments against the doubts that might come to earnest believers—a task that remains for all times and contexts. The primary concern of this phase of Western Christian theology was to justify a particular way of appealing to revelation to establish the data with which a theological construction would be concerned. Thus the Reformers based their construction of a Christian theology on the unique inspiration and revelatory character of the text of Scripture, while those on the Catholic side tended to ground their theology in an ecclesiology that demonstrated the continuity of the tradition and its consequent trustworthiness.

It was not surprising that Catholic theologians should develop their fundamental theology along those lines. Their theology used as its data church teachings developed in the course of the centuries for which there was often no explicit warrant in Scripture. Moreover, these church teachings and the theologies that elaborated and explained them were often points of dispute between Catholics and Protestants. The Reformers and their later followers, keenly aware of corruption in the history of the church and pledged therefore to turn to Scripture alone as the ultimate criterion, questioned the use of past hierarchic teachings just as they refused to accept the authority of contemporary hierarchic, conciliar, and papal pronouncements. Hence the most fundamental questions for sixteenth-century theologians were questions about the proper foundations in Christian history for constructing a Christian theology. From the Catholic point of view that put questions about the church at the center of the effort to justify the claims of a normative tradition. From the Protestant point of view it put the Bible and its relation to revelation and to faith at the foundation. As is well known, this debate became bitterly polemic, and that fact may have obscured foundational questions that were in themselves more important and logically prior, such as those which came to the fore again with the Enlightenment.

The Modern Period

English-speaking scholars have called the latter half of the seventeenth century and most of the eighteenth the Age of Reason. German and French scholars have referred to the eighteenth century as the Enlightenment. They all seem to have had more or less the same developments in mind when they used this terminology. The basic characteristic of this cultural and intellectual movement was an appeal to reason as the ultimate authority in all human affairs and a consequent rejection of the authority of tradition and of official status. Concomitant with this was a great interest in natural sciences and in empirical method as a way of finding the truth about anything. Typically, thoughtful people of the Age of Reason tended to think that there must be a God who was a first cause and who kept things operating like clockwork. But they also tended to reject any sort of claims of privileged knowledge about God through a particular revelation beyond the ordinary knowledge that we have of the universe, including ourselves.

This called for a new approach to justifying a Christian theology, and it affected Catholics, Anglicans, and Protestants alike. The challenge was a difficult one: to ground a claim for revelation, and the theology that would be built on that asserted revelation, in a way that would prove adequate in terms of Enlightenment categories of demonstration. Only two kinds of argument were really acceptable: a demonstration of the logical necessity of a proposition or a demonstration of its empirical verifiability. Demonstrations of logical necessity are those that are operative, for instance, in mathematical formulae. They work independently of any specific events under observation. One knows them to be correct simply by thinking. Some have offered proofs of the existence of God by a demonstration of logical necessity, starting out only from the assumption that anything at all exists. A demonstration of empirical verifiability, however, depends directly on the happening of particular events in succession or concurrence, more frequently on the possibility of repeating the same pattern every time the same conditions obtain.

By definition a claim to particular revelation cannot be directly justified by either of these two methods. It cannot be a matter of logical necessity, for then there would be no need for revelation; the matter would be adequately covered by reason. And it cannot be a matter for empirical verification, because, likewise, there would be no need for revelation; the matter would be adequately covered by science and common sense. The foundational theology of the time therefore used an ingenious combination of these methods through an indirect approach. The arguments focused on the resurrection and the miracles of Jesus. The goal was to show first that the events reported in the gospels were well enough attested to qualify as already empirically verified, and then that their occurrence was so far beyond the course of nature that they constituted incontrovertible evidence of an extraordinary intervention by the transcendent God. This, in turn, was offered as an undeniable guarantee of the claims made by Jesus and for Jesus by his followers.

There are fatal weaknesses in this type of argument. In particular, it begs the questions that it claims to have answered. A number of eighteenth-century writers in Britain, including the Scottish philosopher David Hume, exposed this circularity in the argument. A little later in the eighteenth century the German philosopher Immanuel Kant offered such an incisive critique that Christian theologians even in our own day have to take his arguments into account in establishing theological foundations. He himself was willing to allow a kind of rational faith based on the analysis of experience—in particular, the experience of moral conscience in human persons.[7] By contrast, the German Pietist Protestant writer, Friedrich Schleiermacher, writing at the beginning of the nineteenth century, wanted to show that the foundations for theology are neither in the rational nor in the moral realm, but in the experience of piety that is rooted in human affectivity.[8] This was not an entirely new idea, but corresponded to the reflection and understanding of the devout throughout the ages. It is, for instance, a basic principle in the *Spiritual Exercises* of Saint Ignatius of Loyola, in which an intensifying and focusing of affectivity is used as the foundation for shaping convictions and understanding. What is interesting in Schleiermacher's nineteenth-century writings, however, is his formal use of the phenomenon of piety to ground theological discussion.

Contemporary with Schleiermacher was the liberal German Protestant theologian and philosopher, Georg W. F. Hegel. Hegel developed a foundational theology that might in retrospect be considered more an attack on theology than a defense of it. He proposed his great evolutionary description of all reality as a comprehensive, universally valid philosophical explanation into which all the particular religious traditions could be fitted as partial and provisional. What theologies had been able to grasp only in inadequate representational forms, he claimed, philosophy (his particular philosophy) could grasp comprehensively in its rational necessity.[9] This proposal really eliminates the possibility of a particular revelation and a language of mysteries that can be glimpsed but never fully grasped. Therefore it also undermines Christian theology. Yet this perspective has been very influential in subsequent Protestant writing and more recently in Catholic thought also.

The advent of modern atheism, however, changed the focus once again. It now became necessary to ground any theology by showing adequate reasons for the assumption that there is a God. Actually, taking into account contemporary consciousness, the foundational task might be expressed in an even more exigent way. We need to show that what we can infer about the ultimate horizons of reality justifies the kind of assumptions common to "God-talk." To make a good case one must show, for instance, that it is reasonable to infer that the universe has a unified purpose, that human beings are important in that purpose, that morality is ultimately meaningful, that human freedom is not a bad joke, that human community is possible, and so forth. Not all of this is new. It has always been necessary for theology to show reasonable grounds for asserting a benign, all-powerful God. Anselm and Thomas made it part of their foundation. But in the modern age this has arisen not from the need to be thorough and coherent in order to understand a generally accepted faith, but from the need to counter direct attack from real atheists.

During this modern phase, Catholic theologians have, of course, not been silent, though they were prevented until very recently from free exchange with Protestant and antireligious scholars. The typical Catholic approach to fundamental theology prior to the Second Vatican Council was to treat it as a systematic defense of the Catholic faith based upon reason and revelation.[10] Thus it would probably begin with a defense of religion in general and move to a defense of the notion of revelation, followed by an identification of particular revelation as the Christian one. This would lead to a justification of both Scripture and tradition as trustworthy witnesses of that revelation. Then the claims attributed to Jesus Christ would be validated by his miracles, prophecies, and resurrection. Finally there would be much evidence adduced to show that the Catholic Church as it exists now is in authentic continuity with the apostolic community commissioned by Christ himself. A detailed defense of papal teaching authority, hierarchy, and priesthood would perhaps be offered as well. This approach doggedly addresses all levels of the argument accumulated through the centuries, though not perhaps with any great awareness of the philosophical nuances that that argument had acquired since the Enlightenment.

The Changing Focus of the Questions

It will be obvious from the foregoing that the foundations that need to be established for a Christian theology depend very much on the context in which that theology is being constructed. The selection of foundational issues depends on the assumptions, starting points, and ways of argumentation that seem reasonable and satisfactory in each historical and cultural context. In modern Catholicism this led to controversial but very important developments. Theologians of the Tübingen school in the nineteenth century[11] discovered the unavoidable hermeneutic circularity of claims to found theology upon a particular revelation. While the theology is based upon the revelation, the revelation is only recognized and interpreted as such by the very theology for which it is supposed to be the foundation. An equally important development that influenced Catholic theology was the many-faceted self-critique of human knowledge. This surfaced particularly among the thinkers loosely gathered under the designation of "Modernists."[12] Thus Alfred Loisy, for instance, writing about the turn of this century, showed that theology is always necessarily grounded in human language and understanding that grows and changes in the course of historical and cultural developments. This means that the whole Christian project and its theology cannot be defended on the grounds of their immutability. Maurice Blondel and George Tyrrell emphasized the role of experience in revelation and the inadequacy of propositional formulae to express revelation directly or completely. The earlier writers, as often happens, may have overstated or oversimplified their discoveries. However, they have continued to be influential in spite of official condemnations of their writings. They gave rise to a number of new beginnings from old resources, and these new beginnings continue in our own time to refocus the whole matter of a foundational theology.

The question of the "hermeneutic circle," as raised by the Tübingen theologians, is one that we cannot escape nowadays. We interpret our source texts and founding events according to our own contemporary expectations and understanding; therefore, we necessarily read our expectations into the text to some extent, although the text should also correct what we bring to it. A common example today is that Christians frequently approach biblical texts about salvation with the prior understanding that these texts are concerned with something that happens only after death, and this causes a misreading of the texts themselves. Awareness of the hermeneutic circle makes theologians sensitive to such risks and helps them to become explicitly aware of distortions and to correct them. But the hermeneutic circle also operates in a wider sense. We base our theology on a claim of revelation, but it is because of our theology that we recognize it as revelation. Thus, from the perspective of Christian theology, the death of Jesus is revelatory of God's love. From the perspective of Jewish understanding the death of Jesus is not recognizable as such a revelatory moment. Revelation does not exist as revelation in such a way that it compels recognition by all in the way an experiment in the natural sciences can. This realization undermines the apologetics of the Age of Reason completely. It demands a new kind of foundation for theology—a foundation acceptable to reason and experience in our times.

The self-critique of human knowledge had been pervasive in secular scholarship since Kant. It penetrated theology more slowly because there was great resistance to any movement that seemed to threaten the certainty of the faith and its theological explanations. But thoughtful believers could not continue indefinitely fending off questions about the conditions for knowing anything at all, and the conditions for knowing any religious truth in particular. These questions persistently arose in the second half of the nineteenth century, even in Catholic circles where doctrinal censorship was much more effective. At the same time there was a burst of new scholarly investigation which showed that the documents of the New Testament (as well as many authoritative texts of the church) were less obvious in their meaning and authorship than they had seemed. A deepening historical consciousness demanded critical dating, recognition of complex redaction histories, and interpretation of texts and events in their own cultural and historical setting.

These are only some of the challenges to which twentieth-century fundamental theology must respond. Theologians have approached these challenges in various ways. Karl Rahner, for instance, grounded Christian theology in reflective human self-awareness brought into confrontation with the claims of revelation as these are found in Scripture and tradition.[13] Paul Tillich did something similar, also using contemporary existentialist thought as Rahner did.[14] Both Rahner and Tillich made their fundamental theology more or less coterminous with their systematics because they proceeded in this way with every question they raised—a procedure which Tillich called the method of correlation. Bernard Lonergan, meanwhile, showed that in the new context of our times a foundational theology is not the beginning, but follows on research, interpretation, history, and dialectic by distinguishing horizons of understanding within which particular religious doctrines can be meaningfully discussed.[15]

In such a context Rahner also proposed an answer to the modern atheism of Ludwig Feuerbach and Karl Marx. These authors had contended that while we speak of God creating human beings, the reverse is true: God is a projection of the human mind, made in the likeness of the human person but bigger, more powerful, invulnerable, and so forth. To this Rahner replied that our theology is indeed anthropology; what we attribute to God is certainly dependent upon our experience of the human. But this does not invalidate theology. On the contrary, the most reasonable way of trying to understand something about the source and ground of our being and of all being is to look at the creation that arises from this source. But what makes Christian theology specific is that it shapes its anthropology by looking at the person of Jesus. It is from his representation of the fully human that Christian theology forms an understanding of the ultimate source of the human, namely, God.

Even as this kind of reflection was going on, political forces and events in the latter half of the twentieth century were already posing a different set of questions as foundational to Christian theology. In the post–World War II intellectual world, Marxist and other voices were asking whether Christianity had any serious hope to offer for this world and for people's lives in history. Given the very real sufferings of whole populations in the postwar world, it was difficult for anyone to take seriously a theological discussion of redemption/ salvation that did not deal with any of the issues that could critically affect people's lives. In response to this a new kind of fundamental theology emerged from the German "theologians of hope," notably Jürgen Moltmann and Wolfhart Pannenberg.[16] For them the foundational issues concerned the relevance of the Christian message of hope to any of the serious human tasks in the public arena of the twentieth century. This understanding of the foundational task was taken up in an even more directly and concretely political sense by J. B. Metz in his call for a "political theology."[17] Metz insisted that the questions for fundamental theology in our times were not in the first place questions about the relevance and specific meaning of ancient texts for the contemporary world, but questions about whether faith and theology make any difference in real decisions about the shaping of our world.

This line of questioning has been taken further in various movements and developments loosely gathered under the term "liberation theologies."[18] These theologies begin with the acknowledgment that all theory comes from the reflection on praxis and that theology (and church doctrine) are no exceptions. Praxis is action in the world that effects some result or change. The preoccupation of liberation theologies is to uncover the particular experience and praxis out of which any theological position has emerged so that the cultural and social bias of that doctrine or theory will become evident. The intent is to strip particular formulations of any pretense to transcend their special bias and be universal in their outlook. Positively, the liberation theologies want to make explicit the particular experience and praxis out of which they themselves are drawn—which is in every case an experience of suffering, exclusion, humiliation, or deprivation. They see as foundational the issue of the gospel as good news to the poor. They ground and weigh every claim of a Christian theology to be taken seriously and to be in fact Christian in its commitment to this imperative.

The Questions for Our Times

The changing focus of the fundamental questions asked by thoughtful persons about life and meaning calls for a changing focus in the shaping of a fundamental or foundational theology. Through the ages what people have considered reasonable grounds for taking a discussion seriously has depended on their cultural, social, and political context. It has depended on their language and technology, their social structure, and on the particular philosophies and scientific assumptions that influenced their society. In response to the expectations prompted by all these factors, the scope and focus of fundamental theology has changed. It has ranged from concerns related to the natural sciences, through those related to human introspection, to those related to the great societal questions that arise in human history.

Looking at the development from another angle, the scope of fundamental theology has ranged from a concern to resolve the problem of evil by explanation to a concern to resolve the problem of evil by critical analysis leading to transformation of society. From a third angle one might say that the scope of fundamental theology has ranged from an effort to construct ways of knowing God by more rigorous rules of rational thought, through an effort to establish proper conditions for accepting textual authorities and interpreting them, to a quest for ways of knowing God through faithful reflection on human experience in which the work and invitation of God are seen. Finally, this last endeavor has ranged from observing the microcosm of human experience in the inner life and consciousness of the individual, through various ways of taking the interpersonal seriously, to observing the macrocosm of human experience in the large structures and systems of human society.

If we ask what are the questions for our own times, or what falls within the scope of fundamental theology for our times, we find that the plurality and rapid transformation of our world are inescapable. The questions of all past generations are still with us in some form, but the answers will never have the same appearance of absolute certainty or unshakable permanence. We must still be prepared for the doubts of the thoughtful and committed believer; we cannot offer freedom from search and risk. It is still necessary to establish the rationality of our endeavor, to show that theology really is a way of arriving at a better understanding of ultimate reality in its call upon us here and now. But we now recognize the tentative, figurative, broadly analogous character of anything that we can say. Certainly we must still show the grounds on which we base the conviction that there is a God such as we describe, but we have to acknowledge that we are not building a case of logical necessity. We must still show grounds for taking claims of revelation seriously, especially the claim that Jesus Christ is the definitive self-revelation of the divine. But these can no longer be based on miracles as an empirically verifiable proof of the truth of such claims.

Along with these traditional tasks we face the all-pervasive contemporary challenge to show that our claims of redemption are relevant to all those sufferings, oppressions, deprivations, and fears from which the peoples of the earth know they really need to be set free. This last demand is interrelated with that other subtle and difficult task: to establish clearly and self-critically out of whose experience, and out of which concrete circumstances, a particular theological position or presentation can emerge. This calls for a new kind of awareness of the unnoticed privileges of the classes of society to which theologians and church representatives more usually belong, of the linguistic and cultural biases we normally fail to recognize, and of motivations of self-interest that often lie hidden behind apparently disinterested arguments.

Increasingly today there is yet one more dimension: we must clarify where we stand in relation to other religious traditions and other claims to offer human salvation. In a society where exclusive truth claims have less and less credibility, any theology that is to be taken seriously must first come to terms with the competing truth claims and ask how they are to be met. This is no longer merely an intra-Christian discussion as it was for centuries, but now takes in all the great religions of East and West, as well as the varieties of Marxism and many types of secular humanism. We may respond to this need by acknowledging a certain complementarity in approaches to the transcendent or by debating or making a friendly wager between competing claims.[19] But in some way the question must be considered and resolved as a foundation for further exposition of a particular theology.

The complex task of fundamental or foundational theology in its many dimensions is spelled out in this book in its subject matter and in the methods by which that subject matter is approached and developed. However, that should not obscure the need for everyone working in theology to be critically and constructively engaged in foundational questions.

Recommended Readings

Haught, John F. *What Is God? How To Think about the Divine.* New York: Paulist, 1986.
   This book pursues characteristically contemporary questions and gives them a philosophical grounding.
Metz, Johann Baptist. *Faith in History and Society: Toward a Practical Fundamental Theology.* New York: Crossroad, 1980. An important statement of a "political theology" which seeks to overcome privatizing tendencies in theology and to emphasize the social and historical mediations of Christian faith.

O'Collins, Gerald. *Fundamental Theology.* New York: Paulist, 1982. A basic textbook on the subject, by a well-known professor at the Gregorian University in Rome.

Schüssler Fiorenza, Francis. *Foundational Theology: Jesus and the Church.* New York: Crossroad, 1984. This recent study presents constructive reflections on the resurrection of Jesus, the foundation of the church, the mission of the church, and the historical development of fundamental theology as a distinct discipline.

Sokolowski, Robert. *The God of Faith and Reason.* Notre Dame: University of Notre Dame Press, 1982. A philosopher offers philosophical foundations for a contemporary theology.

T W O | Defending Our Hope: On the Fundamental Tasks of Theology

Joseph A. Komonchak

Always be ready to make a defense to anyone who asks for a reason for the hope that is in you, and make it with modesty and respect. (1 Pet 3:15–16)

Since the Middle Ages, this biblical text has been considered to state the fundamental charge given to the theologian. Although in recent centuries it was often assigned to a particular theological specialization called "fundamental theology," a little reflection shows that it actually represents a basic requirement of all theological activity.

First, note that we are told to provide a reason for our *hope*. During the Middle Ages, a textual mistake sometimes added or even substituted the word "faith" in this text, so that theology was classically conceived as *faith* rather than *hope* seeking understanding. But giving reasons for hope differs from giving reasons for faith. Hope is the existential direction of one's whole self toward an expected or promised future. It has, thus, a practical orientation more immediate than the orientation toward meaning and truth usually associated with faith. "What may we hope?" is a different question from "What can we know?"

Second, in its context, the charge has a quite specific practical reference. The author is addressing a Christian community already threatened with persecution. Between two exhortations—that they do nothing to deserve punishment and that they learn even to rejoice in suffering for doing what is good—he counsels them against fear and toward trust in Christ. To supply reason for hope, then, is to defend a life that willingly endures unearned persecution. It is their hope that has set these Christians apart from others and prompted the request for an explanation of their extraordinary lives.

Third, the account is to be a response to others who seek a reason for the hope and who are to be addressed "with modesty and respect." The exhortation thus presupposes the right of the others to ask for a reason and the possibility for Christians to find some common *logos* that can serve as an *apologia*.

14

But, fourth, the author also implicitly legitimates the request that Christians themselves may make for rational explanation. Through the example of Christ's patience he himself provides a justification for the hope and endurance he expects of them. Their hope, in other words, is because of and for the sake of Christ. As much as the hope is a subjective reality "in them," its ground is found "outside of them," objectively, in Christ the Lord. In that respect, the Christians themselves stand in a certain sense also as "others" vis-à-vis the basic Christian message that comes to them from without: it is not only *fides* (faith) but also *spes ex auditu* (hope [which comes] from hearing).

Certain fundamental features of theology thus appear in this passage: (1) it is an articulation of the ground of one's hope; (2) it arises as a response to questions about the way Christians live their lives; (3) the norm for that hope and practice is Jesus Christ; and (4) reasons may be given for that hopeful practice, whether those addressed are fellow Christians or others. This essay will attempt to explore the implications of this description of the task of theology particularly by discussing the contexts or audiences to which it attempts to give reasons for Christian hope, by exploring the particular challenges this task faces in the modern world, and by outlining the major features of a theology adequate to the task.

The Ecclesial and Cultural Tasks

Taking the text of First Peter as a fundamental challenge, theology may be conceived as the mediation of the Christian gospel within a cultural context.[1] Addressing two not entirely distinct audiences, those who have already accepted the gospel and those who have not, theology faces two tasks, one primarily ecclesial and the other primarily cultural. How these tasks are conceived and interrelated is a basic question for the conception of theology.

For most of the Catholic tradition, both dimensions or roles of theology have been visible. Early Christian "apologies" were defenses against accusations of capital crimes, and their catechesis stressed both in practice and in theory the countercultural implications of discipleship. But even then, Christians were able to find in the surrounding culture germinal intelligibilities *(logoi spermatikoi)* with which both to make their belief in the *Logos* made flesh culturally accessible and also to permit them to begin the long task of an expression of their own faith outside the cultural matrix of Judaism. The success of that effort by the great figures of the patristic period resulted in a theological, liturgical, spiritual, and juridical synthesis, which, bequeathed to the Middle Ages, was received as the taken-for-granted vision of a Christianized culture.

So powerful was this integration of the cultural and the ecclesial roles that more than a few churchmen and theologians interpreted the challenges represented by the introduction of Aristotelian philosophy and Arabic science in the twelfth and thirteenth century and by contemporary economic and social developments as an omen of the last days. Even then the church responded by establishing universities as instruments of the required cultural engagement, and there emerged a few heroic figures, most notably Saint Thomas Aquinas, who not only took up the challenge of writing new works *contra gentiles* (against the pagans) but even borrowed from the new languages and methods to construct the great new *summae theologicae* (theological syntheses). As short-lived as the Thomist achievement was, it remains an ideal instance of a cultural challenge to traditional Christianity that was met head-on, without fear, and with modesty and respect.

Unfortunately, the same thing cannot be said about the succeeding ages when the challenges became far more radical and fractured over centuries the social and cultural unity of Christendom. In the face of the complex developments that occurred during the Renaissance and Reformation, the scientific revolution, the Enlightenment, the economic and social revolutions of the eighteenth and nineteenth centuries, and the rise of historical consciousness, the church desperately needed imitators of Aquinas, people with his ability, confidence, modesty, and respect. But it seldom found them. Instead, particularly after the French Revolution, most of these developments were interpreted as a demonically inspired apostasy from the former ideal, and this apocalyptic diagnosis substituted for critical analysis of the forces that had caused the cultural transformation. The church mourned the loss of its cultural hegemony and its political and social supports, and it opposed the liberal reduction of religion to the realm of the private. But instead of launching a confident evangelizing effort, it created a distinct Catholic subsociety, inspired by a distinctly antimodern subculture.

Within this closed world, theology now had a different role. Moving largely from the university to the seminary, it was conceived primarily as a discipline for the training of the leaders of the subsociety. Its cultural engagement was often little more than the refutation of "adversaries" (the term under which most of the molders of the new culture were lumped) and a defense of the formal authority of the revealing God and mediating church. This refutation and a rational demonstration of the claims of authority were assigned to a separate discipline called "apologetics" or "fundamental theology."[2] On that basis, theology proper could begin its task of explaining, within and for the church, what authority requires one to believe. An occasional "corollary" was devoted to the inner intelligibility of the Christian message. Never before had the task of explaining to Christians the reasons for their hope been so separated from the task of defending it before others.

The cultural alienation of this theology was nearly complete. Even after the church itself, at least from the time of Leo XIII, began to launch a counteroffensive to "restore all things in Christ" (to use Pius X's motto), most theologians remained remarkably deaf to the appeal. How intramural their horizons were can be demonstrated by the absence from their works of any indications, apart from the regular addition of new adversaries, that they had been written during a period of extraordinary economic, social, political, and cultural change.[3] Theologians appeared to be asking their questions principally because they had once been asked before, and they approached them with a method and in a language familiar only to them. Theologians ceased to take seriously questions that were raised by those outside the church. It was as if, with the rise of modernity, Christians were for the first time unable to approach "with modesty and respect" those who ask them for a reason for the hope that is in them. Few theologians even bothered to look for *logoi spermatikoi*, and those who claimed to find some were more often than not rebuked for their claims and told that they were engaged in a fruitless and dangerous quest.[4]

Encountering Modernity

The Second Vatican Council was the great moment in which these modern attitudes and strategies were seriously challenged. Pope John XXIII in his opening address declared his disagreement with "prophets of doom" who see nothing in the modern era but prevarication and ruin. He expressed his confidence that humanity stood on the verge of a new and providential order of human affairs. This appeal for hope instead of fear displayed a rediscovered modesty and respect for the modern age which struck at the heart of modern Roman Catholicism's basic self-image.

The achievements of the council in undercutting the typical attitudes and strategies of modern Roman Catholicism were prepared principally by a group of scholars, such as Yves Congar, M.-D. Chenu, and Henri de Lubac, who had worked in earlier decades largely at the fringes of the Catholic cultural world. They were at the fringes because the suspicions of ecclesiastical authority kept them there and because there they encountered "the others" who might ask a reason for their hope. Through a host of remarkable historical studies, they restored to Catholic consciousness the memory of the two great efforts to face major cultural challenges, the patristic and the Thomist, both of which differed so remarkably from the modern retreat into what Newman called a new Novatianism.[5] Implying that what had been accomplished then could be attempted again, these scholars helped to legitimate the council's challenges to the strategy dominant for the previous one hundred and fifty years.

The theology that underlay the council's achievement represented a new reading of the cultural context. It ceased to interpret it in exclusively religious terms as a diabolically inspired apostasy. Instead it sought to analyze modern culture critically in the economic, social, and political developments from which it had arisen. This permitted the council to differentiate among the principles of those developments, accepting some, purifying others, rejecting still others. More importantly, it committed the church to participate not only in the "joy and hope, grief and anxiety" of contemporaries (*Gaudium et Spes* 1) but to join them in common responsibility for what humanity would do and become in the future. This represented the council's own acceptance of Pope John's opening challenge to turn from a retrospective and even nostalgic fascination with the past toward a hopeful effort to construct the future. Many people began to speak, without regret, of the "end of the Constantinian era" and of the "passing of the age of Christendom."

Elements of Modernity

The decision to engage modern culture in a critically differentiated manner has required theologians to address sets of intellectual and social developments from which the officially encouraged theology had largely segregated itself for centuries. Three areas particularly have attracted their attention: the epistemological, the historical, and the political.

The epistemological challenge arose from a modern philosophical development initiated by René Descartes but given particularly sharp focus by Immanuel Kant. It is the demand that all knowledge claims be justified critically through an analysis of the structure and dynamics of human consciousness. This "turn to the subject" meant philosophy's passage from metaphysics to epistemology as the grounding discipline, from being to subjectivity as the primary focus, and from nature to history as the primary object. Attempts by Catholic thinkers in the nineteenth and early twentieth centuries to take up this challenge had almost all been condemned by the church. Vatican II represented the recognition, however, that this critical encounter should not be postponed any longer.

The second challenge was posed by another distinctive feature of modernity—historical consciousness. The term is often used vaguely, but here it will be taken to comprise three elements. The first is the awareness of the variability of human cultures across generations and within any single generation. Classical anthropology had focused on what was considered essential, universal, and necessary about the human condition. The differences in its various realizations were regarded as at best accidental modifications of a substantially identical human nature and therefore not the object of a possible science.

The modern human sciences, in contrast, focus precisely on the varieties of the human, and they are very alert to any tendency to regard a particular realization of the human as the norm by which all others are to be judged and evaluated. For theology this poses a twofold challenge. On the one hand, theologians must include within their horizon the undoubted gains this more empirical perspective permits. On the other hand, as a result of this modern focus, they face quite new questions in meeting the age-old challenge of articulating the universal claims of so particular a message as the gospel.

Second, historical consciousness is also an awareness of the need for the critical study of history in order to gain a knowledge of the past constructions of the human spirit. Critical history thus emerges as a competitive mediation of the past, alongside the existential histories mediated by a community's traditions and for some, even replacing those accounts. In theology, of course, this development has raised the acute problem of the relationship between the sacred history provided in the Scriptures and tradition, on the one hand, and, on the other, the new history reconstructed in a host of critical studies.

Finally, historical consciousness also means a sense of responsibility for the history that is being constructed by individuals and groups today. It follows from a sense of the human spirit as embodied, spatially and temporally located, evolving, and directed by free human decisions. Historicity, then, means both that human beings have no choice about the conditions within which they begin the exercise of their effective freedom and that they are, singly and collectively, the constructors of the human future. To deal critically with this element of modern consciousness, theology would have to conceive human freedom with more subtlety and with more distinctions than were common when the natural and social worlds were considered to be the fixed or even fated environment in which people were required to live.

The tremendous social and political changes brought about in the last two centuries represent a third area in which modernity challenged classical Catholic theology. The physical and social landscape of ordinary human existence has been so transformed that the social structures and cultural self-understandings long presupposed by theology have now largely disappeared. These changes, even apart from the antireligious ideology with which they were often promoted, effected a dislocation of the social function of religion as an integrating and legitimating element of culture. The church was keenly aware of this effect of modernization and condemned the privatizing tendencies of liberalism. But its ability to deal with them effectively was impeded by its own retreat into a subsociety inspired by an ideal of the past.

Another side of the political challenge, however, is represented by the Marxist critique of the enlightened reason that was the engine of these developments. Here the political presuppositions and implications of concrete human subjectivity were made central in a sharp critique of the individualism of the "first Enlightenment." This forced attention upon the relationships between social context and consciousness, between social structure or status and personal existence, and upon the tasks of responsibility for a collective future which certain forms of enlightened progress prefer to ignore. In some respects, this challenge to the constructions of liberalism ran parallel to the views of the church, but a critical engagement with the challenge was impossible before the council.

All these developments had in common a much more profound sense of our responsibility for our world, our history, our present selves, and our future than was common in the culture in which classical theology had been constructed. It is this common consciousness, however, which generates requests made to Christians today that they give an account of the hope that is in them. And, unless the reply is simply to be the demand that people choose between their enveloping modern culture and a Christianity mediated in a premodern fashion, theologians have to face the new culture head-on and attempt what the fathers of the church undertook in the ancient Hellenistic culture and what Saint Thomas dared when a new philosophy and science threatened the traditional faith.[6]

New Foundations for Theology

To meet this challenge, theologians before and since the council have sought to make anthropology the focal point of fundamental theology. If modernity is so marked by the epistemological claims that have in succession separated philosophy, the sciences, and history from theology and by the institutional differentiations that have made more and more spheres of life the objects of human decision, theology cannot continue to operate with premodern criteria and goals.

But as much as this "anthropocentric turn" (as it is sometimes called) was made in order to meet contemporary questions, it also can claim deep roots in quite ancient and traditional theological positions. The passage of First Peter with which we began legitimates the demand for reasons for our hope. The hope rests finally on Christ and his example and promise, and in that sense it is, like faith, *ex auditu*. But the "hearing" is itself something more than sound waves impinging upon eardrums. It is a human act of reception and appropriation, the word encountering and satisfying the demands of a questioning mind and a needy heart. Revelation is not an act which ends with the speaking of the word but with its reception and appropriation in human lives.

Classically, the message itself was presented in such terms. The ancient creed places all its great affirmations about God and Christ in an anthropological context: *propter nos homines et propter nostram salutem* ("for us and for our salvation"). The gospel does not present sets of truths about God that he sets before us simply to test our willingness to submit to his transcendent authority. It tells of the God who has acted on our behalf, is *pro nobis* (for us). That is also perhaps why the First Vatican Council placed our eternal destiny among the integrating principles of a systematic understanding of the faith (see DS 3016; N–D 132).

These traditional foundations should be kept in mind today, when the anthropocentric emphasis of theological foundations is coming under criticism.[7] What is needed is a *theological* anthropology, not one elaborated on the basis of a priori philosophical or scientific criteria. It must be *an anthropology of the reception of the Christian gospel*. All the elements of this definition should be kept in mind.

First of all, an *anthropology* is needed. It is not possible to articulate the meaning of the Christian gospel without considering the persons to whom and for the sake of whose salvation it is preached. Christian revelation is itself a dimension of Christian salvation, and salvation cannot be articulated except through an analysis of what there is about the human condition that needs healing. And this analysis cannot be undertaken without some reflection on what it means to be the authentic human being whom God has created and redeemed.

Second, an anthropology of *reception* will attempt to explore the fact that Christianity presents itself as a word and grace from without, from God: *fides ex auditu*. It must articulate, therefore, both the possibility and the need for human beings to hear a word and to receive a favor from God. And its reflection on God in turn will have as one of its primary guides the fundamental conviction that, in complete freedom, the transcendent Creator of all things has chosen to address and to call human beings.

Third, an anthropology of the reception of *the Christian gospel* will be needed. It is not just any revelation which is received, but the gospel of Jesus Christ. The fundamental questions are: "What must be true about human beings if the gospel of Jesus Christ is addressed to them as a message of salvation? What must be true about them if it is *his* word which they have needed and his cross and resurrection which has redeemed them?"

Note that this anthropology of reception does not address solely those who have not yet accepted the gospel. The gospel stands over and against believers as well. Their reception and appropriation of it in faith is an act which occurs within the same cultural context and in terms of the same questions and demands as those of "the others." Believers today have no choice about being late twentieth-century believers. Their faith is their own conscious and free decision to orient their existences *today* in the light of the gospel of Jesus Christ. The articulation of that gospel within and for the church, then, cannot avoid relating its meaning to the contemporary demand for meaning and value.

This does not mean tailoring the gospel to fit the expectations and requirements of modernity. The gospel has its own "objective" demands that need to be heard in their integrity. It has the power not only to meet the questions inquirers bring to it but also to transform their initial horizons, leading them to ask questions they had not considered before. But this does not mean that these initial horizons can be overlooked in a presentation of the gospel, that they can be considered as utterly without value, or that the dynamics of their transformation by the gospel can be neglected in analyzing the situation of faith today. The basic anthropology, therefore, must also be a critical hermeneutics of reception which combines at once respect for the questions which people bring to the gospel and the power of the gospel itself to evoke the questions needed for its own reception.

Elements of a Foundational Anthropology

Theology, on this view, is the attempt to mediate between the gospel and the cultural context to and for which it is preached. At a fundamental level, it attempts this mediation by means of a generalized or fundamental anthropology of reception. If the gospel is to be preached to all creatures, in all generations, in all nations, there must be something about the gospel and about its addressees that can be articulated in basic and general terms. And it is essays toward this generalized anthropology that characterize the fundamental direction of the works of Karl Rahner, Bernard Lonergan, and the younger Edward Schillebeeckx.[8]

These efforts attempt an analysis of the fundamental structure and dynamism of human consciousness in order to show how it opens itself to the question of God and to a possible revelation from God. The chief task of Christian theology becomes that of showing how the central Christian doctrines meet the fundamental needs and desires of the human person which the basic anthropology uncovers. This basic anthropology is an attempt to meet the challenges posed by modern philosophy, which is grounded not in metaphysics but in consciousness analysis and which centers it reflections on the problem of human freedom.

For this theological approach, the human person's project of self-constitution through freedom becomes the horizon within which the question about God is considered to arise. *Liber est causa sui* (the free person is his own cause) said the Scholastic adage, and these anthropocentric approaches seek to exploit this insight by appropriating the personalist, existential, and historically conscious emphases of modern philosophies. Human freedom is understood not simply as freedom from constraint but as freedom for self-constitution. One's intelligence and freedom move in a series of inquiries toward an ideal of meaning, truth, and goodness, which, when reached in reasonable affirmation and responsible choice, also constitute one as an authentic human being. But this movement toward the true and the good has no finite term; what meaning is there that a human mind would not try to understand, what truth would it not seek to know, what good would it not seek to embrace? What could give this restless mind and heart rest except the infinite in comprehensive meaning, absolute truth, and unqualified good? And are not these other words for that transcendent One whom the religions of the world call God?

The question about God arises, then, as an inner moment within the analysis of human consciousness. Beyond the particular horizon of any specific question, beyond the horizons of all particular questions, lies the ultimate horizon. If there is no comprehensive meaning, can any search for meaning be meaningful? If there is no absolute truth, what grounds are there for any conditional truth? If there is no unqualified good, can finite goods, including the good of the struggle for human authenticity, be really worthwhile? Is not God, then, the condition for the possibility of these self-defining strivings of the human person? Must not "anthropo-logy" end by becoming "theo-logy?"

And from some such basic anthropology, this theology conceives Christian revelation as God's redemptive intervention into the history of human self-realization. The transcendent and ultimate goal of human inquiry has not been content to be simply present by his absence. He has chosen to move toward us human beings, to bless us by his presence, to name himself, to give himself in grace, in history, in Jesus Christ. Now the task of human self-realization need not be simply a groping toward the ultimate, unfathomable Mystery; it can also be an encounter with Mystery communicating himself to persons. Our freedom can discover and engage God's freedom, and when this happens, through word and grace, our basic, self-constituting freedom is caught up into the self-constituting freedom by which God gives himself for our sake and for our salvation. Human self-transcendence discovers its true depths by the encounter with divine self-transcendence in Christ.

The Critique of Political Theology

Such a fundamental anthropology addresses particularly the challenges posed by the epistemological and historical dimensions of modern culture. But, especially since the council, political theology and the theology of liberation have posed a basic challenge to this generalized anthropology by insisting that the political dimensions of modernity also be addressed. The criticism is twofold: first, that a merely general anthropology is inadequate to the tasks of theology and, second, that such a theology often represents an uncritical accommodation of theology to the culture of modernity.

The first of these criticisms is not so much a repudiation of the general anthropology as a demand that it be brought down to earth. Just as there is no such thing as "man" in general, but only men and women, so also there is no single context for the reception of the gospel, but only specific and varied contexts. Questions of meaning and value are posed by individuals living in particular places at specific times, confronting concrete personal and social challenges with the resources mediated by their societies and culture. The generalized anthropology is useful as a heuristic aid, an orientation of inquiry that can identify but does not itself exhaust the task of theology. Theology does not mediate simply between the gospel and "culture in general," but between the gospel and specific cultural contexts. It is a mistake to assume that theology works only at the general or heuristic level; "theology" concretely exists only as "theologies."

This view may be illustrated by analogy with preaching. Imagine a preacher having to preach at two funerals on successive days. The first is the funeral of an elderly man who has died in the bosom of his family after having lived a good Christian life. The second is the funeral of a young woman who has succeeded on her third try at suicide. The lectionary presents the same scriptural texts for the preacher to choose. But how differently will any one of them speak to the two situations! And this difference lies, not in the texts themselves, but in the context of questioning grief which the preacher must address. There will, of course, be a common question: What in the light of the gospel is the meaning of life and death? But that question is asked existentially in a very specific way: What light can the gospel throw upon this life and this death? A sermon on the same text pertinent at one funeral will not be pertinent at the other.

The effort, common since the council, to construct local theologies follows a similar logic.[9] Differing cultural contexts require different theologies. The demands for reasons for Christian hope arise out of the differing temptations to resignation or despair. In Latin America, for example, as Gustavo Gutiérrez puts it, a theology of liberation arises by the asking of two indispensable and interdependent questions: "What is the meaning of the faith in a life committed to the struggle against injustice and alienation?" and "What is the meaning of the struggle against an unjust society and the creation of a new man in the light of the Gospel?"[10] A commitment to a quite concrete struggle encounters a commitment to the gospel and vice versa; and the effort to answer those two questions is the mediation of the faith to the Latin American situation. In other places or at other times, other particular questions may legitimately articulate the theological task, but this is what it means to undertake theology in the Latin American context.

This criticism leads to the second critique of a merely generalized fundamental anthropology: the tendency it displays to identify religious questions simply with ultimate questions, with questions asking about the meaning of the whole of existence. The correlation between the gospel and the fundamental needs and desires of human consciousness is articulated in terms of a basic and dynamic drive toward the final, all-embracing horizon which Christian faith identifies with God. This is not a mistake, of course, but it is again inadequate. For the assumption often made in modern culture is that "religion" has to do with this question and even with it alone and that it can safely be left to those attracted by it. The question about the whole, about comprehensive and final meaning, thus becomes, paradoxically, the defining concern only of a particular sphere of a society and culture, the sphere of "religion," while other spheres, it is assumed, can get along quite well without either addressing or answering it. The whole has become a part and a part without public significance. Some individuals may find themselves troubled by it, and they should not, of course, be prevented from indulging their concern. That, after all, is what "religion" is for.

Theologians, of course, are likely to disagree with this modern assumption. But a generalized fundamental anthropology reflects it to the degree that it remains content with this privatizing of the question about final and comprehensive meaning or considers it solely in terms of individual existence and its meaning and value. The banishment of religion from the public sphere is mirrored in its restriction to the sphere of the personal and existential. Where this happens, the two questions analogous to those asked by Gutiérrez become these: "What is the meaning of the faith in a life committed to the struggle for personal authenticity?" and "What is the meaning of the struggle for authenticity in the light of the gospel?"

These are scarcely illegitimate questions, either in themselves or in terms of the audience that the gospel addresses in various parts of our late twentieth-century world. But political theologians argue that too many theologians exhibit an unconscious tendency, first, to assume that such questions exhaust the horizon of theology and, second, to neglect the economic, social, political, and cultural conditions in which the questions themselves arise. Why, it may be asked, do such questions arise so frequently and so urgently? Why is authentic existence apparently so difficult to achieve? Why does this culture abound in so many therapeutic movements and techniques? Why are existentialism and personalism the catchwords of the late twentieth century? Could it be that authentic existence is a political problem?[11]

Such questions relativize the general claims of the anthropology under criticism, and that is precisely the point. Questions about authentic existence arise and theologians appropriately address them in certain parts of the world. But they are not simply *the* religious questions, and to assume that they are suggests a lack of critical self-consciousness in theologians and a suspicion that they have taken over the ethnocentric bias that late twentieth-century modernity represents an inevitable or even an obligatory human ideal. The first step toward a critical theology is a recognition that these questions have not always been asked, at least not in this form, and that they are not the only or even the basic questions to which the gospel may be addressed.

The two critiques represented by the "political turn" in theology should not be seen as complete rejections of the basic anthropology offered earlier. Rather they insist that it consider the human inquirers upon whom it focuses in their full concreteness. Human spirit is not only incarnate in a body but also unfolds itself within social, cultural, and historical contexts which effectively orient and limit its freedom. Only by considering these larger contexts can a theologian develop an anthropology adequate to the full breadth of Christ's redemptive work.

The Threat to Humanity

In this basic critique is implied another that rests upon human experience and upon the fact that the Christian gospel proclaims a salvation brought about by the cross and resurrection of Jesus Christ. The problem of evil has to enter into the basic anthropology of the reception of the gospel. This will not be only a theodicy, exploring the question, older than Job, of reconciling the goodness and power of God with innocent suffering. Religion is not simply a response to humanity's search for meaning in an often incomprehensible world. This incomprehensibility itself is not concretely grasped unless within it is included the absurdities of human infidelity, injustice, and failure. Not only is God absent; humanity itself is absent. The question about God, then, does not simply arise as a question about an absent, transcendent meaning, but also as a question about the threat that humanity experiences and that it itself is.[12]

Paul asked the same question: "Who shall rescue me from the body of this death?" His reply was the exclamation "Thanks be to God, Jesus Christ our Lord!" (Rom 7:24–25). This encounter of the human cry of pain and the most basic Christian affirmation of faith illustrates the intersection of anthropology and theology. They meet in the figure of Jesus Christ, "the Christ who died and, more than that, was raised from the dead" (Rom 8:34). It is in Christ that the full depths of humanity's need for God are revealed, and never more than in his unjust death. It is in Christ that the full depths of God's self-gift are revealed, and never more than in his conquest of "the last enemy, death" (1 Cor 15:26). An anthropology of threatened humanity, then, opens out upon an anthropology of redeemed, renewed humanity, now given a hope which nothing can disappoint.

Conclusion

We return then to the point from which we began, to the attempt to give reasons for the hope that is in us. It is perhaps clearer now why fundamental theology cannot be simply an introductory discipline that might be left behind as one pursues other theological tasks. It addresses the basic question implied in all other theological questions: Why may we hope? And it addresses it not just because some others who do not hope wonder that we do, but because the ability to hope is itself one of the most basic clues to the meaning of the Christian gospel. That the question continues to arise from others is the surest indication that the gospel still has a light and power to bring to the world today. In that question and in the effort to respond to it out of the heart of the gospel lies the great challenge of a theology still conscious of a redemptive mission for the church and for the world.

Recommended Readings

Gutiérrez, Gustavo. A Theology of Liberation: History, Politics and Salvation. Maryknoll, NY: Orbis, 1973. The classic work which paved the way for the effort to construct a theology adequate to the needs and demands of Latin America today.

Lonergan, Bernard. Method in Theology. New York: Herder and Herder, 1972. An effort to lay foundations for theology in a historically conscious age.

Rahner, Karl. Foundations of Christian Faith: An Introduction to the Idea of Christianity. New York: Seabury, 1978. An attempt to present a comprehensive introduction to Christianity on the basis of a fundamental anthropology.

Thomas Aquinas, Saint. Summa contra Gentiles. A classic example of a medieval effort to address the challenges to faith represented by a massive new cultural movement.

Von Balthasar, Hans Urs. Love Alone: The Way of Salvation. London: Sheed and Ward, 1968. A small work that argues against attempting a defense of Christianity on any other grounds than the beauty of its own truth.

T H R E E

"For the Salvation of All Who Believe": The Word of God as a Future for Humanity

Leo J. O'Donovan

At the end of the last century, in a remote village on the island of Tahiti, Paul Gauguin painted perhaps the culminating work of his tumultuous career. On a broad canvas throbbing with his saturated colors and statuesque forms, he reimagined the ages and plight of humankind from infancy in a mother's arms to the infirmities of old age. In the center a vigorous youth reaches for red fruit that may well be forbidden. To the left a mysterious deity, invented by the artist himself, overlooks the scene and its dreamlike religious search. To emphasize the scope of his ambitious project Gauguin wrote three questions in an upper corner of the painting: "Where do we come from? What are we? Where are we going?"

Such fundamental questions about human existence are sometimes disparaged today, or dismissed as impractical distractions. But few visitors to Boston's Museum of Fine Arts who thoughtfully view Gauguin's work will easily set them aside. Indeed, late in our own century, these are questions we may well consider still more insistently our own. Our origin, nature, and destiny are issues to which answers in fact are given daily, through the shaping of our family life, urban policies, and international posture—and with all but irreversible effect on the other inhabitants of our planet.

The Questions of Revelation

Gauguin was an artist of such unusual passion and scope that many of us may feel more intimidated than enthralled by his work. His extraordinary range of interest in human culture led him to excavate imagery from every continent. In paintings, prints, statuary, and autobiographical writing he undertook an uninhibited synthesis of apparently incompatible material. But his appreciation for alien ways and his enormous capacity for inventive self-expression relate him

27

strongly to our time. And his persistent religious sense inevitably awakens our own.

How seriously shall we take such visitations of divinity, expressed in so many different human forms? Religious thinkers from Augustine to Karl Rahner have held that every human heart is restless until it rests in God. Convinced that we have been created not simply for natural ends but to share in God's eternal life, they recall the many ways in which we phrase and practice the most basic questions of our lives. In a real sense, they suggest, we are not merely human persons who may ask about God if we wish. Rather, only when we pose that question do we become truly ourselves.

But as human beings have lived out their concern for the divine, their own humanity has become more and more a puzzle to themselves. At first human nature seems to be the most obvious and available "thing" in the world. Yet gradually we realize that our true desires and identity are often obscure and indeed conflictual. Once the difficulty of true self-knowledge is glimpsed, the personal and social depth of the question comes to seem unfathomable.

For Roman Catholic Christians, the interrelation between these two questions of God and our own humanity was vividly stated during the Second Vatican Council. The opening chapters of *Lumen Gentium*, the council's Dogmatic Constitution on the Church, look to Christ as a light for all nations. God's own Word has taken flesh among us, not only gathering us in the unity of a true humanity but also enlightening our search for the center of our lives. "To carry out the will of the Father, Christ inaugurated the kingdom of heaven on earth and revealed to us the mystery of the Father" (LG 3).[1] Reflecting his light, the church is shaped as "a kind of sacrament or sign of intimate union with God, and of the unity of all humankind" (LG 1). Such a revelation can scarcely be a matter simply for the mind. It also challenges and judges, heals and consoles, renews and transforms. For the depths of transcendent goodness and love have opened; holiness has been named. The truth that time needs for its healing and fulfillment has begun to act among us.

The vision was majestic, bearing a new and practical understanding of God's mystery at work in time. Yet the conciliar discussion also recognized the "other side" of the question. As the bishops in Rome learned to articulate the church's historical mission more clearly, they also came to reflect more concretely on the world for which the church is meant to be "a universal sacrament of salvation" (LG 48). The learning process came to its fullest expression in *Gaudium et Spes*, the Pastoral Constitution on the Church in the Modern World. There the council sought to indicate its "solidarity with the entire human family,"[2] committing itself to conversation about the most urgent questions of the age. One central question focused the discussion:

> What is humanity? What is this sense of sorrow, of evil, of death, which continues to exist despite so much progress? What is the purpose of these victories, purchased at so high a cost? What can human beings offer to society, what can they expect from it? What follows this earthly life? (GS 10)

Having reflected on the mystery of God in its remarkable first steps, the conciliar way of renewal gathered strength as it learned to speak "in the light of Christ . . . to all human beings in order to illuminate the mystery and humanity and to cooperate in finding the solution to the outstanding problems of our time" (GS 10).

This conjunction of the questions about God and humanity may seem obvious to us several decades after the event. Theologians like Paul Tillich, Karl Rahner, and Langdon Gilkey have made the question of human existence an integral part of their theological program. Following the great example of Gustavo Gutiérrez, liberation theologies have taken the suffering of oppressed human communities as the starting point for their reflection. Broader awareness of the great world religions has reminded us that there seem to be as many "ways to the center" as there are human cultures. But the sudden light generated by Vatican II came in large measure from rejoining elements of Christian consciousness that had been sadly separated. Probing the range of real religious experience, the council achieved a whole historical perspective that enabled particular aspects of Christian belief once more to be confessed in unity. Drawing out the dialectic between our views of God and of humanity, it helped us to recognize how a redeeming Creator may be lovingly more interior and immeasurably more transcendent to our lives than any language can express.

For the council, the correlative mysteries of God and humanity meet in the mystery of Christ. Fifteen centuries earlier, the Council of Chalcedon had affirmed that true humanity and true divinity are united in Christ. In a more typically modern way, Vatican II develops this fundamental christological doctrine through its meditation on Jesus Christ as the enduring Word of truth who manifests both God and himself in time. "Only in the mystery of the incarnate Word," it insists, "does the mystery of humanity take on light." For "by the revelation of the mystery of the Father and His love, [Christ] fully reveals humanity to itself and makes our supreme calling clear" (GS 22).[3]

If the mysteries of God and humanity meet in Christ, if questions about divine life and human existence thus become questions about *him*, then naturally we must listen more carefully to him in order to understand the full meaning of those questions. Recall, for example, the pivotal scene at Caesarea Philippi in the eighth chapter of the Gospel of Mark. See the disciples again as they follow Jesus, seeking to be faithful members of the people of Israel and to walk in the fear of Yahweh. In their own ways, they certainly experienced questions about the meaning of God and their own lives. But it is not simply the disciples' questions about humanity or God that Jesus evokes when he presents them with his decisive challenge to their faith. Instead he asks: "Who do the people say that I am?" And when the disciples answer, he presses his question home still more personally: "But who do you say that I am?" (Mk 8:27 ff.).

Could Peter have answered this question for us all, if the Lord had not first questioned him? A moment later he objects to Jesus' sense of the suffering entailed in his mission. Would he, or any of us, be likely to unite our search for ourselves and for God without God's question: What do you make of the humanity of Jesus?

The more one meditates on the scene of Peter's confession and seeks to join Peter's faith, the more one realizes that it is a moment of commitment that God alone makes possible for us in Christ and then sustains in the company of Christ. We see Jesus as light for the world because his figure first comes to meet us, not because we first ask where true humanity and true divinity, light for our darkness, may be found.

Deep within human hearts lies a longing to understand ourselves, our origin, and our destiny. But deeper still, and more embracing, is the longing of God to remain our source and become our home. This is a reversal of the way human logic inclines to put its basic questions. It occurs when we realize that only God's approach to us assures us that we may approach God.[4]

Isn't it predictable, really, that the way human beings tend to put their religious questions will be reversed and enriched by God's questions put to them? When we ask whether God is with us, God seems to ask with whom we ourselves stand. When we wonder about the reliability of God's care for us, the Holy Spirit may question our care for others. When our hope in God falters, we may well be led to practice hope for our brothers and sisters. In this reversal of questions that had seemed first to rise within ourselves but then come still more urgently home from the heart of God, we may recognize that God's word is greater and more powerful than we ever could have imagined, that it comes to us from beyond and before all our time. We may recognize as well that this word of truth and love comes just as much from deep *within* our history, propelling it forward. The initiative of revelation may indeed be ultimately divine. But its form and course are insistently human.

Let us pursue this intimation that it is God's self-revealing word that most intimately directs our human story and offers it a worthy future. In the next section we will consider a fundamental objection to the very possibility or meaningfulness of divine revelation. Then we will review some of the forms in which God is revealed and, in a further section, the unity of the dialogue that God's revelation initiates with humanity. If God's word is living and active, we must also reflect more explicitly, in our final sections, on its pragmatic effect and the future it opens.

Revelation in Question

Addressing the theme of revelation specifically in *Dei Verbum*, the Dogmatic Constitution on Divine Revelation, Vatican II once again chose biblical language, emphasizing God's personal address to humanity and the climax of that dialogue in Jesus Christ. The Constitution includes all particular expressions of divine truth within the convenant relationship which revelation expresses; it speaks of the divine "plan of revelation . . . realized by deeds and words having an inner unity" (*DV* 2). Revelation is handed down from Christ to his apostles and from the apostles to the church which "in her teaching, life, and worship perpetuates and hands on to all generations all that she herself is, all that she believes" (DV 8). The text rejects the notion that Scripture and tradition are separate sources for revelation; it speaks of them as "flowing from the same divine wellspring" (DV 9) so that they form "one sacred deposit of the word of God" (DV 10). This the church seeks to practice and profess, guided by the authoritative teaching of its bishops, who stand not above the word of God but in its service. In the gospels pre-eminently we have "a perpetual and divine witness" (DV 17) to the prophetic ministry and paschal mystery of God's own Word made flesh for us, giving his life on the cross and now mysteriously present through his Holy Spirit poured forth on all the earth.

Vatican II presents this teaching on revelation in a direct, doctrinal mode. It appears to assume that the very idea of a self-revealing God is credible to its hearers. For almost all traditional religious cultures, in fact, theophanies or manifestations of the divine were thought of as frequent if unusual occurrences. The Bible itself offers a record of revelation rather than a defense of its nature and possibility. Only with the rise of a critical historical sense in Western thought was the very possibility of revelation questioned. The existential question had earlier been predominant, namely, whether one could live in fidelity to God's word. But then a more theoretical question became urgent, whether it made human sense to speak of a message from a transcendent God to a historical world.[5]

While it is true that Vatican II does not directly address the theoretical question, it nevertheless contributes an important, indirect response to it. If one compares its teaching on revelation, for example, with the statements a century earlier in Dei Filius, the First Vatican Council's Dogmatic Constitution on the Catholic Faith, one notes significant differences in approach. Whereas Vatican I had sought a middle path between the extremes of fideism and rationalism, Vatican II attempts a more dialogical contribution to the questions of contemporary men and women. Dei Filius (Vatican I) adopts an abstract philosophical perspective, distinguishing natural and supernatural knowledge of God and arguing the necessity of divine revelation; Dei Verbum (Vatican II) speaks more biblically and historically, evoking the transmission of the Christian message through time and its expression in the pages of Scripture. Dei Filius points to humanity's ultimate end in the beatific vision, while Dei Verbum centers our attention more forcefully on Christ as our way. Dei Filius states the relations between natural and revealed knowledge abstractly, insisting that in principle there can be no conflict between reason and faith; Dei Verbum recommends the word of God by seeking rather to manifest its inherent value and attractiveness, its splendor illuminating our human need. Dei Filius seems to move from confidence in reason to a recommendation of faith; Dei Verbum, on the other hand, takes its start from a sense of grateful responsibility for a message the people of God has received in the course of time. In brief, while Vatican II certainly had no intention of departing from the teaching of Vatican I, it did propose, "following in the footsteps of the Councils of Trent and of First Vatican," to make progress in the understanding of revelation "so that by hearing the message of salvation the whole world may believe; by believing, it may hope; and by hoping, it may love" (DV 1).

Between the two councils, in fact, the theme of revelation had become central for Christian theology. Whereas nineteenth-century Protestant liberal theology expected the gradual progress of the human species, authors like Johannes Weiss and Albert Schweitzer rediscovered in the preaching of Jesus a message of judgment and finality. Later, when the First World War threatened the complete disintegration of European society, theologians such as Karl Barth insisted on the sovereignty of God's word over human affairs. American theologians influenced by the new dialectical or neo-orthodox school reflected its sense of divine intervention in history.

H. Richard Niebuhr was an eloquent representative of the new emphasis on God's word, and his masterful essay of 1941, The Meaning of Revelation, invited readers to search in their common memory for the foundation of a rational moral life. In response to the historical and religious relativism of the day, Niebuhr rejected subjectivist and skeptical responses to the questions posed by a world of radical historicity. He argued instead for a critical historical theology in which revelation could "mean both history and God," pointing the human community more effectively toward both the divine and the temporal.

Niebuhr proposed a pregnant distinction between history written by disinterested, scientific reason on the basis of observation from without (external history) and another form of history recorded on the basis of lived participation in communally valued experiences (internal history). He held that the transition from the first to the second could only be made by decision and faith. The perspective of internal history is justified by "practical" rather than by "pure" reason. From it, however, a unified point of view becomes possible "which makes the God of Jesus Christ the measure of all things."[6] Living from that perspective, which is what Niebuhr meant by revelation, "we seek to conquer the evil imaginations of the heart,"[7] not merely the adequate images of an observing mind.

Niebuhr's distinction between pure and practical reason may have been overly Kantian. His moving reflections on the human condition, both individually and communally, were necessarily foreshortened. But the general direction of his proposal has retained its value and cogency, relating the great tradition of Christian faith in God's word to the needs of a pluralistic, historical world.

Some four decades later, similarly concerned for historical fidelity and contemporary adequacy, Avery Dulles has offered another magisterial and still more comprehensive treatment.[8] Dulles first anatomizes the five most typical approaches taken by twentieth-century theologians: revelation as doctrine, as history, as inner experience, as dialectical presence, as new awareness. After comparing these models, he then develops his own constructive view of symbolic communication as a dialectical perspective that allows one to discern what each model can contribute to recognizing revelation at its present value. Like Niebuhr, he may be said to be postcritical. He recognizes the rational criticism of the idea of revelation. But his response does not argue for a permanent and unassailable rational starting point or foundation for theology. Rather, he takes the continuous confession of the Christian community's faith in God's revelation as a reasonable perspective from which to reflect faithfully on the human prospect. As theologians, both authors make revelation more plausible by showing its inner coherence and its historical fruitfulness.

In that respect they pursue in more formal theological terms a course similar to what we find in the church's public teaching in *Dei Verbum*. The council document does not in the first place argue that revelation is possible. Instead it makes sense of the rational possibility of revelation indirectly, in the course of its direct teaching on the meaning, transmission, and biblical expression of revelation. In the text the historical experience of God's word is narrated; some of its basic structures are described; implicitly, an argument is made that this revelation discloses the true depth and possibility of time. Whoever believes, or comes to believe, is thus invited to listen more carefully to God's word and to stand more confidently in the company of those who celebrate it. Further, if a community responds in faith to an address from God, then it will proclaim its good news to other men and women who are invited to join the healing circle of belief.[9]

In our time, marked as it is by historical relativity, economic inequity, and nuclear threat, it would be simplistic and in fact irreverent to turn to divine revelation merely as a divinely prescribed remedy for our personal and social predicaments. But the urgency of our situation may alert us to the need for a guidance surer than our own. I suggest not simply that we *risk* believing in what God may have communicated to human history, or place a wager on revelation that could be worth everything if it proves true and yet would lose little if proven false. Rather, I suggest that the course of history, for all its failures and folly, is most adequately imagined and shared by seeing it fundamentally as a dialogue between created time and its Creator; still more, it is a dialogue between a frequently unfaithful people and a mysteriously steadfast God of covenanting love.

Let us pursue this intimation that it *makes sense* to trust that we are addressed by God's revelation and may in turn entrust ourselves to it. Let us live a while with the claim that the Holy Mystery called God has spoken to our world and that this address lives among us still, constituting the most fundamental exchange in existence. In the next section I shall consider some of the forms in which the address occurs. I shall ask how they are related to each other and whether they suggest a single story. Throughout, I want to suggest that we consider opening ourselves to God's word coming to us from the center of time and appearing in various forms that can transform our lives, so that we may not only learn the truth but hope to do it. My approach will not argue for the possibility of revelation from the point of view of pure reason, nor will I urge its acceptance on the basis of tradition and authority alone. Rather, I shall try to let its own historical expression commend itself again to a human reason open enough to accept a future reason itself cannot assure.

Human Form for Revelation

It is difficult if not impossible to distinguish adequately between the forms of revelation and the course of its inner life.[10] Still, we may gain a greater appreciation for both if we attend first to the ways it appears and then, in the next section, to the story of its unfolding as a whole. One may question precisely whether there is a wholeness, an integrity or unity, to the various manifestations of divinity in human history. But this question has its full import only if one realizes the great variety of ways in which the divine has been revealed. Historians of religion, philosophers, and biblical critics, among others, have studied these modes of revelation in great detail. I shall recall some of their findings before asking then whether the various experiences communicate a single spirit or simply many.

Among historians of religion perhaps no one has been more influential for American readers over recent decades than Mircea Eliade. Eliade's study of traditional societies repeatedly drew attention to the distinction between the sacred and the profane as distinct modes of being. One primordial experience, he found, was the sense of sacred *space* associated with such places as the "holy mountain." Such space confers form, reality, a center to the world of archaic societies. Another primordial experience was the conviction of sacred *time* grounded in a longing for "the perfection of beginnings" and memorialized, for example, in temples where the annual renewals of the world were celebrated. For religious people, Eliade showed, time, like space, is not homogeneous; sacred time can be reversed and repeated, and the myths that interpret it celebrate regeneration through return to "the time of origins."

For religious peoples, *nature* is always sacred too; the essential structures of the natural world—sky, water, trees, sun, moon—reveal sacrality, speaking through their coherent symbolism to the whole person. Finally, Eliade held, if "the appearance of life is the central mystery of the world,"[11] then *human existence* itself reveals the sacred most of all; the human being is a microcosm of the larger world, opening to the divine especially through those rites of passage that initiate their participants into knowledge of sexuality, death, and the sacred. As diverse and extraordinarily rich as the religious expressions of humanity have been through history, Eliade nevertheless found them regularly patterned or formed in ways such as these.

Now for Judaism and Christianity, as religions of the Book, the revelatory manifestations of God range from Moses' experience at the burning bush to the cross of Jesus some twelve or thirteen centuries later. While the original events comprised a living disclosure of divine intentions for human life, the meaning that originated then is faithfully witnessed now in the biblical text that is sacred for both Jews and Christians. And the Bible's rich variety of literary presentation itself reflects the depth and power of the divine disclosure.[12] In a seminal essay "Toward a Hermeneutic of the Idea of Revelation," Paul Ricoeur has argued that a proper approach to the notion of revelation should consider not first the level of theological assertion but rather those more "originary" modes of speech used by a people in its fundamental confessions and professions of faith. In the Bible, he writes, "these originary expressions are caught up in forms of discourse as diverse as narration, prophecy, legislative texts, wisdom sayings, hymns, sup-plications, and thanksgiving."[13]

Prophetic discourse, the basic referent for the biblical idea of revelation, declares itself as spoken "in the name of Yahweh," whose word comes to the people through the prophet. But the biblical revelation would be seriously foreshortened, Ricoeur points out, if narrative discourse did not accompany prophecy. In narrative, those historical events are recorded that both constitute Israel as a people and liberate it from slavery. In addition, the prescriptive discourse of the Law significantly develops the practical dimension of revelation, not so much in the sense of a higher, external command but rather as the ethics of a redeemed people; Torah is concerned with the perfection of a new covenant, not primarily with "moral submission." The Wisdom literature of the Bible, furthermore, expresses revelation in another way, reaching out beyond the covenant relationship between Yahweh and Israel to all human beings and binding together the sphere of human action and the sphere of the world at the very place they are most discordant, namely, in the experience of innocent suffering. Finally, in the lyricism most familiar to us through the Psalms, hymns of praise, supplication, and thanksgiving transform the story of salvation into an invocation of salvation's author.

For Ricoeur, as I have noted, prophetic discourse is the prime analogue for our understanding of revelation. But by emphasizing its interrelation with narration, instruction in the Law, wisdom sayings and biblical hymns, he constructs a genuinely analogical concept of revelation that refers internally to its various forms and many meanings. His approach also gives full value to what he calls the nuclear dialectic of revelation, "the dialectic of the hidden God who reveals himself."[14]

Eliade's study of ancient religion concentrates on natural forms of revelation, whether cosmic or personal. For a hermeneutical philosopher like Ricoeur, the Bible as a religious text offers a panoply of literary forms for interpretation. But biblical scholarship as such has been concerned not only to read Scripture correctly but also to respond to deist and rationalist critiques of revealed religion. For over two centuries scholars have been developing methods of interpretation that combine literary examination of the texts and their genres with historical criticism of their reliability as historical documents.[15] While the nineteenth century saw the emergence of the historical critical method, uniting literary and historical modes of analysis, the twentieth century witnessed the refinement of form criticism, distinguishing the larger and smaller forms employed by biblical authors to convey their message. The form-critical method especially has made us more aware of the very different ways in which God's care is expressed for the world, whether through gospels or letters, parables or stories of healing.

Naturally there was a wide range of opinion among Protestant authors on the adequacy of form criticism for interpreting Scripture. For Catholics, however, the reaction was cautious in the extreme, largely as a result of the supervisory vigilance exercised by the Pontifical Biblical Commission in Rome. However, with the publication in 1943 of Pius XII's encyclical, *Divino Afflante Spiritu*, a major breakthrough occurred, and the new encyclical served as the Magna Carta for modern Catholic biblical studies.[16] The pope held that biblical interpretation begins by discerning the literal sense of biblical texts and by seeking their full "spiritual significance, intended and ordained by God."[17] But he went on to insist that such interpretation can succeed only through accurate determination of the "modes of writing," the "forms or kinds of speech" used by the sacred writers, "whether in poetic description or in the formation of laws and rules of life or in recording the facts and events of history."[18] He thus authorized a responsible use of form criticism and the historical method among Catholic exegetes.[19]

We see, then, that various approaches help appreciate the different forms in which revelation appears. For historians of religion like Mircea Eliade, the sacred is manifested in shapes of this world which refer beyond it. For a hermeneutic philosopher like Paul Ricoeur, it is important to recognize the different forms of discourse in which a people makes its fundamental religious confession. For biblical critics specifically, careful methods have been developed to distinguish the distinct forms in which God's word has been expressed. But in each case a range of definite forms, with their origin in experience of this world, are understood to bear meanings about the world's origin and destiny that transcend its own capacities.

The question then arises about the interrelation and reliability of these many perspectives on the deepest reality and future of the world's history. The issue is as far-ranging as the very phenomenon of religion, but I shall focus it here by considering how it is posed in terms of Scripture. Since the Bible is the privileged record of God's revelation for Israel and the church, the various literary forms we find in it may stand for manifestations of the sacred in other religious cultures as well. The written expression of God's self-disclosure is not identical with the disclosure itself; the words witness to that event. Nor do words convey meaning without reference to the human images and actions they express. Still, the different forms we have learned to discern in Scripture can raise for us in an especially clear and illuminating way the fundamental question about the unity of revelation in its various forms through time.

Let us ask, then, whether the scenes and sayings we find in Scripture together constitute a single story. Does one new life or spirit, in other words, come to expression in the many forms? As we shall see, the question will also lead us to reflect on the historical character of revelation.

Revelation as God's Story

For many Christians, and certainly for Catholics, their encounter with Scripture coincides especially with the experience of worship. Usually our liturgical readings comprise one or more literary units or literary forms. The congregation may not advert to the distinct stylistic character of the word proclaimed, nor is it likely to reflect on how a particular reading evokes the rest of the writing from which it is selected, and ultimately the Bible as a whole. Still, by reason of their reverence for Scripture and their attention to it through the course of the liturgical year, the gathered people in a real sense hear the whole story in its parts and understand that whole story as their own. This sense of the faith among Christian people may offer us a clue to the unified truth of revelation whose various forms we have just been considering.[20]

With the rise of historical consciousness in Western culture, students of the Bible had to consider more carefully how God's absolute word could be expressed in the relativities of human history. That issue as much as any other prompted the development of the historical critical method for interpreting Scripture. It likewise affected subsequent study of the editorial work of the sacred authors (redaction criticism), the formation of a normative canon (canonical criticism), and, more recently, renewed appreciation of the Bible as a literary creation (rhetorical criticism).[21] Revelation might be related to particular historical circumstances (such as the Exodus from Egypt); it was often expressed in terms of them (as in the Deuteronomic confession of faith). But the Bible offers profound variations on the theme of God's covenant fidelity recreating God's people in word and spirit; it does not *argue* the modes of possibility for divinity's participation in time. Thus, it remains for subsequent theological reflection to consider how thoroughly revelation is to be identified with history and how really the eternal and the temporal can be found in unity.

In our own century, some of the most prominent Scripture scholars have minimized or attenuated the relationship between Scripture and history, God's word and the course of human time. For Gerhard von Rad, for example, historical data strictly speaking were irrelevant to an understanding of God's traditions. Rudolf Bultmann thought that revelation should be located in the kerygma of the early church rather than in the actual life of Jesus.

By contrast, however, some major Protestant theologians such as G. Ernest Wright and Oscar Cullmann have emphasized the historical activity of God as the essence of biblical revelation.[22] Other theologians have been concerned that approaches like Wright's and Cullmann's separate redemptive history from the ordinary human experience of history. Thus, Wolfhart Pannenberg has proposed a more thoroughgoing historical understanding. He argues that revelation is not restricted to any single part of history but occurs in every age as the world moves toward its final end. That consummation, he holds, has been universally assured only by the resurrection of Jesus, through whom God's divinity has been proven and the transformation of the world anticipated.[23] Langdon Gilkey summarizes the perspective of these latter authors when he writes that two basic certainties have guided all the movements of twentieth-century theology: "Revelation or illumination—whatever its content—is *historical* and comes to us through historical events, and (secondly) all events and their meanings are *interpreted.*"[24]

On the Catholic side, while Vatican II was still in session, the Pontifical Biblical Commission in 1964 published an important "Instruction about the Historical Truth of the Gospels."[25] The Instruction was of major significance not only because it officially accepted biblical criticism but also because it clearly distinguished three stages of the gospel tradition: (1) the origin of the gospel material in the life and teaching of *Jesus;* (2) the transmission and formation of that material in the early preaching of the *apostles;* (3) its shaping by the *evangelists* into the written gospels. Shortly afterwards, *Dei Verbum* recapitulated the basic teaching of the Instruction and thus gave it conciliar authority (*DV* 19). Yet neither the Instruction nor the Constitution on Revelation intended to decide precisely how the gospels, and by implication the rest of Scripture, are historical. Rather, as is typical in official church teaching, they adopt a position which excludes erroneous extremes—in this case, either fundamentalism or ahistoricism—while remaining open to further development.

In addition, in a particularly important passage which we have already cited, *Dei Verbum* states that the divine "plan of revelation is realized by deeds and words having an inner unity." This means, the council continues, that "the deeds wrought by God in the history of salvation manifest and confirm the teaching and realities signified by the words, while the words proclaim and clarify the mystery contained in them" (*DV* 2). Thus, while not settling the question of biblical revelation's historicity, the council strongly adopts a mediating position that neither words nor events alone can be understood as revelation but only the two together with an "inner unity."

In a practical way that remains open to further theoretical development, we might say that the simplest and most traditional answer to the historical unity of Scripture is still the best: God's multiform address to us in time has its focus through God's own Word, eternally born of God in a union of immeasurable love and born also of Mary for the sake of our salvation.[26] In all the passages of Scripture (as in so many aspects of other religions), we hear not simply stories about God's dealings with us but God's interpretation of our lives and our selves. It may well be that we seek meaning and purpose, structure, and direction for our world. But in the stories we hear about Jesus of Nazareth, a promise of light and life *presents itself* to us, enshrined in a sacred text but coming ultimately from a source who is not merely sacred but Holy. This is the way, we realize, that the human story should be told, as God's own. The many things said to us are also one, through a life lived wholly in love.

It is clear enough in the New Testament that Jesus Christ's way to God is the center of all that is said there. The early Christians also saw his revelation as fulfilling in one way or another what the Hebrew Scriptures had promised. On further reflection, we recognize that the teaching and life of Jesus remarkably exemplify what Vatican II called the inner unity of divine deeds and words. Though we will always struggle to reach some understanding of what is meant by eternity, and though the meaning of time also remains mysterious for us, still in faith we see that time and eternity are united in Jesus. In his life history we recognize the care of an everlasting love for us. The many scenes and sayings constitute more than a single story. They are moments in the one story we most need to hear, initiated, sustained, and promised its completion—told, in fact— by God.

It seems premature at this point, however, wholly to identify revelation with history. While the truth of human life has a radically historical character, even history may not be a category sufficient to contain that truth entirely. Art and science are two other realms of human endeavor that shape the cultures in which they arise but also transcend them. Further, the ultimate effects of free human decision are seldom discernible in their immediate time and often remain obscure to subsequent historians. It is reasonable to speak of "the human story" so as to suggest the projected unity of all human life and also of particular individual lives. But the very term "story" intimates the poetic dimension of an "account" that does not simply coincide with the history investigated by the rational discipline of the same name.

Another way to put the point is to say that neither reality nor truth may be *identified* with history. Humanly speaking, we have no access to either truth or reality that is not historically conditioned. But it is just as important to realize that our historical experience as such cannot reasonably be held to exhaust what is true and real. At the very least, then, following Paul Ricoeur's insistence that we need a genuinely analogical concept of revelation, we should keep in mind its unity in Christ and the great variety of forms through which it is communicated in time. When we speak of the history of revelation, we emphasize the redemption it effects through a sequence of historical events and also the historical faith it awakens. But a poetics and ethics of revelation also enter into an adequate appreciation of how it addresses and assesses us. The scenes and sayings of Scripture, one might say, constitute not only the possibility of a single story but a unified world of imagination and action as well.

For an understanding of revelation that balances its historical, aesthetic, and ethical aspects, Avery Dulles's account is particularly complete and persuasive. In the constructive chapters of *Models of Revelation* he argues that revelation lives, that it is given and transmitted, through symbolic communication. Symbolism in general, he shows, gives us not speculative but participatory knowledge. It has a transforming effect, influences our commitments and behavior, and introduces us to depths of understanding previously unrecognized. Similarly, revelation draws us into a new way of life. It changes our frame of reference, opens us to a new and decisive form of trust, and teaches us to appreciate the fundamentally mysterious character of our lives before God. The qualities of revelation thus correspond to those of genuine symbolism, which serves as the most apt medium for God's communication with the world.

In contrast to universal language or conventional signs, true symbols have a richness of reference that enables them to convey knowledge of God and to impart God's spirit, even though they are distinct from God.[27] In that case

Dulles calls them *realizing* symbols, bearing within themselves what they signify, just as Jesus bore the offer of grace to a dismembered humanity. At once subjective and objective, the symbols in the parables and healing stories offer direction for both thought and conduct. With Karl Rahner and Michael Polanyi, Dulles emphasizes that such symbolic communication depends on tacit awareness, informal modes of inference, and a personal framework of commitment. Here too his approach is postcritical, since it begins not with methodical doubt but with the actually lived context of the interpreter.

The adequacy of Dulles's view may be further tested by asking how well it interprets the three stages of the gospel tradition in the life and teaching of Jesus, the preaching of the apostles, and the writing of our four gospels. For none of these stages can we do justice to the discoveries of biblical criticism by saying that the Bible principally communicates *either* doctrine *or* inner experience, historical event *or* the dialectical presence of the divine. The range of symbol employed—natural, linguistic, personal, social—is too complex and rich, and the interrelation of the stages of the communication is too intimate for any univocal explanation of how they communicate saving truth. The reign of God which Jesus preached is proclaimed by the apostolic preaching as inaugurated in Jesus himself, whom the first Christian communities celebrate as their Lord. Any attempt to sever one stage from another and give it univocal priority disrupts the whole and distorts what Joseph Fitzmyer calls its evangelical truth. But a partly satisfactory account is given when we view this time of foundational experience as symbolic communiction between a created humanity and a Creator seeking to redeem it. Jesus Christ is thus the central personal symbol in a system of symbols through which his God tells the human story as unlimited love means it to be.

A theology of revelation as symbolic communication also corresponds well with a balanced understanding of human reason. Paul Ricoeur, in the essay cited earlier, sought to overcome a false opposition between "an authoritarian and opaque concept of revelation and a concept of reason which claims to be its own master and transparent to itself."[28] Dulles's view implies a symbolic realism of reason as well as of revelation. Far from being fully evident to itself and self-mastering, human reason is dark as well as light, radically receptive as well as freely active. It *realizes* the world neither by the pure exercise of itself nor simply by prompting practical decision. Although radically rooted in history, reason is also instinct with scientific experiment and poetic creation. Through it, human beings most adequately participate in the world when it guides their symbolic communication in a variety of ways rather than in any univocal one. Our reason's longing for symbols that will really satisfy us is revealed at the same time that God reveals God's eternal care for us.

The Risk of Revelation

But one moment of revelation above all tests the adequacy of conceiving it as symbolic communication, and that is the cross of Jesus. No account of God's address to the world can hold our attention unless it also offers some understanding of this central fact in Christian experience: the cross standing at the center of all our worship as the sign of our salvation.

We construct our theologies too soon if we do not allow their primordial symbols to claim our imagination and freedom. Without true meditation on the cross, the truth of revelation will seem too easy. And it will not satisfy the mounting sense of historical relativity and the horror of human suffering that mark our late twentieth century.[29] To address the growing skepticism of a relativisitic world, Christian faith must be centered on the moment in its confession which is utterly particular in reference and yet universal in appeal. To live compassion for people who are struggling not to forget the Holocaust but also to avert nuclear disaster, faith must know how to speak of God's word at the darkest and most helpless place. With Christ on the cross we have that word, the embodied story of how close God comes to time, the imagining of the event through which eternity, seeded in the human heart, begins to bear its fruit.

Indeed the cross remarkably unites both event and word, story and symbol, the concrete and the universal. As the most indisputable fact about the life of Jesus, namely, that he went to a criminal's death in consequence of a mission accepted from God, it represents an event whose full salvific meaning appears only through the living interpretation of confessing disciples. With the cross, the form and spirit of revelation, its outer expression and inner life coincide. Through this dynamic symbol, uniquely referring to the time of Calvary and to all of time, God's care for the world is expressed in an utterly personal, historical way that nevertheless allows the most diverse appropriations and interpretations by martyrs and contemplatives, artists and social reformers. Although situated at an entirely particular time and place, the cross has shown its power for every time and place. It calls all men and women to its foot, first for them to see who else is gathered there and then to look up on the one whom they have crucified.

How can this symbol have such a dynamic effect? Because it embodies a word which is at once God's word, addressing all of time, and our word, asking for the truth of our lives. With the cross the contrast between saving historical event and prophetic interpretation is superseded. Here the prime analogue for revelation becomes more than the prophetic word which illuminates the divine action; here God's own personal Word, incarnate in Jesus, reaches into the darkest depth of the human situation, from which only a redeeming Creator can rescue him.[30] The cross is not raised simply as a response to individual questions of meaning, nor even in response to a people's cry for justice. Rather, it is lifted up so that all things—heart and history, story and science, every human achievement and suffering—may be drawn through Christ to God.

"Human history" may be the most adequate category to express the full range of the action of the cross. In the previous section I offered a qualification on that view, suggesting that no one expression of human activity—history, science and technology, or art—can satisfactorily summarize it, but only all of them together. If we understand revelation as symbolic communication, furthermore, we may give full weight to its unfolding in history without neglecting its other manifestations, for example, in myth and poetry. But in any case, when we ask what the full scope of revelation is, the symbol of the cross will always remind us that revelation is an *action* that involves us ultimately. Revelation has variously been understood as illumination and self-disclosure, judgment or promise, a call to conversion or the beginning of a transformation. But the cross above all expresses the salvific truth that we must lose our lives to save them. The cross is at once the central and most practical symbol of Christianity, claiming our freedom and imagination for its living truth and embracing us in the new world it effects. If any historical or artistic symbol possesses us more than we possess it, then surely it is the cross of Christ.[31]

This final, practical truth of revelation is the other side of the questions about divinity and humanity that we discussed earlier. There we saw that God's word in Jesus reverses and radicalizes the questions we suppose we have about God and ourselves. Now we may recognize that when the crucified Jesus asks us who we think he is, we are not far from finally hearing his new command of love. The more we recognize him truly, the closer we come to his self-sacrificing love for God and humankind in one. His is a word of risk that we cannot hear without being drawn to do it as well. Karl Rahner's theology of this unitary love of God and neighbor applies to both the incarnation and the passion.[32] Other theologians have emphasized that Christian faith must always have a double dimension of "political" care for human welfare and "mystical" contemplation of God's glory. But whatever one's theology, the cross will always be a summons to recognize that we trust our fellow human beings most effectively by entrusting ourselves to God entirely.

The question and command of which I am speaking address our imagination as much as our intelligence and freedom. When God questions our lives through Christ and calls us to love, we hear the address in particular statements of Scripture, to be sure, but we sense still more a whole new way of life, the advent of a redeemed world. In the synoptic Gospels, it is called the kingdom of God; in Saint John's Gospel, eternal life; in the letters of Saint Paul, new creation and life in Christ. But always it is entered only by the narrow way of the cross.

The symbolic communication of revelation thus involves practice and risk. God's word to the world is an action. Only because it is wrought by the true and costly disclosure of God's love can salvation mean the liberation of human love. *Living this revelation* that we have been given is far more than simply applying it to our lives. It means *letting it be*, again and again, for ourselves and the world. The cross will remain the great question for us: Will we let the suffering of our time turn us to the passion of Jesus, or will we seek to sustain our griefs on our own?

In this sense, the cross is the center for a process of continual conversion, the fulcrum for a new way of living that originates with God's word offered lovingly to the world. In the dialogue between time's origin and its course, revelation is symbolic action as well as communication.

The Future of Revelation

If the cross is the clearest expression of revelation as symbolic communication and action, still the whole truth of revelation is not told until the resurrection of

Jesus is proclaimed. Catholic thought has sometimes in the past moved too quickly to its theology of glory. Today liberation theologians as well as critics of religion refuse to allow the ideology of "another world" to serve as a palliative for the poverty and injustice suffered by so many human beings in this world.[33] But the full scope of any Christian theology is only stated when it reflects Saint Paul's hope to "gain Christ, and be found in him, . . . that I may know him and the power of his resurrection, and may share his sufferings, becoming like him in his death, that if possible I may attain the resurrection from the dead" (Phil 3:8–9, 10–11). Without recommending resignation or passivity before the work of being human, Paul nevertheless insists that whatever we do to shape our earth in the image of its Creator, still our hope is finally in God alone, who works the redemption of all that happens in our story through joining it with the risen Christ.

Biblical theology helps us to hear the message of resurrection in all its richness. Christian doctrine recalls its proclamation and interpretation through the ages. Systematic theology tries to express it in today's language. But the foundational question about the meaning and credibility of God's self-revelation must also be qualified in a final way by the primordial confession of Jesus' eternal life. The revelation of God, which is sealed in the passion, death, and resurrection of Jesus, is at the same time a revelation of the new creation God is working through Christ in the Holy Spirit. As with the idea of revelation itself, this transcendent goal is not a truth to which we can argue with purely rational means. But neither is it an opaque statement *imposed* upon us. First and foremost, it is an appeal to our imagination to see the world in a new way, so that with intelligent responsibility we may labor for the reign of God in it. Revealing the mystery of our own lives and of the God from whom they come, revelation opens us to God even beyond the time in which we receive it.

The word of God gives us our true future. There is no blessing simply in having one's "calendar" predicted. Nor can revelation give us a true future if it is only a provisional communication of God's care, to be supplemented by future revelations or further truths. For God's word to be authentically *saving*, it must assure us unmistakably that our world is indeed addressed by God's own life and that our response will enter materially into the outcome of the dialogue. This is precisely what the church confesses when it says that "there is one God, and there is one mediator between God and human beings, the man Christ Jesus, who gave himself as a ransom for all" (1 Tim 2:5–6). At an entirely particular time and place the love that bears and embraces the world has made itself unmistakably present. At a singular point in history the astonishing hope was born that just as Jesus lived and died into the holy mystery of an ever-watchful God, so too runs the course of the world of which he is the "first fruits" (1 Cor 15:20). That hope in no way cancels other hopes that arise in human hearts. On the contrary, it can certify and purify them all.[34]

Thoughtful people may rightly ask whether the revelation that is "complete" in Christ continues after him. They may wonder how to relate the particular revelation attested by Scripture and God's universal presence in the world and its history. They may ask, too, whether the "private" revelations of holy lives add to the "public revelation" entrusted to the church for authentic teaching. But these and other such distinctions are secondary in comparison with the realization that if God is indeed revealed to us in time, then time is also revealed, "unveiled" to eternity.

Sometimes this "opening" of time is understood as referring to what is "above" time. Then revelation is said to have "come down" to us, and God's initiative in self-revelation is interpreted as a descent. But this spatial metaphor is only one among many that are possible. It is equally true to say that God's word comes to us from the depth of our being, or in the forgiveness of our sin, or through the empowerment of our love; in the restoration of a broken people, for the guarantee of human dignity, through the overthrow of despotic authority. The truth of the gospel into which the Holy Spirit leads us, in other words, has no adequate analogue except human life itself.[35] And that life, as I have suggested above, is both a history we enact in the course of time and a work of art we daily create.

Most radically, revelation gives us our future because it is the communication of God's life itself—our absolute future, as Karl Rahner liked to say. The prospect of that fulfillment works within all our imaginings and activities, lifting them up, healing them, guiding and refining them. When a people struggles for the fundamental conditions of justice and dignity or when a culture strains to recover its spiritual identity, it is the hope of a home with God that will call forth their deepest truth; the promise of dwelling with God will inspire their truest freedom.

In a real sense, then, we may say that there will never be an end to the revelation that accompanies every created act of God and that becomes, as it redeems us, a share in God's own life. Looking to Jesus Christ, crucified and risen as one of us and one with God, we may dare to say that *we are God's dialogue with time*, the living language God lets be so that it may share eternity. Or, in the conciliar terms of Vatican II's Constitution on Revelation: "Just as the life of the Church grows through persistent participation in the Eucharistic mystery, so we may hope for a new surge of spiritual vitality from intensified veneration for God's word, which 'lasts forever' (Is 40:8; cf. 1 Pet 1:23–25)" (DV 26).

In this essay we have first asked whether it is we who raise questions about God or God who calls us in question. Since rationalist and Enlightenment thought had challenged the very possibility of revelation, we considered the forms in which it is expressed and the sense in which the various modes of revelation point to a single life within them. Then we tested our idea of revelation as symbolic communication by relating it practically to the experience of the cross and to the promise of resurrection. None of our assertions stands on reason alone. But if together they shape a view of human life in conversation with God, and grounded in God's love, then room has been made for God's word to work its way.

Then too, perhaps, the sense of life I have tried to communicate will harmonize with Vincent van Gogh's great late painting of the reaper in the wheat field. There Paul Gauguin's sometime friend, self-admitted to a mental hospital, could still imagine the world as an undulating buttery field of yellow wheat through which a reaper works his way, intimating the harvest of death and yet peacefully suggesting that the outcome will be blessed. Van Gogh could not, alas, sustain his own personal existence through his art, which has so immeasurably enriched the lives of others. But as Christians we are blessed to believe that the word of God is still greater art, and possesses lasting power in time, "for the salvation of all who believe" (Rom 1:16).

Recommended Readings

For several chapters in this book it will be useful to review *Dei Filius*, the First Vatican Council's Dogmatic Constitution on the Catholic Faith (1870), and *Dei Verbum*, the Second Vatican Council's Dogmatic Constitution on Divine Revelation (1965). The former can be found in *The Christian Faith in the Doctrinal Documents of the Catholic Church*, edited by J. Neuner, S. J., and J. Dupuis, S. J., rev. ed. (New York: Alba, 1982); the latter in *The Documents of Vatican II*, ed. by Walter M. Abbott, S. J. (New York: America, 1966).

Dulles, Avery. *Models of Revelation.* Garden City, NY: Doubleday, 1983. A survey of modern theologies of revelation and a constructive presentation of Dulles's own method of symbolic realism.

Niebuhr, H. Richard. *The Meaning of Revelation.* New York: Macmillan, 1941. An eloquent neo-orthodox essay on the starting point, historical context, method, and content of revelation.

Rahner, Karl. "History of the World and Salvation History," in *Theological Investigations 5*, pp. 97–114. Baltimore: Helicon, 1966, and "Profane History and Salvation History," in *Theological Investigations 21*, pp. 3–15. New York: Crossroad, 1988. Middle and late essays in which Rahner discusses the distinction between profane history and the history of salvation.

Ricoeur, Paul. "Toward a Hermeneutic of the Idea of Revelation." In *Essays on Biblical Interpretation*, edited with an introduction by Lewis S. Mudge, pp. 73–118. Philadelphia: Fortress, 1980. Seeks "to recover a concept of revelation *and* a concept of reason that, without ever coinciding, can at least enter into a living dialectic and together engender something like an understanding of faith" (p. 73).

Faith in the God of Jesus Christ

Brian O. McDermott

God's revelation in history involves a human response in history, a response called faith. Revelation and faith are two sides of the one dynamic relationship between God and creatures, so it is appropriate that we turn our attention to the relationship of believers to the God revealed in Jesus Christ. We will begin by looking at the place or milieu where faith flourishes and then examine the process of coming to faith, the dimensions of living the faith, and the relationship between faith and unbelief.

The "Place" of Faith

Christians bear the name they do because they belong to, believe in, and share the mission of Jesus Christ. They believe in someone who lived in Palestine almost two thousand years ago, someone they proclaim died and was raised by God from the dead and lives now in the glory of God never to die again. This Jesus is no longer visible. He cannot be found among the physically existing human beings of our experience. There was a time when he was one of our number, or, better said, one of the number of his contemporaries. But we cannot encounter him that way now, and Christians who profess that they belong to Christ and believe in Christ are making a rather unusual assertion.

When a husband and wife say that they belong to one another, or parents say that about their children, such belonging has flesh and bones to it. Such people have nourished their relationship over time by face-to-face interaction, and even when they are forced by work or other reasons to be absent from each other their mutual belonging relies on the time spent in close, physical contact with each other.

Stressing the physical interaction between people who belong to each other does not imply by any means that one person's belonging to another is reducible to the physical. Nor does true belonging of one person to another involve one person's becoming the property of another, or one person's trying to control the other. Authentic belonging to other persons grows as we are able to let the other persons *be* themselves, giving them space to flourish as well as being open to the

46

gifts they can offer us. Belonging to someone involves allowing oneself to be known as associated with, a friend of, in special relationship with x or y. "She's Jim's wife" or "He's going with Paula." When I belong to someone I willingly enter into the sphere of influence of that person, I expose myself to another's values and view of the world. Belonging to someone, I begin to recognize the goals that person is striving for and to learn about that person's past, the past that has shaped the person as I presently know him or her.

Ordinarily, a Christian belonging to Christ involves a belonging to the church.[1] We may also say that Christians are followers of Christ through being members of the faith community. Whether born into the faith, as the vast majority of Christians in the United States are, or converted to the faith, followers of Christ are members of a community. The belonging to Christ "shows up" in the world and ordinary life as a belonging to a community, being a member of the church. This is not to say that faith in Christ is simply identical with membership in the church, viewed sociologically or theologically. But the most obvious "face" of faith in Christ is this belonging to a group called the church.

Why? Because the crucified and risen Jesus Christ in whom Christians profess faith continues his presence in the world in and through the church which believes in him and follows him. We cannot see Jesus' individual body, or hear his voice, or ask him questions and physically hear his answers in ordinary conversation. Any belonging to Jesus Christ that is possible for us today will ordinarily involve our having to do with the church, hearing its voice, watching and participating in its behavior, joining in its profession of faith and praying its prayer.

Belonging to the church acquires its deeper significance from the fact that Christians believe in the God of Jesus Christ through believing the church and believing in the church. Christians' faith in God and in God's incarnate Word does not descend, as it were, from God upon the individual. The church's witness, preaching, and activity nurture the faith that the Spirit plants in each individual's heart. We come to be believers through the activity of the church, whether it be our parents' faith, that of a friend, or a parish's faith. We learn our prayers from the church, we participate in the celebration of the church's sacraments, we are nourished by God's word and instructed by the church's teaching. Our faith is formed by the church, supported and challenged by the community. Thus the church is the milieu, the home or "place" of our faith.

The church exists by the grace of God offered in Christ. The life, death, and resurrection of Jesus culminated in the sending of the Holy Spirit upon the disciples that marked the birth of the church. The church lives through the saving act of God and our faith lives by that same grace. From another perspective, the church exists through the faith of believers, not in the sense that they create the church but in the sense that if there were no faith there would be no church (and vice versa). The church is not some entity existing apart from believers and their faith; it consists precisely in the fellowship of believers.[2]

Believers are persons of faith *because* of the church as well. The church is sinful, broken, unfaithful, at times excessively bureaucratic or downright mediocre, to be sure. But the one church is also the work of the Holy Spirit (the "holy church"). It can be relied upon to speak God's word, proclaim who Christ is, witness in the power of the Spirit. The reliability of the church in its teaching regarding faith and the conduct of Christian life ("morals") is ultimately due to the Holy Spirit's guidance of the community.

Christians do not believe in the church the way they believe in God the Father, Jesus Christ, or the Holy Spirit. The triune God is the ultimate and only "object" of full faith, that is, the One who can rightfully receive our full self-surrender. It is only to God that we creatures may surrender ourselves totally. Neither another human being nor the church may be the object of faith in this total sense. An ancient baptismal question indirectly states the matter succinctly and correctly: "Do you believe in the Holy Spirit in the holy church for the resurrection of the body?"[3] In other words, we are called to give ourselves over to (believe in) the Holy Spirit totally, that Spirit who works most explicitly within the church to renew and fulfill all things (a fulfillment which Christian faith expresses in terms of the resurrection of the body).

We do not see Jesus Christ or God, but through the faith that is invited, nourished, and supported by the community of believers, Christians are able to enter into relationship with the risen Jesus and the God whom he reveals.

In belonging to and believing in the God of Jesus Christ through belonging to and believing in the church, Christians also experience themselves called to share in Christ's mission. The focus of the mission of the church is basically the same as Christ's mission in his earthly life: proclaiming and preparing the reign of God. Christians participate in Christ's mission through their participation in the church's mission. The reign of God is that decisive act by which God acts as God on behalf of the created world. The reign of God formed the center of Jesus' proclamation and activity while he lived on earth.[4] He did not preach himself nor did he ask people to turn all their attention to himself. Jesus referred people to the God who was seeking to break upon the world in Jesus' activity.

Through parables Jesus turned the world upside down—the good Samaritan, the betrayed Father who goes out to wait for the son to return, the mustard seed that becomes a spacious tree. He provoked people to take a fresh stance toward God and to allow God's action, rendered present in the parable, to uncover and discover them.

Jesus spoke with authority and called people to a more radical, person-oriented understanding of the law. He cured the sick and spoke words of forgiveness. He called people into a relationship of discipleship with himself with an astonishing authority. All these activities—preaching, teaching, parable-making, healing, forgiving, calling into discipleship—are activities of both Jesus and the church.

What is the difference? Besides the fact that the members of the church are not identical with Jesus of Nazareth of two thousand years ago, the situation for the church now and for Jesus then is different. Jesus preached the reign of God and anticipated its benefits in his healings, acts of forgiveness, and challenges to the religious authorities of his time. But that reign did not occur in any definitive way through those activities. Only in and through his death and resurrection did the reign definitively happen as an irrevocable dimension of human history. Jesus' own acceptance of God's reign was the way it arrived among us, and that acceptance did not come to completion except in and through the totality of his life into death.[5] In the period of the church, Christians give living witness to the power of God's reign now definitely at work among us. That reign is the presence and activity of Christ in the world to which the presence and activity of the church witnesses—without ever circumscribing it.

Those who believe in Christ and who belong to the church thus share in Christ's mission in a situation different from Christ's before his death. But Christians differ from Christ in another way as well. They are redeemed sinners who need to be drawn further into Christ's paschal mystery through experiences of forgiveness and healing. Jesus during his life and now in glory was not and is not a forgiven sinner but the perfect bearer of the Spirit, the one who was rooted so completely in God as Abba that all he did and said reflected and expressed that relationship with Abba.[6]

Christians share in the church's mission insofar as they are drawn into witnessing to the reign of God in human affairs through personal example, through active service of their brothers and sisters, and more broadly, through the promotion of justice and peace in our world. They let that witness be nourished by corporate and personal prayer, sacramental worship, and openness to the Holy Spirit's guidance in their lives.

Belonging, believing, sharing in mission: These are three principal ways by which the Christian believer relates to the God of Jesus Christ by relating to the church.

Coming to Faith

Christian faith is not an eternal reality, although it bears on the eternal reality who is God, Creator of all. Nor is Christian faith something fixed and stable in itself, although it comforts many believers by giving them a firmness and courage when all else in their lives seems to fail them. The faith of Christian believers lives and moves in history, capable of growth and decline. It can assume the focus of one's consciousness or move to the periphery. It can become more determinative of our way of thinking and feeling, our loving and deciding in our world, or it can become a shadow and mere memory of past conviction.

The ways one comes to Christian faith, or to more mature Christian faith, are varied. One can be born into the faith in the double sense of being born of Catholic parents and then baptized and raised in the faith through formal and informal Christian education. In this situation an individual and indeed family can go through life without any major crises, depending on their own personal stories and the kind of support or incentive the surrounding community and culture provides them. Some people's faith develops or unfolds in tune with their own developing psyches, moving from childhood through adolescence into mid-life and old age without any apparent dramatic moments or periods of radical reorientation or recommitment.

The famous psychologist William James would call these people once-born believers; they proceed on their way with a quiet and firm conviction in the midst of the church community.[7] These people do not need to look for fresh evidence of Christianity or Christ's claim to assure their minds or hearts of the truth and believability of the Christian message. The faith functions for them more like the air they breathe or the ground they walk on than like a problem to be focused on or a question to be pursued.

For these people the life journey basically affirms and confirms their faith relationship to Christ and the church. They accept the church's teaching that faith is a gift freely given by God and wonder at times why they have received the gift while others, apparently, have not. The intellectual reflection they have absorbed from others, the spiritual sustenance that helps them in time of difficulty or transitions, the moral life that gives a sense of direction to their lives, all these come together to convey a sense of truthfulness, coherence, and consistency to their lives. Any thought of seriously calling the church of Christ into question or leaving it would seem like an invitation to betray themselves.

Others who are born into the faith do not find faith supported by their environment. They may find themselves assailed by serious doubts or experience crises of meaning such as the sudden death of a loved one.[8] Perhaps a cynicism or skepticism from the world around them insinuates itself into their faith, or they become more critical about what we can know and how we know it. It may be the increasingly secular and technological character of our understanding of things that forces new reflection on one's faith.[9] However it may happen, the result is that the faith of such people cannot be a simple process of unfolding or development but calls for examination of evidence, a risk of deeper commit-ment, a search for resources for greater trust. Unless some kind of "coming to faith" occurs in a new way, their faith could well weaken and atrophy.

The ways by which people with such threatened faith may come to deeper faith are many, depending on the personality of the believer and the kind of crisis affecting the faith. For some the most important challenge is to examine the beginning of Christianity and the life of Jesus, the veracity of the gospels, or the signs of Christ's relationship to the church through a consideration of its history. Perhaps one's understanding of God, particularly in relation to free human beings and the suffering and injustice that mark so much of human history, needs to be the focus of reflection. The reality of Jesus Christ as the personal unity of God's definitive self-gift to humanity and humanity's full-bodied acceptance of that gift may be what needs exploration and clarification.

For others it will be personal religious experience that must go deeper. The experience of God and Jesus Christ in prayer, both personal and communal, may be the arena where more will be ventured, if they are fortunate to receive help to do so. Having heard "about" God and Jesus from others they may not be able to appreciate that their knowledge of and relationship with God and Jesus can deepen through prayer. Another way in which people in such a crisis may deepen their faith is by trusting themselves to Jesus' way of witness and service to others, struggling for peace and justice in the world in the Spirit of Jesus. By following Jesus in conscious and deepened discipleship they can hope to come to know and love him more maturely and authentically.[10]

Sometimes even when one has attempted to deepen one's conviction through study and critical reflection, to increase one's personal relationship with God through prayer and discipleship in the following of Jesus, the darkness does not lift; rather one feels abandoned, alone, and lost. It may be necessary for such people to remain faithful to their commitments, the duties of their state of life, and let themselves be carried, as it were, by the rituals and prayer of the larger church community, trusting that God will visit the darkness and change it from burden to blessing.[11]

Coming to faith has received much attention in recent years in terms of evangelization, the propagation of the faith to nonbelievers or those estranged from the faith.[12] Ways have been explored and discussed by which the church through her members might reach out to those in American society who are unchurched or who, because of some unhappy experience, no longer participate in church life. The primary approach involves communicating the message of the gospel in as clear and forthright a way as possible, particularly the good news of God's unconditional love, the humanity of Jesus as the most reliable revelation of God's reality, and the Holy Spirit's action in the church and world. The aim is to focus on the values and the life that the church as institution is meant to serve, since many departures from the faith involve clashes of personality, disagreement over law or doctrine in church life.

Evangelization seeks conversion of the nonbeliever or the half-believer. Conversion in the area of faith cannot be equated with the development or unfolding of the human personality. This is the case not only because God's grace, God's own life and love communicated to human beings, far exceeds in value and being the structure and dynamisms of the human psyche, but because development as ordinarily understood by psychologists is a process of maturation in which the person moves from one level of functioning to another (say, from adolescence to young adulthood) without consciously choosing the transition. The changes that occur in the ordinary growth of the human psyche from stage to stage appear to many scholars to be structurally natural to the human person, given the proper internal and external conditions.[13]

Conversion, on the other hand, involves more than structural unfolding. Conversion is marked by a person's conscious appropriation of growth. If the conversion is intellectual, then the individual assumes responsibility for all intellectual operations; if moral, the person chooses to respond to values because of their intrinsic goodness and not merely the subjective satisfaction they may offer. If the conversion is religious and Christian, then the converted person chooses to view the world of fact and value in the perspective opened up by the experience of being unconditionally loved by God and responding "in kind" to the gracious God's self-offer.[14]

Christian religious conversion involves both conscious and unconscious motives, influences, and changes. Because Christian faith is a response of persons from their center to the self-communicating God, all the personal dimensions of body, mind, will, and affections are brought into play. To the notion of development conversion further adds the engagement of the individual's freedom in response to God's self-offer. The Catholic tradition has maintained that the act of faith in the revealing God must be a responsible or prudent act as well as free (not coerced), an act ultimately made possible by God's illuminating and inspiring grace.

The tradition appeals to the role of signs in people's coming to faith to clarify the free—yet responsible—character of the assent of faith. A sign functions as a pointer or representative for a reality that is distinct from the sign. In faith a sign offers partial evidence for the truth and meaningfulness of faith, but the reality ultimately assented to, namely, the living God revealed in Jesus Christ and the Holy Spirit, is infinitely more than the finite signs that partially disclose that ultimate reality. There are external, or publicly available, signs which can invite and aid reason to offer assent to the truth revealed by God. Such signs are the holiness of the saints and the church, the ways in which Jesus Christ fulfilled the promises made in the Old Testament, and the good contributed to the human family by Christians.

Internal signs of the believability of Christian revelation show themselves within our consciousness, for example, the understanding of human nature offered by Christianity, the sense of reverence for the created world instilled by Christianity at its best, the feeling of peace and consolation and coherence when assenting to the truth of Christianity.

These signs of God's revelation—both external and internal—are not of such a nature that they compel the assent of the mind or commitment of the will and heart, but they are indications of Christianity's truth and validity. Just as in a human relationship one only truly and fully knows the lovability of someone else by letting oneself love him or her, so too one appreciates the credibility of Christian revelation in a satisfying way only when one *ventures* the surrender of self to the self-revealing God.[15]

Evangelization, in an extended sense of the word, can apply to the effort to bring Christians from a culturally mediated faith (from family or community) to a subjectively mediated one, that is, a faith that is the free response stemming from the person's own responsibility for his or her own relationship to ultimate reality and value.

Since the Second Vatican Council new attention has been given to the way adult converts should be initiated into the faith. This renewal forms part of the wide-ranging liturgical renewal of the church, with a deepened appreciation of the ancient church's concern to lead people into the faith through a graduated series of rites, instruction, and religious experiences. The program of initiation is called the Rite of Christian Initiation for Adults (RCIA), and it has proven to be a fruitful source for reflection on the meaning of adult Christian conversion and membership in the church.

In the RCIA catechumens, as they are called, are gradually led into an appreciation of the sacramental and doctrinal dimensions of the faith, all with a view to helping them enter into a lifelong path of discipleship of Christ as a Roman Catholic Christian. One of the strengths of this program of initiation is that it emphasizes the symbolic dimensions of the faith in relation to the catechetical and doctrinal so that the formative influence of the program touches the affective as well as intellectual and moral aspects of the person.[16]

Living the Relationship That Is Faith

Because every human being and every relationship involve the unity of body and spirit, faith has an embodiment or form and a spirit to it as well. Neither of them can be separated from the other when they are both truly alive. Yet we will need to consider first one, then the other, so that we can give each dimension its due.

The Forms of Faith

The Christian community embodies itself in a visible way most emphatically when it celebrates the Eucharist, the memorial of the passion and death of Jesus in which that saving event is rendered present and effective for the participants by its being expressed as Jesus asked that it be expressed. The way the Eucharist is celebrated today shows both continuity and change in relation to its celebration in the early centuries of the church's life or even just prior to the reforms of the Second Vatican Council. Over the many centuries there remains a basic dynamism to the Eucharist: the church proclaims God's word, the community brings forward its gifts, the Spirit transforms them, and then the gifts are returned to the community to be shared among them. This is an embodiment or form of our faith, a way of proceeding with God in Christ that is enacted time and again whenever Eucharist is celebrated.

People come to the Eucharist in varying moods and attitudes of mind and let themselves enter a flow of life that is liturgy. They do not reinvent it each time nor are they called to be passive spectators in relation to it. Rather, they are invited by the call to worship at the beginning and the proclamation of the word which follows to participate in the power of the dynamic that Christ's life, death, and resurrection have provided for the community. This is an example of tradition in its most vital form.[17] Liturgy is a process of prayer and worship in which the Christian community as a group and as individual persons are borne into the central thrust of the church's life. By listening, carrying gifts forward, standing in prayer around the alter with the priest, and receiving the gifts now transformed, the community gives body to its faith, its belongings, its believing, and its participation in the mission of the church.

Each of the seven sacraments involves the word of God proclaimed and the offering of gifts (one's self for baptism, for example, or one's desire for forgiveness and confession of sins in reconciliation, or one's growing maturity in the faith in confirmation). Through the church Christ blesses the gifts and makes them fruitful for the community. Liturgy, the church's public and official sacramental worship, is a privileged form of Christian faith, for here the church says who it is to itself and to the world but most centrally to the God who draws the community into new and more abundant life.

While liturgy is a privileged expression of Christian faith, there are other forms as well. The creed, or Profession of Faith that Christians recite within the liturgy or apart from it is an ancient statement of the basic faith of the church. There are many creeds but the most frequently used one comes from the Councils of Nicaea in 325 and Constantinople in 381. The creed brings together a number of beliefs that express various dimensions of the faith: God as Creator, the incarnation, the life, death and resurrection of Jesus for our salvation, the sending of the Spirit and the role of the church, the consummation of all things in the resurrection of the body and life everlasting. The creeds Christians usually use in public worship are ancient ones, but that has not prevented modern-day theologians from proposing briefer, more contemporary professions of faith.

The forms of faith vary greatly, from church architecture to grace before and after meals; from agencies of the church, such as the papacy and the U. S. bishops' conference, to the teachings which proceed from them; from rituals such as blessing oneself with the sign of the cross to praying the Liturgy of the Hours; from actions such as sheltering the homeless or feeding the hungry to uniting one's unavoidable suffering with the suffering of Christ. To be sure, all these forms can become mere externals, devoid of any heart or spirit, but when they are truly forms of faith, they express in space and time the tradition of faith into which Christians were baptized, a tradition that is a process of transmission of the faith created and sustained by the Holy Spirit and by those who, adult in their faith, are called to pass it on to the next generation.

History also shapes the form of faith. Just as there are constants with regard to form (the Eucharist and other sacraments, the creeds, certain traditional prayers, the works of mercy), so there is the shape, style, or form that faith possesses, depending on the particular period in history when it flourished. Avery Dulles, for example, has identified seven changing forms of faith: Old Testament, New Testament, patristic, medieval scholastic, Lutheran, existential, and contemporary.[18] Each of these ways of believing in the God of Jesus Christ in the context of the church grew out of the historic needs and opportunities of its epoch, involving intellectual, affective, aesthetic, and religious elements. Each form of faith has something lasting to offer Christians of later ages. Yet each form is limited just as the respective culture was limited. Only certain ways of seeing the world and its relation to God were possible for the people of that particular cultural epoch.

Another way of viewing the forms of faith in addition to the public, external forms and the cultural, historical forms is the distinction between Western and Eastern churches, where the differences in liturgy, prayer, architecture, and church policy express different Christian and Catholic sensibilities at work over the centuries. We can expect an increase in forms of faith as we witness the emergence of Catholic Christianity in the so-called Third World countries of Africa, Asia, and Latin America. Coming into their own voice and giving expression to their Christian faith in their own distinctive ways, they are contributing to a World Church that is more than a church in which the West holds sway.[19]

Yet a further manner of considering the forms of faith is the distinction between sacramental faith and prophetic faith. Insofar as faith is sacramental it is aware of and responsive to the already offered presence of God through the humanity of Jesus, the shared life, symbols and doctrines of the church, and the goodness of creation. Sacramental faith is attuned to the presence of God already at work in nature and in the beneficial accomplishments of human civilization and culture. The God of sacramental faith is Emmanuel, God-with-us. A poet like Gerard Manley Hopkins gave all his life and talent to exploring and expressing the sacramental character of life. Insofar as Christian faith is prophetic it is alert and responsive both to God's word as challenging the community to further the reign of God that has not yet fully conquered sin and evil and to the ways the latter work themselves out in personal and social history. Prophetic faith feels keenly the ways in which God has not yet arrived among God's people. It suffers the absence of God's justice and peace in our world and works, prays, and longs for the God-who-is-to-come. Martin Luther King and Dorothy Day each in their own way devoted themselves to fostering the justice and peace that God longs to bring about in *our* time.

Authentic Christian faith must be both sacramental and prophetic, but, depending on the gifts of nature and grace operative in people and communities, the form of faith may emphasize one dimension more than the other.[20]

The Spirit of Faith

Christian faith has a habitation and a name. The habitation is the church and the name is Jesus Christ. Faith has a body as well, not only in the sense that it is found living in the members of the social body called the church, but inasmuch as it has all the kinds of external expression we have reviewed above. Ritual, language, doctrine, institutions, sacraments are spatio-temporal realities that are public forms of the faith.

But faith has a body and a soul, flesh and spirit. The externals of living faith are not merely externals, they are the expression, the coming-to-be, of the interior of faith.

The gift of faith comes from God in Christ through the working of the Holy Spirit. Because faith is our response to God's self-communication to us by which we participate in God's relation to God's own life, the ultimate dynamic principle at the root of our faith is God as responder to the abundance of divine life, that is, the Holy Spirit. The Spirit is the divine self-acceptance in person, the fully adequate, joyous, loving welcome of the divine truth and life in person. The Holy Spirit poured forth into the hearts of believers affects their minds and hearts in such a way that they begin to resonate to the life of God and the values of Jesus Christ. Classical theologians such as Saint Thomas Aquinas have called this growing resonance a process of connaturalizing, whereby we come to know and love the things of God, draw nourishment from God's revelation of divine truth and love, and experience our neighbors and God's good creation as lovable because created by God and gifted by the divine self-communication.[21]

God's self-communication to persons is the most intimate exchange of life possible. God is the Creator and Gift-er of the human person, and no finite reality is able to touch the human mind, heart, freedom, and affections the way God can. God can transform the core of the person and at the same time respect him or her. An axiom of Catholic theology, which admittedly sounds very paradoxical, is that the more God becomes the source and principle of human activity the more that activity flows from the human person.[22]

The Holy Spirit is the divine gift that works faith in Christian believers. The Spirit is the soul of faith. The human spirit is changed by the gift of the Spirit, not in the sense that it becomes a member of a different species but because it begins to walk a path of conversion, discipleship, and mission. Faith, it has been said, involves three dimensions: conviction, commitment, and trust, "a firm conviction regarding what is supremely important, dedication or commitment to that which one believes in, and trustful reliance on the power and goodness of that to which one stands committed."[23] Faith thus involves the intellect, the will, and the affections—all three "elevated" and purified by the gift of living faith.

The Spirit convinces the believer that the gospel and God's revelation are true. Such conviction emerges not through argumentation or reasoning, although, as we saw earlier, these have their proper place in the realm of faith. It occurs most deeply through the power of grace touching the intellect so that it can expand and deepen and then recognize and appreciate the infinite closeness and transcendence of the mystery of God. The human will is, at the same time, affected by grace so that it wants to share the life of God and live according to the values of the gospel. The affections, finally, begin a process of becoming the affections of Christ. In the risen Jesus God draws immeasurably close to human beings while remaining the holy, boundless One dwelling in "inaccessible light." Through the grace of the Holy Spirit the human spirit is in turn drawn toward the self-communicating God, so that the *drive* toward self-transcendence and *being drawn* into the life of God by grace become one movement of faith, wrought by God in the Holy Spirit and desired by the graced human spirit.

The Spirit and the forms of faith constitute a living unity in which the Spirit never becomes lost or simply merged among the forms. Nor do the forms become unimportant because of the Spirit. Rather the Spirit creates and enlivens the forms (the rituals, the prayers, the worship, the doctrine, the public and visible discipleship) so that they express, in young or mature ways, the Spirit's light and life and love, as the divine self-acceptance in person, shared fully with believers since Pentecost.

The most basic gift the Spirit offers is trust in the self-revealing God, a trust that forms the foundation for a full-bodied relationship with the Holy Mystery.

Faith as Relationship

Christian faith reaches out in loving trust and connects one with the God of Jesus Christ in the power of the Holy Spirit. Thus the ultimate structure of the act and virtue of faith is trinitarian. The divine power at work in us rendering us open to God's self-communication is the Holy Spirit. The Spirit knows the heart of God, what God treasures and values, and draws us into God's sense of things. With a bond that is stronger than death and sin, the Spirit unites the believer to God and to God's Jesus and to fellow believers.

Christian faith as an act and a habit of being relates us personally to Jesus Christ. As we have seen, this is a different kind of relationship than the ones we have with those we love who live with us in this world. We cannot encounter Jesus in the usual way now, for he has died and been raised into the glory of the Father. At the beginning of this chapter we discussed the fact that we are able to come into contact with Jesus through belonging to and believing in his church. At this point we can focus more specifically on the kind of personal relationship with Jesus that faith makes possible.

There are several dimensions to this relationship with Christ that can be viewed as a pattern. We deepen our relationship with Christ through prayer and praxis. In both these activities we let Chirst influence us by exposing our minds and hearts to his presence in the Spirit and conforming our actions and our sufferings to his.[24]

In prayer we let ourselves experience Christ's love for us as we seek liberation and healing from him in those places where we are broken and sinful. We dwell with the New Testament stories of his life, passion, death, and resurrection to let the Spirit of Christ refashion us in his image. Even though Jesus is not physically present with us now, he is present as the risen One. Becoming attuned to his presence in our life depends on our willingness to share our own feelings, desires, hopes, and fears with him, entrusting ourselves to the silence of his presence and listening for his presence to us in that silence. Even though there is a great difference between relating with Christ and relating with another who is physically present, there is a similarity as well. For just as presence to other persons is not ultimately attention to their face or hands or body but attention and response to the presence they offer us, so it is with prayer to Christ. Faith risks entrusting itself to that offered presence without prior proof that Christ is present to the pray-er. Only in the entrusting of oneself to that presence will there be a mysterious assurance that Christ is there to be trusted. Just as in relationship with those still alive and physically present you only know their love for you through extending trust to them and coming to know them truly in that trust, so we come to know Jesus in learning to believe in him.[25]

This believing in Christ in prayer finds nourishment and direction when we begin to live as Jesus lived. While the gospels do not give us the sort of biographical information about Jesus' earthly life that we would expect from a modern biography, the gospels do offer us a sense of Jesus' values and way of proceeding with people. Firmly rooted in God whom he called Abba, Jesus reached out to those who were oppressed by guilt, by illness, by social disgrace and marginalization. He offered them freedom and a sense of dignity before God and their neighbors. His words and actions were intended to be anticipating signs of the reign of God he preached. Christians come to know Jesus in faith when they enter into a prayer relationship with him but also when they follow him in discipleship, relating to their world in a way analogous to the way Jesus related to his.

Praxis is a word contemporary authors use to designate activity which seeks to transform the conditions of human life. Jesus' activity was praxis in this sense. Jesus did not simply contemplate the world in its beauty and ordinariness (although his parables let us know that he did do this); he sought to ignite people by challenging them in their cozy goodness, freeing them from the prison of disease, sending them out as adventurers on mission. He adapted himself to their needs while at the same time keeping as the focus of his ministry the saving reign of God.

We learn how to be disciples of Jesus not by slavish imitation of the stories about him in the gospels but by learning what discipleship in our own time and place require. We need to read and meditate on the gospels in the light of the signs of the times and can be helped in this, for example, by studying the church's teaching on peace and the economy and finding how to live in a way that is guided by that teaching. In chapter 10 more will be said about the living out of Christian existence, but now the point is that coming to know Jesus involves following him as his disciple as well as praying to him as his friend.[26]

Faith as Structure

When Christians relate to Jesus Christ and the God of Jesus Christ there are two dimensions to the structure of that faith—transcendence and beliefs. This duality flows from the very makeup of our human consciousness. At the root of the human intellect, will, and affections there lives a fundamental drive or thrust toward fuller life which some philosophers and theologians call self-transcendence. Self-transcendence is the dynamic process by which the human spirit seeks to go beyond what it already knows, loves and relishes, moving toward greater truth, life, love. I experience myself as a transcending self, called forward beyond my present limited situation of knowledge, love, and rela-tionships. God's self-communication as revelation and salvation reaches into that root of my human spirit and brings it within the sphere of the divine in a process which simultaneously makes me yet more human, more true to my own self. What God wants for me—for us—is what we most deeply want for our-selves.

The Christian experiences God as the ultimate goal of all striving and all desire, beyond all the concepts and images and words which are otherwise helpful and necessary in a fully human relationship with God. Theologians called God "the Holy Mystery" to suggest several things: that God cannot be grasped, encompassed by the human mind and heart; that God is infinitely rich in being and love so that for the believer God is always greater, always more than hitherto experienced; that God holds sway over human life and all creation as its source and term and is met best in love and worship, in joyful praise and service.[27]

As necessary as the transcendental dimension is the belief structure of faith, the many particular convictions which express in specific ways the content of one's faith. Not only does the Christian relate to God and Christ in faith but the Christian believes *that* God is good, or holy, the eternal Creator and Father or Mother of us all; the Christian is convinced *that* Christ forgives his or her sins, is head of his body, the church, is the liberator of oppressed people, is one person in two distinct but inseparable natures, and so on. For Christian faith to be human and historical it requires both these dimensions: the transcendental dimension (faith in its ultimate structure) and the dimension of beliefs (faith as expressed and lived in specific discernments and convictions). Both the ultimate faith relationship and the belief structure of faith undergo changes in the sense of deepening or deterioration or shift of horizon. It is impossible to have faith without beliefs and vice versa.

Faith and Unbelief

Traditional theology maintained that faith's assent was entirely certain. Look-ing to God as the revealer of that to which we assent, it emphasized that what we believe in is true and thus "objectively certain." In faith we rely on God's reliability. Naturally our trust in God and believing "on" God's word is open to growth. Personal reliance on God's truthfulness admits of degrees and is tradi-tionally called subjective certitude. Indeed, we can and must pray for greater trust in God's word as well as for the courage to embrace the mystery of God more than the fragmentary lights that illuminate our life's journey.

There can be times when a shift in beliefs through a process of doubting or outgrowing certain beliefs can suggest that one has lost one's relationship to God and Christ. Yet that need not be the case. In older Catholic theology, "doubt" was a term used to refer to deliberate rejection of Christian doctrine when the person knew the truth of the doctrine. But in more ordinary language "doubt" refers to a condition of mind that is often sincere and unavoidable and which can be an occasion for an individual to grow in conviction and commitment, provided that one meets the crisis with patience, prayer, and honest searching.[28] The light that faith offers us is a dark kind of light. The obscurity of faith rarely leaves us, and the holy men and women of history attest that the obscurity increases the more we surrender to God's ways in our lives and in the world. Doubts are thus inevitable and unavoidable as we follow the path God opens up for us in life. The crucial question is whether we let these doubts acquire a false power in our life, or bring them into our relationship with our God.

There are times when a denial of beliefs can seriously affect one's faith relationship with God and Christ. There have been times in the history of the church when certain beliefs were ruled incompatible with authentic communion with the church or authentic belief in Christ. Such beliefs or doctrinal positions are called heresy because they involve cutting oneself off from the church's mediation of God's truth. Not all statements, discernments, and convictions nourish and authentically express the fundamental faith relationship to Jesus Christ and his and our God. When the church declares that certain positions are heretical, it affirms that giving one's mind and heart to that way of thinking will lead one away from the primary faith relationship and possibly undo it.[29]

In the fourth century, for example, there was a strong sense among many Christians influenced by Middle Platonism that God could not become involved in human affairs and brokenness. It was thought that a mediator, someone less than God yet more than an ordinary creature, would come in God's place. Jesus Christ was supposed to have been this mediator. As God's Word he was a supercreature who became incarnated in Jesus' humanity. The church discerned this understanding of Jesus Christ and of the salvation effected by him and found it grievously wanting. In response to that view (called Arianism) the church affirmed at the Council of Nicaea that Jesus as Word was one in being with the Father and was fully divine. This doctrine of consubstantiality has imprinted itself in Christian faith ever since. But it was in relation to a specific challenge that this belief, or expression of faith, was formulated.

Traditional theology reminds us that faith is a necessary gift. Faith is absolutely necessary for salvation and is a supernatural act, that is, the work of the self-communicating God in us. Nothing can substitute for faith as a prerequisite for salvation, because faith is the way we participate in God's self-communication, salvation, and revelation. Living faith, as we said above, is the acceptance on our part of what God is offering us for salvation. Being necessary does not mean that we can or must produce the act of faith on our own. Faith is necessary, but it is also a supernatural gift; it is a gift that exceeds our powers and capabilities as creatures on our own and can come to us only by God's sharing of that divine life with us. We humans are indeed paradoxical beings. We are created for something we cannot come to by ourselves. We are made for that which only God can give to us as sheer gift.[30]

Sometimes Christians encounter people who consider themselves agnostics. These people do not want to take a position either for or against the belief that

God exists and is providentially involved in a divinely created world. Many Christian thinkers would maintain that such people can be very sincere. If they probed their own agnosticism, they might well find an ultimate concern in their lives that shows itself through their way of thinking and acting in relation to other humans. Atheists, on the other hand, are those who deny the existence of God and who try to live according to that conviction. Sometimes atheists are people who reject a false or very inadequate understanding of God, or who believe that a God's power would compete with human freedom; accordingly, they resolve to live in a godless world.[31] An Albert Camus, for example, was sensitive to the false gods that people have worshipped and preferred to serve humanity in a "godless" way rather than to give allegiance to "gods" that did not seem to have humankind's well-being in mind.

Conclusion

Christian faith is a journey. Like any journey it unfolds in time and moves toward a destination. Faith changes its shape at various junctures in human life, either because we humans pass through various stages of growth, or because of particular crises which confront us, or because God invites us into new and deeper life with the Holy Mystery.

Our image and understanding of God or of Jesus can undergo significant, even radical change in our lifetime, and yet our faith can deepen through such changes. There can be times when we do not think that we are still believers. Perhaps at such times we are learning to let go of underdeveloped or inadequate or even untrue images of the God our hearts are seeking. Surely times of loss can turn out to be seasons of purification, as we seek deeper trust in the revealing God and more adequate signs to guide our path.

For our way to God must be marked by signs and symbols. As long as we are living our earthly life they can be precious lights on a mysterious journey. In the next chapter let us turn our attention to the symbolic structure of faith and revelation.

Recommended Readings

Dulles, Avery. "Faith and Inquiry." In *The Survival of Dogma: Faith, Authority and Dogma in a Changing Church*, pp. 15–75. Garden City, NY: Doubleday, 1971. These chapters treat the relationship between Christian faith and religious inquiry, recasting some of the traditional concerns of apologetical theology.

Dunn, James D. G. *Jesus and the Spirit: A Study of the Religious and Charismatic Experience of Jesus and the First Christians as Reflected in the New Testament.* Philadelphia: Westminster, 1975. A comprehensive yet readable exploration of the role of the Holy Spirit in the life of Jesus and of the early church.

First Vatican Council, *Dei Filius*, Dogmatic Constitution on the Catholic Faith. In *The Christian Faith in the Doctrinal Documents of the Catholic Church*, edited by J. Neuner,

F I V E | Knowing by Heart: The Symbolic Structure of Revelation and Faith

Justin J. Kelly

Jesus sat down opposite the temple treasury and watched the crowd as people contributed their money; many rich folk put in large sums. And a poor widow came and put in two small coins worth about a penny. And he called his disciples around him and declared: "Believe me when I tell you that this poor widow has put in more than all the rest. For they all gave out of their abundance, but she out of her poverty has put in everything she had, her whole livelihood."

Mark 12:41–44

How can I know what I mean till I see what I say?

—Anonymous

This little episode from Mark's gospel may serve as well as more dramatic or didactic passages to illustrate the symbolic character of revelation. In it, Jesus highlights a small, momentary gesture and the person who makes it, and declares both to be of great worth. As he does so, he reveals himself, and the heart of God.

As Mark narrates the story, Jesus' "metaphorical eye" scans the crowd of people approaching the treasury, watching and waiting until one simple situation lights up for him. Then he calls his disciples around him and interprets what they have witnessed. As he speaks, the situation itself speaks to him: the woman and her deed become a living parable. The words he utters are not prepared in advance—part of a script written in heaven which Jesus, like an actor, merely delivers. The little scene is first of all a revelation *to him*, its meaning illuminated by his own interior awareness of God. That awareness is made actual in this specific moment, seen or realized in the outward event and in Jesus' emotional response to it. Beginning as an intuition, it is completed in the act of being uttered. Jesus learns about God anew as he speaks, and becomes again, in the instant, God's Word.

Thus the woman's gesture, Jesus' intuitive reading of it, and his outward proclamation of its meaning, all belong to the symbol whereby God is manifested. Through the spontaneous movement of Jesus' human heart, new knowledge arises. It is a knowledge of what God approves or likes, and hence "is like": "Tell me what you like and I will tell you who you are," runs an old saying. Obviously, the story is a revelation of Jesus as well. From the heart's fullness the mouth speaks; in singling out the poor widow and praising her generosity, he shows what his own heart contains. Thus the words he utters, while directly concerned with someone else, are a manifestation of himself. They are a Christophany that is at the same time a theophany—a revelation of God.

Such manifestations are by nature symbolic. If symbol is understood (following Karl Rahner) as the self-expression of one reality in another, distinct from it yet one with it, then Jesus' behavior in the passage quoted is a symbol.[1] So, in a larger sense, is the New Testament itself, and the whole revelation of God in the Scriptures and in the church. In them all, a graced awareness of who God is finds tangible expression in human and finite forms. Only in this way—only through symbols, in other words—can this reality "get through to us" without ceasing to be God's reality. For symbol alone is capable of bridging the infinite gap between transcendent divine truth and limited human awareness; it alone can unite the depth and suggestiveness of metaphor with the particularity of the historical and concrete.

Among other authors, Avery Dulles has developed this theme of revelation as a symbolic mediation of God. In Models of Revelation, he first analyzes (and critically evaluates) five major approaches to revelation: as doctrine, as history, as inner experience, as dialectical process, as new awareness. Then he offers his own model—revelation as symbol—and argues that it preserves what is most valid in the other models while avoiding their defects. Defining symbol as "an externally perceived sign which works mysteriously on the human consciousness so as to suggest more than it can clearly describe or define," he notes a parallelism between the properties of symbolism and those of revelation. Both give knowledge that is not so much speculative as participatory; both tend to transform the person of the knower; both powerfully affect commitments and behavior; finally, both introduce us to "realms of awareness not normally accessible to discursive thought."[2]

The present essay will try to show somewhat more concretely what it means to call revelation symbolic. It will also provide a simple psychological model for understanding the process of revelation.[3] That is, it will try to describe what happens in certain typical "disclosure situations"—the manifesting of an otherwise hidden divine meaning. When this occurs, faith is transformed—momentarily, at least—into vision: a hopeful seeking is rewarded by a glimpse of the one it longs to see. In this process, as I hope to show, a heart-knowledge of God "by anticipation" realizes itself in outward signs. Such signs are self-expressions of faith as well as self-revelations of God, through them we know God and ourselves at the same time.

Instead of proceeding immediately (in defiance of the subject-matter) to abstract definitions, it may help to look first at another example of the symbolic character of revelation. The story of Moses' encounter with the burning bush in Exodus 3 can serve both as a primary instance of revelation and as an illustration of the qualities Dulles assigns to symbolism. For if ever there were an external sign capable of working in mysteriously suggestive ways on the mind, surely it is the blazing bush and the words "I Am Who Am." Beyond precise definition or delimitation, this revelatory sign powerfully affects the "commitments and behavior" not only of Moses but of the Israelites and countless later generations. But while its influence is discernible in the external events of history, its deeper meaning discloses itself only to those who participate in the event by sharing in the faith-tradition it engenders. The knowledge it gives, "not speculative but participatory," opens the mind to realms of awareness not available to purely rational thought.[4]

Like the biblical revelation as a whole, the theophany at Horeb comprises many elements: image and word, action, command, and promise. The Exodus narrative is almost a paradigm of the archetypal religious experience, the encounter with "the Holy" as described by Rudolf Otto. Moses, tending his father-in-law's sheep, is first attracted by the "strange sight" of the bush that blazes up suddenly and is not consumed. Yielding to the fascination of the mysterious object, he draws closer, only to be overwhelmed by feelings of awe and dread. These sensations are given voice in the words that seem to emanate from the bush: "Approach no nearer; take off your shoes, for you are standing on holy ground" (Ex 3:3).

Taken simply as an image, the blazing bush powerfully symbolizes that "harmony of contraries" (coincidentia oppositorum) which Mircea Eliade called "the most basic definition of divinity" in the world's religions.[5] The law of finitude obliges nondivine beings to be this or that—male or female, light or dark; God alone transcends such oppositions. In this case, fire, an element from above, associated with sun and sky, is linked with vegetation, whose life is rooted in the earth. Fire itself is paradoxical and mysterious, combining as it does continual movement with apparent permanence of form. It suggests restless, superhuman energy, at once fearful and fascinating. The bush, in contrast, represents organic life with its quiet continuity and slow incremental growth. It unites flexibility with strength and limitedness with unlimited potential. If its roots clutch the soil, its branches reach into the sky. Fire and bush together, "indivisible but unmixed," neither negating the other, reveal the divine as both transcendent and immanent: "wholly Other" and yet already familiar and close. For "I am the God of your fathers, of Abraham, Isaac, and Jacob" (3:6).

The words Moses hears coming from the midst of the bush involve a still further reconciliation of opposites, one which links this exotic, naturist phenomenon with an existing tribal tradition. Nonpersonal things are given a voice, a personal identity; the divine has the power to say "I." However, even this "personalization of the *numen*" (to use Otto's terms) does not remove the eerie sense of mystery. When, a few verses later, Yahweh responds to Moses' request for identification by saying "I Am Who Am" (or "I Am That I Am"—3:14), the words have a mystical resonance that goes far beyond their simple, yet elusive, literal sense. (Indeed, one of the many plausible exegeses for this riddling statement interprets it as a refusal to answer—"I Am Whoever I Am"—implying the denial that the divinity can be named at all, and so held and possessed.)

Even as uttered by a human being, the words "I am," used absolutely, have something unfathomable about them. They point to the primal mystery of personal existence, its underivable originality and uniqueness, its inability to account for itself. "I cannot truly say how I came here"—the words of the young lover Demetrius as he awakes in the forest beside his beloved (in Shakespeare's *A Midsummer Night's Dream*[6])—are full of rapturous wonder. They can be spoken with equal truth—and equal amazement—by every man and woman. The reduplicative "I Am That I Am," occurring here in the context of this fiery theophany, only enchances that mysteriousness. The words even open up, for the imaginative hearer, a kind of intuition of divinity—a sense, that is, of what it must mean to be God. For though primarily a declaration of power and presence ("I Am" = "I Can Do"), the words contain a hint of joyous astonishment. They suggest a being who instead of taking existence for granted, wonderlessly, exults in the disclosure of an inexhaustible fullness. It is as if the self-explanatory, self-justifying existence which is God's—which is Love—were experienced as sheerly and only miracle, even by God. Could "I Am That I Am" be a cry of infinite surprise?

This reading of the text, whether exegetically sound or not, may indicate one aspect of what it means to call revelation symbolic. Images like the burning bush and the cross, events like the Exodus, words like "I Am" and "the Christ," persons like the prophets and, above all, Jesus himself, manifest God and God's manner of acting in their very concreteness. That is, they say more in their concrete totality than abstract doctrines derived from them can ever convey. They contain a mysterious "overplus" of meaning that can be known only by participation, and this, along with their literal sense, is their revelatory heart. Even creedal statements which express revelation, such as "I believe in one God" or "Jesus Christ is Lord," are essentially symbolic, in that they point beyond themselves to the "unspeakable" realities to which they refer—which is ultimately one reality, the saving presence of God.

These statements reveal God, therefore, in their very density and mystery-laden obscurity; they are verbal symbols for what necessarily surpasses human comprehension and conceptual articulation. To say this is not to say that revelation has no intelligible content; as Dulles notes, the symbols of revelation are not "indefinitely pliable."[7] But their literal meaning is not their whole or even their primary meaning. For them to be truly a revelation *of God*, they must "say" more than human language as such can ever convey.

The following excerpt from an extrabiblical source may serve to indicate how image and literal meaning work together to reveal the divine. In a famous passage in her *Revelations of Divine Love*, Juliana of Norwich describes a vision granted her during an illness in the year 1373:

> Also in this he showed a little thing, the size of a hazelnut, which seemed to lie in the palm of my hand; and it was as round as any ball. I looked upon it with the eye of my understanding, and thought, "What may this be?" And I was answered in a general way, thus: "It is all that is made." I wondered how long it could last; for it seemed as though it might suddenly fade away to nothing, it was so small. And I was answered in my understanding: "It lasts, and ever shall last; for God loveth it."[8]

The wonder aroused in Juliana by the sight of the tiny object lying in her hand makes it a thing of awe, full of a mysterious signficance, even before the words "It is all that is made" form themselves in her conscious mind. Like the author of the Wisdom of Solomon, she experiences the world through the eyes of its Creator, in all its delicate fragility:

> For the whole world, before you, is like a speck that tips the scales,
> And like a drop of morning dew that falls upon the ground.
> But you are merciful to all, for you can do all things,
> And you overlook our sins that we may repent.
> For you love all things that exist, and despise nothing of what you have made.
> For you would not have made anything, if you had hated it.
>
> (Wisdom 11:22–24)[9]

As in the passage from Mark quoted above, something apparently transitory and insignificant is revealed as being of enduring worth. And in both it is the specific image, the actual story, which gives the word-revelation much of its force. The vision of the universe as a hazelnut may continue to tease and to teach even after the specific message associated with it has faded from the conscious memory. Like the seed in the gospel parable "growing by itself," it suggests at once the nurturing powers of the earth and the expansion of life from tiny, insignificant beginnings. (It may even, for the twentieth-century reader, conjure up the cosmologists' picture of the universe's original state—a tiny clump of incredibly superdense matter, no bigger, perhaps, than a hazelnut, an infinitesimal millisecond before the Big Bang threw the makings of all future galaxies, including our own, out into space.)

The participatory power of symbolism thus permits a kind of God's-eye view of things. To see the world as a hazelnut, or a speck of dust, a drop of dew, is at the same time to know God, to sense how God "feels" about creation. To know one is to know the other—to perceive the cherishing of the infinitesimally small by the infinitely great. Paradoxically, we know God by entering into God's experience of us. The concreteness of the symbol enables us to participate in the experience of another (here, a divine Other) in ways that are beyond the scope of ordinary discursive speech, which tends toward separation and abstraction. Symbols do not merely instruct us, but invite us to share a feeling, a perception of reality through the heart.

Does knowledge like this really require a revelation—that is, an act of God to make it known? Some will say that the value of the universe (or even of the poor widow's act, in our first example) is obvious and needs no divine endorsement— only the testimony of the human heart. Perhaps. Yet in another way, isn't it just such fragile human truth that stands most in need of witnessing, that seems unsupported by much of our life experience? In this sense, revelation occurs precisely to give assurance to our wavering heart-testimony, to put the weight of God's truth behind it. Revelation occurs to show us what God loves.

The Nature of Symbol

Heart speaks to heart—but it must do so through signs. For them to be true transmitters, conveying the contents of the heart, they must be signs which contain what they signify—in a word, symbols. Real symbols differ from merely representative or empty signs by *being* the very presence of the reality they signify. This presence can occur in different forms with different levels of intensity. For instance, a sand dollar found on a beach can stand for the memories of a happy day by the oceanside: it makes present the whole of which it was a tangible part. Moreover, it is not just *any* part; if it were, a pebble or a grain of sand might do as well. The whiteness of the shell, its almost perfect symmetry, the delicate tracery of the five-leafed design on its upper side, its associations with the sea, with life, and with death, its fragility—all these elements and more may enter into its symbolic meaning, enabling it to stand for a host of personal realities. Similarly, a wedding ring can symbolize not only the ceremony in which it was given and received, but all that is implied in the pledging of two persons to one another in lifelong fidelity. Its gold color makes the value, the preciousness, of that loving commitment visible, even as its circularity embodies the ideal of mutual self-giving without end. And on a higher (and more intimate) level of symbolization, the kiss of two lovers *is* the tangible presence of their love. Though more transitory than the sand dollar and the ring, it is more truly a part of the very love it expresses, and that love realizes itself anew in each kiss.

Real symbols thus involve a paradoxical presence-in-absence, an identity and a difference. A person's deeds, for instance, are a real symbol of the person. I am in my words and actions. They are not just external signs of me (like a black, curving arrow on a sign announcing a coming bend in the road), but literally *me*. I exist in them and by means of them. And yet in another way they are not me, but something I do. I exist at other times apart from these particular signs through which I reveal myself now; it may even be that my words and gestures are misleading, deceitful, seeming to show what is not really there. A handshake can be a real symbol of friendship, as a kiss is of love. Yet political enemies often shake hands, and Judas kissed Jesus in the act of betraying him.

This is the primary parodox of symbols, that they both are and are not what they represent. In a certain way they overcome what in logic is called "the law of the excluded middle," whereby a statement is either true or false (just as a thing is or is not). Valid for propositions, this logical rule is untrue for signs—at least for the special signs that symbols are. What follows from this? Not that symbols are not to be trusted; if we cannot trust them, we will never gain access to the most important of realities—the interior, the heart of another. Nor does it mean that they are not true, that they have no valid, intelligible sense that can be translated. But it does mean that they must be read symbolically, as the man-ifestation of something other than their literal or obvious contents. Their meaning is in them, but it is not confined to them; a too literal approach to them distorts that meaning.

It would be a mistake, for instance—even an idolatrous error—to identify Yahweh too simply with the bush and the fire, or even the words, of the passage quoted above. Yahweh is not literally "in" the bush, nor does God utter (at least as human beings utter) the words that Moses hears. They are the symbolic expression of a transcendent experience—an experience, precisely, of God's saving nearness. Through their encounter with Yahweh mediated by these signs, the Israelites are invited (and challenged) to go forward, to trust in the unseen. As they move into the unknown future, they know that Yahweh will be with them—but in God's own way, not necessarily in theirs: "as who I am I shall be with you." That divine presence will be no more tangible than the images of "cloud by day and fire by night" attending them in their trek across the desert. It will often be, in the words of Samuel Terrien, "a presence in absence."[10]

Faith as Openness to Symbol

Recognizing the symbolic character of revelation, then, requires an awareness both of the unity and the difference between the reality symbolized and the forms which mediate it. To apprehend its true meaning, one must *pass through* the symbol to what it makes present (re-presents). This is true to an extent of all types of communication, even the indicative signs of ordinary language. To read a text (such as this one, for instance), one must pass through the printed shapes of the letters to grasp the words and the meanings for which they stand. Still further, one passes through individual words to comprehend their joint meaning in sentences and paragraphs; finally, one may sense and come into contact with the author's mind and outlook expressed in a whole essay or book. Such comprehension is already symbolic, and involves a measure of participation. But in dealing with real symbols, as Dulles notes, "a deeper degree of indwelling is required":[11] we enter into a relationship with the reality expressed in the symbols in a way that requires a greater surrender of intellectual control.

This yielding of control, which already contains the kernel of what is meant by "faith," involves an opening of the mind to meanings which are beyond it. It consists of a nonintrusive awareness, an active receptivity (like the *wu wei* of Taoism, or the therapist's "listening with the third ear"). This open and impressionable attitude allows the symbol in its concreteness to work, informing the mind and heart, changing consciousness, altering expectations. One learns from the symbol what it means, instead of allowing one's prior knowledge to dictate to it what it must (and must not) mean. When Jesus in the gospels says that becoming like little children is prerequisite to entry into the kingdom of God (Mk 10:15), he points to such trustful openness as an essential condition for receiving the gifts of God. For the gift that is revelation is not merely knowledge *about* God; it is the very being of God, symbolically bestowed.

Revelation is a symbolic process, therefore, in that the concrete signs through which God is manifested are necessarily other than God. Moses truly encounters Yahweh in the burning bush, yet the bush is not Yahweh, nor is the fire, nor are both together. The divine cannot be identified with a specific object or pinned down to a certain locale. The parallels between the Mosaic experience and theophanies found in non-Judaic religions point to components of the event which derive from the human religious imagination. The burning but unconsumed bush itself may be a natural phenomenon of the desert (analogous to "St Elmo's fire" at sea), if not a narrative invention. There is even a sense in which Moses clearly *brings to* the encounter with Yahweh the essence of the revelation he receives there: the God he meets in the bush is precisely the God of his fathers, the God whose earlier covenants have manifested a special care for this people. Through the extraordinary event, Moses perceives that Yahweh is still present, still caring, still powerful—and therefore that the same God is active and acting now, in a new way.

Thus the call Moses hears as emanating from the bush also has a basis in himself. The commission he receives is a response to already existing conditions—social, historical, personal. On the one hand, Yahweh is truly present in the strong sense of injustice felt by the most "conscienticized" of the Israelites. God is likewise present in the impulse he obeys to do something about it, in his own profound and growing sense of mission. On the other hand, more is at work here, obviously, than a divine mandate fallen out of heaven. Yahweh speaks and acts through human elements which have their own independent, quasi-autonomous existence—in a word, through symbols. The call to liberation which Moses hears comes ultimately from within. It involves *the conjunction of an already existent faith with an external sign*—a sign which is the outward reflection of that inner reality. A faith which seeks the saving power of God finds assurance in a symbol which renders the believed-in reality present. Through the symbol, that faith both realizes (recognizes) and transcends itself.

The Symbolization of Faith

Revelation is thus a symbolic process in a second sense. It is not only the self-expression of God but the self-realization of faith. Revelation designates the process by which faith, as a trustful foreknowledge of God, comes to explicit self-recognition and objectification. In that process, as the example of Moses indicates, faith transcends itself through its encounter with external signs, arriving at a new knowledge both of God and of itself. It comes to know experientially what it formerly believed only notionally, or at most half-knew. Thus in meeting Yahweh and receiving the assurance "I will be with you," the faith of Moses is both confirmed and transformed. As the God who was far off and remote becomes close, without ceasing to be mysterious, so the faith that was once passive becomes active and dynamic. The God who *is* becomes a God who *acts*, acting precisely through those to whom the revelation takes place.

Moreover, what is revealed to Moses and through him to the people of Israel is not only the identity of Yahweh but their own identity and destiny. The God who shows Godself to them in the covenant of Sinai shows them at the same time who they are and what they are called to be. They are those whom God loves and chooses to be present to; they are the people of Yahweh, obliged in consequence to imitate Yahweh's justice and holiness. "Be holy, therefore, for I your God am holy" (Lev 19:2). The burning bush and the decalogue are thus symbols not only of Yahweh but of the faith of Israel; through them that faith recognizes itself and goes beyond itself.

Not only revelation, therefore, but faith too has a symbolic structure. It realizes itself in and through external signs, signs mysteriously both distinct from and one with itself. The Christian believer of today who prays the creed, or gazes upon the image of Jesus in the crib or on the cross, finds his or her own faith there given external or symbolic form. In such forms faith both knows itself and is led beyond itself. One knows God in contemplating the signs of God's redemptive presence in human life and knows one's deepest self at the same time.

Faith enters, then, into both the original constitution of revelatory symbols and their later reception and communication. Does the believer's faith *create* that revelation—that is, simply project into these external signs the knowledge it claims to find there? This is a difficult question, to which no simple answer is possible. On the one hand, faith (in the sense of the openness and trust described earlier) is clearly an essential condition for receiving revelation. Certain symbols, perhaps all symbols, are meaningful only to those who come to them with a receptive, faith-disposed attitude. Jesus was said to be unable to work many miracles in his home town of Nazareth "because of their lack of faith" (Mk 6:6). But in another (and more important) sense, the answer is no. Revelation is experienced as divinely disclosed rather than as humanly created (see Mt 16:17). If in one way the believer, like the prophet, brings to the disclosure situation the knowledge that he or she finds there, in another and more immediate way the knowledge is received anew in the encounter. A preexisting faith is confirmed, but at the same time fresh knowledge is given, a new level of awareness is attained.

This is precisely the power of symbols, that they are able to present and communicate knowledge which exceeds the receiver's conscious awareness. Dreams, for instance, convey knowledge through narratives with symbolic import. The dreamer learns about himself or herself by means of fragmentary, emotion-laden images, words, and events. These express things already "known" to the dreamer, but excluded from waking consciousness. Artworks such as paintings, poems, and musical compositions, are symbolic in the same way, or at least in an analogous way. According to the philosopher Susanne Langer, they formulate in visual, verbal, or auditory forms "patterns in human feeling"— awarenesses too complex and elusive for discursive thought, yet a familiar and important aspect of life.[12] A literary work may be called a symbol, according to R. P. Blackmur, when "it stands for that within me the reader which enables me to recognize it and to illuminate it with my own experience, at the same time that what it means illuminates further corridors in my sense of myself."[13]

An Illustration: Peter's Confession

The gospel narrative describing Peter's recognition of Jesus as the Christ shows both aspects of this process at work: revelation as an act of divine self-disclosure, and revelation as an act of human self-discovery. In the familiar (and controversial) passage from the Gospel of Matthew, Simon responds to Jesus' question, "But who do you say that I am?" with the ringing declaration: "You are the Christ, the son of the living God." In turn, Jesus responds: "Blessed are you, Simon, son of John, for flesh and blood have not revealed this to you, but my Father in heaven." He goes on to give Simon the new name Peter, assuring him that "on this rock I will build my church," and conferring on him the keys of the kingdom of heaven (Mt 16:15–19).

Whatever the historical provenance of this account—pre- or post-resurrection, historical event or creation of the community (or some combination of both)—the use of the word "revealed" (apekalypsen) is itself revealing. The parallel account in Mark (8:27–30) perhaps brings out more starkly the sudden, surprising character of Peter's recognition of Jesus as "the Messiah." It is as if two hitherto unrelated things—Peter's experience of the man Jesus, the wonder-worker from Nazareth, and the concept of messiahship—suddenly came together; there is a moment of insight, in which a new meaning is disclosed. Peter's perception of Jesus is altered, transformed, by the application to him of the word "Christ"—a word already laden, even for the first disciples of Jesus, with such multiple and diverse associations and preconceptions that it can only be called a symbol. To see Jesus and his actions through the lens provided by that symbol is to experience him differently, as a (or perhaps the) primary agent of God in the world. It is also to begin to alter the image, the concept, the ideas associated with messiahship, to read them in the light of Jesus and his ministry.

Exactly when, where, and how this took place are questions open to scholarly dispute; what is beyond doubt is that the early followers of Jesus came to perceive him this way and made Peter's confession their own. No less certainly, the making of that connection, the moment of fusion between the experience of the living Jesus and the notion "the Christ," was felt as a moment of revelation. That is, it was perceived not as something reasoned to or immediately obvious, not learned from hearsay, but as a gift given and received. "Flesh and blood have not revealed this to you, but my Father in heaven." The essence of revelation lies in this sense of knowledge as the result of a divine initiative—a meaning not made but disclosed.[14] However much human inquiry, observation, and effort have paved the way for it, it occurs freely and unexpectedly. It is beyond human control, and the halo of wonder surrounding it is already a glimpse of God.

In Matthew's narrative, Simon's awestruck recognition of Jesus as the Christ leads to a further recognition, of which he is the object. Jesus looks on his eager, earnest, often bumbling disciple with new eyes, and confers on him a role and an identity which were not his an instant before. "Jesus is himself astonished by Peter's confession," says Rudolf Otto, suggesting that in their dialogue Jesus discovers something new about himself.[15] True or not, in the scene as depicted something new is disclosed about Simon. His faith in Israel's God and his openness to that God's action in Jesus find expression in his enthusiastic, daring proclamation. It sums up all that has been implied by his following of Jesus and carries it to a new level. Jesus recognizes this in choosing Simon as the foundation stone of his new community, symbolizing it with a new name. The passage suggests that this choice, while free, is anything but arbitrary. It is precisely Jesus' response to the revelation of God's grace alive in Peter. The scene is one of mutual wonder and dual recognition: a revelation of each man to the other—and to himself. Like the word "Christ," it implies a bonding of the human with the divine.

The process of revelation, therefore, involves a kind of self-realization also on the part of the one who receives the revelation, a symbolic self-recognition. There exists in every human being a hunger for God that is already a dark foreknowledge of the one sought. In Peter's case, this "a priori of faith" finds its objective correlative or answer in the person of Jesus. Peter's experience of the latter as one of his disciples leads to deepening trust and a more active faith. Finally, under the pressure of the question about Jesus' identity, an interpretation occurs that has the force of certainty: Jesus is the Christ, the long-awaited Messiah. However long a time this interpretation may have been gathering form as a tentative hypothesis or a wild hope, its occurrence and the assurance which accompanies it are unexpected. It makes sense of Jesus, while Jesus makes sense of the concept. In it Peter's groping faith is given symbolic expression: it comes to itself through its objectification. As it does so, Simon, son of John, becomes "the Rock."

Seeking, Symbol, and Significance

The psychological pattern involved in this process can perhaps be more clearly indicated in the following contemporary example. Viktor Frankl, in a memorable passage from his partly autobiographical *Man's Search for Meaning*, gives this account of an experience he had as a prisoner in Auschwitz:

> Another time we were at work in a trench. The dawn was grey around us; grey
> was the sky above; grey the snow in the pale light of dawn; grey the rags in which
> my fellow prisoners were clad, and grey their faces. I was again conversing silently
> with my wife, or perhaps I was struggling to find the *reason* for my sufferings, my
> slow dying. In a last violent protest against the hopelessness of imminent death, I
> sensed my spirit piercing through the enveloping gloom. I felt it transcend that
> hopeless, meaningless world, and from somewhere I heard a victorious "Yes" in
> answer to my question of the existence of an ultimate purpose. At that moment a
> light was lit in a distant farmhouse, which stood on the horizon as if painted there,
> in the midst of the miserable grey of a dawning morning in Bavaria. *"Et lux in
> tenebris lucet"*—and the light shineth in the darkness. For hours I stood hacking at
> the icy ground. The guard passed by, insulting me, and once again I communed
> with my beloved. More and more I felt that she was present, that she was with me;
> I had the feeling that I was able to touch her, able to stretch out my hand and grasp
> hers. The feeling was very strong that she was *there*. Then, at that very moment, a
> bird flew down silently and perched just in front of me, on the heap of soil which I
> had dug up from the ditch, and looked steadily at me.[16]

The basic constituents of this moving account are very simple. On Frankl's side there is a desperate hunger for meaning in the gray, hopeless world of the camp. This search takes two distinct but related forms: one is his anguished question about whether there is a purpose for all this suffering, for life itself; the other is his longing for the presence of his wife. He knows that she is far away, perhaps already dead, but his need for her and his experience of the reality of their continued love is so intense as to create at times the sense of her actual presence. Just when this longing is most extreme, he experiences a victorious "Yes" from somewhere beyond. It says: yes, there is meaning; yes, your wife's love continues to exist. The specific symbols associated with this revelation are almost pitifully slight, transparently inadequate to the meaning they convey: a light turned on in a farmhouse, the sudden descent of a bird on a small hill of dirt and its unwinking, silent stare. Yet despite their triviality and apparently coincidental occurrence, they bring conviction. Frankl is reassured; he knows that Meaning exists, even in the midst of this desolation, though he cannot say how.

The critically minded person may be tempted to "demythologize" this account. Is this "revelation," one might ask, any more than the confluence of intense human need and some chance events? In an environment so barren, the human imagination is bound to be given free play, creating presence out of fantasy and seeing design in happenstance. A Freud would almost certainly interpret it this way, as the projection upon outward reality of infantile cravings, needs which create their own illusory object. Is Frankl's experience anything but an exercise in unconscious wish fulfillment?

I believe it is possible to give it a more sympathetic (and less reductionist) interpretation, one nonetheless grounded in human psychology. Could it be that here an inchoate yet real faith—a seeking which preapprehends its own object— finds external confirmation and fulfillment? For Frankl's question about the existence of ultimate purposefulness is clearly no mere speculative inquiry; it is a passionately personal quest in which his whole self is involved. Such questioning by its very nature implies and presupposes a partner in the dialogue, a Thou who can both listen and respond. (This remains true even though it is also a *cri de coeur* wrung from him by the pressure of his anguish—an expression of feeling which is at the same time a call for help.) It is a prime example of that need for meaning which Frankl sees as a (perhaps *the*) major constituent of human motivation—a need which is at once the wish or hope that meaning should exist, and the conviction that it does.

As Frankl describes it, this need for meaning does not so much "push" people from behind, like a drive, as it draws them from ahead, like a goal or value. I would argue that it is therefore already faith—even faith in its deepest and most original form. For the latter is nothing but an elementary and instinctive trust in the goodness of life, in the meaningfulness of existence. It is present not as a thesis or a theory, but as the dynamic operating principle implicit in all human action. Without it, as psychologists like Erik Erikson have pointed out, no human growth or development is possible. This basic trust, rooted in the life processes of the organism, finds its fullest objectification (and ultimate justification) in explicitly religious faith, in the knowledge that God exists.[17] For as Peter Berger and others have argued, in a world of suffering bounded inescapably by death, the meaningfulness of life is logically tenable if, and only if, the transcendent exists.[18]

In Frankl's narrative, the three elements composing what I call the symbolic structure of faith are presented with unusual distinctness: they are, respectively, seeking, symbol, and significance (meaning). The seeking is a hunger for meaning which, like all faith, involves a tacit foreknowledge of its own object. This hunger is satisfied, not so much by the patently inadequate symbols it encounters—the light lit in the farmhouse, the descent of the bird—as by the significance they convey, the meaning of which they are the imperfect embodiment. For all their inadequacy, they are appropriate to that meaning: light, a primary symbol of divinity, is identified with the Logos in the line from the Johannine prologue quoted by Frankl ("and the light shineth in the darkness"— Jn 1:5); a bird, symbolic of transcendence, freedom, and communication from on high. In the total situation, a "presentiment goes out to meet the 'revelation' to which it belongs":[19] a questing faith finds its correlative answer in signs, signs which make present the reality it foreknows.

Granted that these specific symbols are somewhat more loosely bonded with their revelatory meaning than in the biblical examples we are considering, they nevertheless share with their biblical counterparts the power to point beyond themselves to transcendent and personal meanings.

Revelation to Jesus, Revelation by Jesus

Exactly the same pattern of seeking, symbol, and significance can be found in the synoptic accounts of the baptism of Jesus (an episode which nearly all authorities accept as historical). According to Mark's version, after Jesus comes from Nazareth to be baptized by John in the Jordan, "no sooner had he come up out of the water than he saw the heavens torn apart and the Spirit, like a dove, descending on him. And a voice came from heaven: 'You are my son, the beloved; on you my favor rests'" (Mk 1:10–11).

In this case, the element of seeking which looms so large in the Frankl narrative is left unspoken. It is implicit in the impulse that leads Jesus to ask for baptism at the hands of John. Whatever form that impulse may have taken, the action suggests a radical humility which accepts human existence as a question—and with it, accepts the need for tangible mediations of God. Like the most profound human questions, its true meaning only becomes clear in the answer which it receives; it discovers itself in the revelatory event.

Jesus' descent into the water and his emergence out of it symbolize a change in consciousness, the birth of a new awareness. It is new in that Jesus appears to experience with a new intensity and greater explicitness his own condition as beloved of God. It is an awareness born "from above," as Mark's image of the dove descending from the torn-apart heavens suggests. It is a divinely given answer to that most basic of human questions: Who am I? Do I count? Am I worthwhile? The voice, which in Mark's account Jesus alone hears, puts into words the content of an inner experience of approval, of being the object of another's love. It is the clear realization of a mutual relationship, not simply as a fact, but as a cause of delight. Through that experience, Jesus passes from the universal human state of relative uncertainty and ambiguity about one's status and worth, to one of assurance: "You are my son, my beloved." Such knowledge is the very heart of revelation.

It is no accident that this knowledge given to Jesus becomes the core of the revelation given by Jesus. Biblical scholar James Dunn, among others, has argued that it is the sense of being beloved—the "Abba" experience—coupled with an impulse to proclaim a message and the power to heal others as a sign of it, that convinced Jesus that the last days were now occurring.[20] "The time has come, and the kingdom of God is now at hand. Repent, and believe the good news" (Mk 1:15). As all commentators agree, the kingdom (or reign) of God is a dense symbol for a rich and complex spiritual reality. The multitude of parables Jesus tells to express what this kingdom is like testify to its having no one, simple definition. But for all its richness, the phrase primarily designates the dawning of the end-times, the drawing near of the holy God in full power and love. Even now, Yahweh is becoming Lord in the house of Israel; from now on the Lord will reign, not just in principle or in theory, but in fact. The arrival of the kingdom thus means "God's rule in love" (Walter Kasper); it is this which makes it "good news."

In this perspective, the question asked by the people in the synagogue at Nazareth—"Where did he get all this?" (Mk 6:2)—can be given a relatively clear answer. Jesus speaks with the absolute assurance that only direct experience can give. "Ask, and you shall receive: seek, and you shall find; knock, and the door will be opened to you" (Lk 11:9). In such sayings, which seem to fly in the face of common sense, Jesus enunciates a fundamental law of the spiritual life, based on his own experience of God. It would contradict the character of God, as Jesus intimately knows it, to fail to give all good things[21] to anyone who asks. For the God he knows is a God of unbounded love and generosity. In Jesus, faith has become knowledge; or more exactly, it becomes knowledge again and again as he speaks.

This may help clarify what was said at the beginning of this essay regarding the story of the poor widow. Jesus learns about God in the act of speaking about God; what becomes revelation to others is also, in a primary way, revelation to Jesus himself. For it is the making explicit, and hence available to consciousness, of what Jesus already knows about God in the depths of his being.[22] In talking about the behavior of earthly fathers, Jesus discovers, and so reveals, what the Father is like (Lk 15:11–32). Similarly, in the process of responding to a question about the Law, he learns, as well as teaches, that there is no commandment greater than the love of God and the neighbor (Mk 12:28–34). His symbolic realization of the meaning of God is an ongoing process which continually transcends itself as he speaks and acts.

This accounts for the originality of what Jesus says and does, that caused people to remark "Here is a teaching that is new" (Mk 1:27), in contrast to the teaching of the scribes. It has a freshness and a force that makes it memorable, unlike things learned by rote and repeated. The spontaneous self-symbolization of the "faith" of Jesus makes it not just a record of revelation, but actively revelatory. It continually brings people into the presence of God.

Thus when Jesus tells a parable or heals a sick person, he opens up a window through which God may be glimpsed. His realized (or, better, self-realizing) faith enables him to perfect or complete the faith of others.[23] The revelatory sign magnetizes the spontaneous faith of his listeners—awakening it out of its dormancy, drawing it up into a relationship with itself. In a familiar passage, Jesus calls attention to the nourishment of the birds and the beauty of wildflowers. He uses these instances of the harmony and beauty of nature to reveal what the Creator is like. "If God so clothes the wild grasses . . . will not the same God much more clothe you, o you of little faith?" (Mt 6:30). Essentially Jesus appeals to a faith knowledge of God latent in the hearts of his hearers to ground the truth of his observation. At some deep level they already *know* that they are of greater worth to God than the birds and the grasses. Jesus invites them to recognize this consciously, to feel and claim it, to stake their lives on it. Their inner faith is brought to life by encountering its own likeness in the outer sign, and the result is a revelation of God.

Jesus *gives* that revelation insofar as he makes the connection explicit for his hearers; he first *receives* the revelation insofar as he sees the connection—that is, allows it to be made in him.[24] The revelation or message, therefore, does not preexist the symbol that conveys it, as if the latter were a wholly indifferent, external channel. Instead, it emerges into full clarity in the act of being told. Its language and imagery, its narrative structure, even its historical context are intrinsic to the revelation itself. So too the person and life history of Jesus are intrinsic to what he reveals, belong to what make him the perfect and final revelation of God. For it is in saying what he says and in doing what he does—in living and dying (and rising from the dead)—that he becomes the Jesus we know: that is, the Christ.

The Cross: An Ultimate Symbol

The crucified and risen Jesus is, accordingly, the ultimate Christian symbol. First, the crucifixion, as a historical event, is a symbolic summary of Jesus' whole life and ministry—his passionate commitment to the Father and to truth, his identification with the poor and the outcast. In the world of Jesus, as in ours, such a commitment could only lead to the cross. The way Jesus met the entrenched resistance to his liberating good news, his whole manner of dying, made it the symbol of his faith. In dying as he did, without hatred or recrimination but in utter fidelity, Jesus gave expression to the truth he lived from the center of his being. The cross became the symbol of his open-ended trust in God, of love poured out in sacrifice. That sign at the same time reveals the redemptive power of God, the mysterious God who "so loved the world that he gave his only Son" (Jn 3:16). We know who God is above all in contemplating this image of loving and total self-abandonment.

If all real symbols involve mystery, the supreme symbol is the supreme mystery. Even its literal sense is profoundly obscure; Karl Rahner observed that it is not easy to understand, from a theological point of view, what our redemption by the death of Jesus means.[25] The specific images involved here are ones of unsurpassed richness, density, and depth; the very word *blood*, for instance, with all it evokes (e.g., convenant, blood sacrifice, death); the notion of redemption, at once full of meaning and difficult to define; the image of Jesus crying out "My God, my God, why have you forsaken me?" and yielding his spirit into his Father's hands. To perceive the meaning of these signs, nothing is so necessary as a reverent silence, a worshipful attunement to the embodied mystery. Only in this way can the symbol speak—and, in speaking, darkly reveal the true meaning, not only of the death of Jesus, but of all other human deaths as well.

The resurrection of the crucified belongs intrinsically to this symbol, for it vindicates Jesus' whole manner of living and dying. It makes clear not only the truth of Jesus but the truth of God, for "whom God vindicates, discloses the character of God."[26] It interprets the dying of Jesus, not as one more instance of human blindness and cruelty, but as the victory of God's power in the midst of human weakness and sin, the sign of a divine will to life that is stronger than the human will to death. Because of this sign, we know that nothing, not even death, can separate us from the love of God made visible in Christ (Rom 8:38–39).

The arising of resurrection faith is the supreme instance of the symbolic process described here. For it is to the seeking heart that the revelation comes—whether that seeking be overt and explicit, as in the story of Mary Magdalene going to the tomb on Easter Sunday morning, or tacit, as in the case of Jesus' discouraged, fearful, and demoralized disciples. The good news which breaks through to them in the form of visions and proclamations comes as a total surprise, an unexpected discovery. At the same time, it corresponds to and expresses the deepest longings of their own hearts; their wavering and almost shattered faith discovers itself anew in the symbol of Jesus risen. That knowledge, as the various New Testament accounts suggest, is mediated multiply: in direct experience, in the witness of others, in the very act itself of proclaiming to the world that Jesus has been raised from the dead by the power of God. The sign of resurrection is thus both the object of faith (that which is believed) and its motive (the reason for believing). It gives assurance to the very hope it calls into being.[27]

"I have to know that as a thinking, finite being I am God crucified," wrote Simone Weil. "God is crucified from the fact that finite beings, subject to necessity, to space, and to time, think."[28] The cross of Jesus, therefore, presents the believer with the image of his or her own self. If so, the resurrection reveals the full meaning of that symbol, turning the vision of death into an assurance of life. Through it we know that our efforts and sufferings *matter*, that our death-bound lives have eternal significance. Here above all, revelation occurs to show us what God loves.

The Church, Scripture, and Sacrament

The symbolic expression of revelation and Christian faith does not come to an end, of course, with the resurrection. The community of believers that that event brings into being, the *ekklesia*, is itself a symbol. Jesus continues to live in his body, the church, which is the proleptic presence of the kingdom whose coming he announced. The radical oneness of Jesus with those who make up this symbolic body is expressed in the words heard by Paul at the moment of his conversion: "This is Jesus, whom Saul persecutes" (Acts 9:6). That continuing presence is realized first of all in the behavior of Christians, whose relationship to Jesus and God will be known above all by their love for one another (Jn 17:23). It will also be rendered tangible in sacrament and word. Each in their different ways incarnates the continuing presence and influence of Jesus. The revelation of God goes on in and through the faith of the community—for, as Dulles observes, without the church "we would not be able to know Christ as he really is."[29]

The transmission of this revelation is not a static repetition, but an ongoing reexpression and resymbolization. The unfolding of Christian faith through the early centuries, from the New Testament era to the time of the great church councils, shows this process at work. What Jesus announced as the coming reign of God is resymbolized in the first disciples' proclaiming him as risen and as Lord. The apostle Paul reexpresses the good news in ways that appeal to his increasingly gentile audience, in the process helping transform the Christian movement from a Jewish sect into a world religion. Later still, the Fourth Gospel radically transposes themes from the synoptic tradition in its narrative reinterpretation of Jesus' life and message. The early Christian creeds attempt to formulate the contents of Christian belief, leading in time to the patristic theologies and the conciliar definitions that express that faith in terms very remote from the world of first-century Judaism.

Underlying these repeated transformations, nevertheless, is a process at least analogous to that which brought the original revelation into being. I have suggested that when Jesus utters a parable (for instance), his tacit knowledge of God, operating through the imagination, "gives itself a body." That is, it marshals images and narrative materials drawn from daily life to express (or realize) an intuition. This is the conscious form of a process that occurs unconsciously in moments of religious vision—in Juliana's vision of the hazelnut, for instance (or, still more dramatically, in Saul's encounter with Jesus on the Damascus road). In such an event, a truth already in some way *known* to the seer, but hitherto not recognized, breaks through into conscious awareness. The medium of the breakthrough is always something concrete or capable of being sensed, such as an image or a sound, usually conjoined with a statement which explains its meaning. The knowledge conveyed only comes to be, fully, in the symbol which embodies it.

Something similar occurs, I believe, whenever the faith-knowledge of God or of Christ is expressed again under the impulse of grace. This process underlies the composition and editing of the gospels, for instance. Very many factors go into that process: historical recollection and theological reflection, community controversy and personal faith, literary models and creative fantasy (to name only a few). But besides the authors' responses to issues being debated in their communities, it is their living awareness, in faith, of who Jesus is that above all directs their presentation of stories and sayings furnished by the tradition. The result is a series of *true but symbolic* portraits of Jesus, inspired stories that are and are not the historical presence of the reality they express.[30]

This perspective, which can be extended to the whole of the biblical revelation, provides an alternative to fundamentalism. The view which Dulles calls "symbolic realism" shares with fundamentalism the conviction that the Bible is truly the word of God. But, in contrast to fundamentalism, it recognizes a difference between human and divine speech. It insists on the genuinely human and historical character of God's self-expression. Thus it sees revelation as a unity-in-difference of the God who reveals and the signs which reveal God. This holds true even when, in the person of Christ, symbol and symbolized are so intimately one that Jesus is truly the presence of God in human flesh. For the Logos or Word of God contains more than even Jesus can fully express.[31]

Language and Action

The symbolic understanding of revelation liberates the language of Jesus—. both the images he uses and his moral teaching—from the narrow literalism with which it has often been interpreted. Jesus' address to God as "Abba," for instance, clearly expresses his own sense of God's tender care, and Jesus' corresponding feeling of filial responsibility. It is itself the product of an original, revelatory insight, a fusion between his unique experience of belovedness and the image of ideal human fatherhood. Today's use of inclusive language and occasional substitution of feminine images (such as "God our Mother") in public worship does not contradict the meaning intended by Jesus. Instead, it restores that meaning by making clear the symbolic, nonliteral character of Jesus' own usage—a fact which almost two millennia of Christian patriarchalism have tended to obscure.

Jesus' ethical teaching is also symbolic, insofar as it is the expression of his awareness of God's overwhelming and transforming love and the impact it ought to have on human behavior. Such "commandments," for instance, as the admonition to "offer no resistance to injury" or the prohibition of divorce and remarriage, are not the publication on earth of eternal divine decrees. Like the parables, they are meant to startle their hearers into a new awareness. It is an awareness above all of who God is, and of how different human life would be if lived in the full light of that knowledge. Their primary function is to reveal "the character of God" rather than to prescribe (or proscribe) certain specific behaviors.

To say this is not to empty Jesus' moral teaching of all practical bearing, as if it need not be taken seriously. Each ethical injunction, from the advice to cut off the "offending" hand or eye to the commandment to "love one another," needs to be considered in its own right, for they obviously vary greatly in degrees of literalness. Their applicability to individuals varies as well, a fact which points to a further reason for recognizing the symbolic character of this teaching. For Christian moral behavior, no less than the Christian revelation itself, is symbolic. It is the expression in loving action of the believer's response to the God whose love Jesus makes known. What that response requires in the concrete is ultimately for the individual to discern—in dialogue with the community of believers at large, the individual's own conscience, and the God revealed in Jesus. This implies a personal and communal "listening in faith," which hears individual teachings in the context of revelation as a whole. Only in the light of this total symbol are they read and heard truly, as the revealing word of God.

Such reformulations or re-symbolizations, linguistic and practical, continue the mission of Jesus within Judaism. His preaching purified, enlarged, and transformed existing Jewish symbolism for the God of Moses and the prophets, freeing it from the encrustations of centuries. Likewise his teaching about the unconditional primacy of love put the Law on its true footing—at once transcending it and bringing it to completion. Jesus' symbolic speech "resurrects" the true God of Judaism from the tombs of language and religious custom. "For it is not of the dead, but of the living, that Yahweh is God" (Mt. 22:32).

Symbolism and Belief

To be aware of the difference, as well as the unity, between the living God and the symbols which reveal that God, is important also for the act of believing. For faith too has a symbolic structure, comprising both a subjective and an objective dimension. The subjective aspect is an openness, a reaching out in hope to the unknown and unlimited—an act of cognitive trust which is already a precognition of God. To say "I believe in you, God, holy mystery," is to give intellectual form to this most basic of human dynamisms. The objective aspect is the concept or doctrine which mediates the divine, providing that subjective movement with an external pole (as the word "God" does in the statement above). Thus it makes possible an act of recognition, whereby the believing person senses a correspondence (or connaturality) between the movement of faith-trust and its external symbol. To say, for instance, "I believe that Jesus is Lord, and that we are saved by his death and resurrection," is to proclaim that one finds in that faith the justification and confirmation of one's instinctive (and finally inescapable) urge to trust in being, ".no matter what." Believing in the lordship of Christ and in the saving power of Jesus' death and resurrection bestows an assurance that this ineradicable hopefulness is not an illusion. Even more; to the one who believes, the true scope and goal of the act of faith stands revealed for the first time.

In such faith, in other words, I come to know where my spontaneous, biologically based faith is headed. I know what its goal is, and thus I know what it means. Still further, through it I come to know what I mean. The object of faith reveals my self to me: the true bearing of that activity which I do not simply perform, but am. The symbols of faith, therefore, not only reveal the mystery of God, but in so doing reveal believers to themselves, as persons oriented to the mystery. This brings with it the invitation—and obligation—for them to commit themselves in freedom to the mystery and to that which reveals it: to affirm it, to rely on it, to recreate its presence continually so that its influence can permeate their lives. For faith requires one to let oneself go, in trust and love, to what is beyond oneself; in drawing me out of myself, the signs of faith reveal to me my own transcendence. When I believe, I put myself consciously and freely at the disposal of that over which I have no control, trusting in a wisdom and a goodness greater than my own. The supreme expression of such faith is found in the final words of Jesus on the cross: "Into your hands I commit my spirit."

Even as belief, therefore, faith's structure is symbolic in that is moves beyond the explicit object of its professions to the mystery contained in them. The conceptual content of faith (for example, the kingdom of God preached by Jesus, and proclaimed by the church as present in Jesus' own death and resurrection) is always symbolic, in that it contains more than the believer in it can comprehend. The creeds which formulate such transcendent realities are meant to provide a window on the mystery they symbolically represent. They lead the mind and heart of the believer beyond their explicit statements to the contemplation of the realities they refer to, the divine mystery of which they are the partial unfolding.[32] This is why it has sometimes been said that the creed is fully true "only in the act of worship." That is, only as pronounced by someone—in fact, by the whole church—in full awareness and reverent surrender to that mystery, do its statements take on their authentic meaning. We know who God and the Christ are in the worship of them.

Christian faith, therefore, requires a dialectical awareness analogous to the experience of the disciples in the gospel accounts of the transfiguration. It is an awareness that moves between the revealed glory of the Christ and the ordinary humanness of the man from Nazareth. "And looking around, they saw no one with them, but only Jesus" (Mk 9:8).

Conclusion

If there are two ultimate questions in human life—who, or what, is God? and who, or what, are we?—revelation may be seen as God's answer to both of them. Unlike other answers to more limited questions, this one does not put an end to the questioning—though it reorients it, giving it both a new direction and the assurance of finding its goal. For the divine answer infinitely surpasses the human question: it is the very being of God, symbolically bestowed. To hear and receive it fully requires faith and a lifetime's labors—and even they are only a beginning. One hears it by listening faithfully to the word spoken in nature, in experience, in Scripture, in the church; one hears it in prayer and action, living and thinking, suffering, loving, and above all in dying.

These symbolic acts, in which each human person must find himself or herself, are both a response to and a realization of God's revelation in Jesus. In that revelation God shows us who and what God is, even while making known to us who and what we are. Our real identity is thus simultaneously our achievement and God's gift: "To the one who overcomes, I will give . . . a white stone with a new name written on it, a name known only to the one who receives it" (Rev 2:17).[33]

Recommended Readings

Besides Dulles's *Models of Revelation*, the following books and articles are particularly recommended.

Dulles, Avery. "Revelation and Discovery." In *Theology and Discovery: Essays in Honor of Karl Rahner*, S.J. Edited by William J. Kelly, 1–29. Milwaukee: Marquette University Press, 1980. Overcoming the traditional opposition between "acquired" and "revealed" knowledge, Dulles shows how human effort and the psychological dynamics of discovery enter into the revelatory process.

Eliade, Mircea. *Patterns in Comparative Religion*. Translated by Rosemary Sheed. New York: Sheed and Ward, 1958. A classic study which interprets basic "natural symbols" (sky, sun, moon, vegetation, stones, water, etc.) used in the world's religions so as to make clear how they manifest the transcendent.

Langer, Susanne K. *Philosophy in a New Key: A Study in the Symbolism of Reason, Rite, and Art*. New York and Toronto: New American Library (Mentor), 1951 (1942). A major twentieth-century contribution to the epistemological understanding of symbolism, clearly written and full of suggestive insights.

McFague, Sallie. *Metaphorical Theology: Models of God in Religious Language*. Philadelphia: Fortress, 1982. A well-written and original synthesis of some of the best contemporary thinking on the topic, which uses "metaphor" in a sense analogous to "symbol" as understood in this article (though stressing the "is not" or nonidentity of symbol and symbolized more than the "is"). See also her *Models of God: Theology for an Ecological, Nuclear Age* (Philadelphia: Fortress, 1987).

Rahner, Karl. "The Theology of the Symbol." *Theological Investigations*. Vol. 4, pp. 221–52. Translated by K. Smyth. New York: Seabury, 1974. Rahner's classic essay in the metaphysics of symbolism, understood as the self-realization of one being (or aspect of being) in another, a category inclusive of both God and creatures.

S I X
The Wisdom that Leads to Salvation: Revelation and Scripture

Peter Schineller

To speak about the meaning of revelation and Scripture today is something like walking into the middle of a mine field. With dangers on all sides, we seem to be living in an age of extremes. In the religious world, on the one hand, there are an increasing number of fundamentalists who take the Bible with utmost seriousness. For many of them it is the *only* important book, containing the answers to all of life's problems. Often they interpret the Bible in a literal sense, forgetting that almost 2,000 years have passed since it was written.

On the other hand are those for whom the Bible has lost its real significance, becoming only one book among many. These persons are shocked by the historical inaccuracies, the seeming contradictions and naïveté of the Bible, shocked so much that some of them have given up their Christian faith and turned to secular faiths or to a God no longer revealed uniquely in Jesus Christ.

In between, however, one finds the majority of Christians for whom the Bible still holds special importance but who have varying degrees of familiarity with it. In Africa, for example, Protestants and Catholics alike show vivid interest in and love for the Bible. But there is a danger of turning to fundamentalist and at times magical interpretations. In the United States too we also find a growing tendency to fundamentalism, yet the deeper and more dangerous tendency may be to secularism, or what some now even call neopaganism. This holds true in the United States, and surely is true of Africa as it is invaded by the forces of modernization.

Where does the truth lie for the Christian? How does one set the steady course between fundamentalism—where the Bible becomes the only book—and secularism—where the Bible is simply one book among many? How does one maintain the central but not exclusive significance of the Bible for human life today? This is the first question to be considered. Second, granted the Bible's significance, how did it arise? How were the various Scriptures assembled into the book that we call the Bible, the Old and New Testaments? Third, is this book the final word of God or could another Bible come into existence? Fourth, how do we understand the Christian claim that the Bible is the inspired and inerrant word of God? Fifth, are all books and parts of the Bible equally important for Christian faith? Finally (and here we return to the first question), what is the relation between the written word of God and the other ways that God is revealed today?

The Bible and Life

How do we come to understand properly the place of the Scripture in Christian life? How do we avoid the extremes of fundamentalism and secularism? The key, it seems to me, putting it rather boldly, is to realize that life is primary and the Bible is secondary. This is precisely what is happening in many small Christian communities throughout Latin America, communities that are deeply Christian and take the Bible with utmost seriousness, frequently in the midst of life-and-death issues. One biblical scholar who has lived with and studied these communities, describes it this way:

> The common people are putting the Bible in its proper place, the place where God intended it to be. They are putting it in second place. Life takes first place! In so doing, the people are showing us the enormous importance of the Bible and, at the same time, its relative value—relative to life. [1]

This may seem shocking. It seems to undercut the importance, the central significance of the Bible for human life. But it serves to remind us that the God who speaks through the Scriptures also speaks to us in many other ways. In the Middle Ages, for example, Saint Bonaventure spoke eloquently of two books, the book of Scripture and the book of nature. To be able to read the book of Scripture, according to Bonaventure, we must also study and find God through the created world, the world of nature that God also gifted us with. Today we speak of the discernment of spirits, seeking God's particular call and will for me and the community in the present that comes through the active inspiration of the Holy Spirit. We can recognize, with Peter at Pentecost and with Vatican II, not only the priesthood but the prophethood of all believers. God speaks a word to everyone, a word for which each must take responsibility.

In short, the God who speaks to us in the Bible has already spoken to us, and is continually addressing us in many different ways, through our personal histories and through the signs of the times.

John Calvin sets forth a helpful image in the first book of his *Institutes of the Christian Religion*. He says that the Bible functions like spectacles *through* which we see the world, God, life, and our neighbor. [2] When our sight is weak and our vision blurred, glasses enable us to see better. Like eyeglasses, we do not look *at* the scriptures, but *with* and *through* them to see God and God's ways. The Bible serves to give us a clearer vision of who God is and how God encounters us in our everyday life.

Why this insistence on the relative value of the Bible? I believe that it helps to overcome the two tendencies or temptations we began with. On the one hand, if we believe that God speaks through events and experiences today as well as through the Bible, then we are on the road to avoiding the fundamentalist narrowing of revelation to the words of the Bible. In interpreting the Bible, we will keep at least one foot on the ground because, as we interpret it, we are also involved in interpreting life around us. This is the approach to which the experience of the Latin American Christian communities attests. We turn to God's word to help us understand and interpret our present situation. This attitude goes a long way toward preventing ungrounded, fundamentalist, and often fanciful interpretations of the Bible.

On the other hand is the secularist tendency. Persons of this persuasion would be more likely to take the Bible seriously if they are supported in their conviction that the Bible is not the only source of truth. While they can trust their own experience, they also need the spectacles or eyeglasses of Scripture to clarify and interpret their experience. In this way they are encouraged to test the waters, to see that the Bible is one key source of truth, a wisdom that does lead to salvation (2 Tm. 3:15), as the title of this chapter indicates. Later we will show how the Bible indeed functions as a classic, a rich treasure or resource for truly human existence today. It is not outmoded or outgrown but a perennial witness to the truth and reality of God's love.

From Revelation to Scripture and from Scripture to Revelation

Scripture is rather easy to describe or define since it refers to that specific collection of writings that the Christian churches take to be their most reliable guide, their basic source. Scripture has a unique, formative, constitutive role in the history and life of the church.

Revelation on the other hand is not so simple to describe or define, because it is a word used in many settings and on many levels. During the Watergate hearings we heard of new revelations. An insight into a friend or a problem can be called a revelation. Not only Christians but many religious traditions speak of divine revelation at the base of their belief. In spite of the pluralism of meanings, for our purposes we quote the following general definition from Avery Dulles:

> Revelation is God's free action whereby he communicates saving truth to created minds, especially through Jesus Christ as accepted by the apostolic Church and attested by the Bible and the continuing community of believers.[3]

What is the relationship between Scripture and revelation? As implied in the previous section on Bible and life, revelation is a more encompassing term, one that extends to religious revelations beyond the Christian tradition and to revelations occurring within the Christian community but not found exclusively in Scripture. Thus the Bible or Scripture, while it may be termed the basic source for Christian life and theology, should not be viewed as the only source. It does not contain the whole of revelation.[4]

So too, while all of Scripture is said to be inspired, and Scripture can be called divine revelation, not every word of Scripture should be considered to be revelation if that is taken to mean truth that is revealed only by God. Many of the factual truths in Scripture, the existence of Pontius Pilate, for example, can be known from other sources. We say therefore that the Scripture contains and points to revelation. It is a record of human testimony to revelation.

To understand better the relationship between Scripture and revelation, we might use our imagination to try to recover how the Scripture came to be written. While the exact dates remain unknown, we are quite certain that the period from the earliest writing of the books of the Old Testament, perhaps in the ninth century B.C., to the latest writing in the New Testament, probably at the beginning of the second century A.D., lasted more than one thousand years. Even within the New Testament there was a span of about seventy years from the earliest writing (Paul to the Thessalonians) to the latest (2 Peter).

The writing of any particular book also took time and effort. Luke points to this in his prologue (Lk 1:1–4). He hints at the toil and care that permeates his own writing. He is familiar with other accounts or stories of Jesus; he knows of eyewitnesses to the events; and then he mentions his own efforts at drawing up an orderly account. In other words, Luke looks back to and depends upon the various revelations of God to Jesus, the various revelatory experiences of Jesus by the apostles and disciples, and the various traditions that already record these revelatory events. Then he writes his own presentation that eventually becomes known and accepted as the Gospel according to Luke.

The Second Vatican Council's Dogmatic Constitution on Divine Revelation (*Dei Verbum*) expresses the process in this way:

> The sacred authors, in writing the four Gospels, selected certain of the many elements which had been handed on, either orally or already in written form, others they synthesized or explained with an eye to the situation of the churches, the while sustaining the form of preaching, but always in such a fashion that they have told us the honest truth about Jesus.[5]

The written Scripture arises, therefore, from a series of revelatory events guided by the Spirit of God. Under the same Spirit, Luke, as author, inherited the story of these events and wrote his story of Jesus Christ for his particular community and its mission.

The revelatory process continues, however, as the writings of Luke become a source of revelation for those who listen to it in faith. In other words, in the faithful telling of the story of Jesus, God again reveals God's saving power and love. We come, therefore, full circle from the revelation of God to Jesus; through the revelation of Jesus to the apostles and disciples; through the inspired written record of these events according to the pen of Luke; to the proclamation of the story of Jesus according to Luke that takes place in churches and homes today. The same God who spoke to Jesus, and to Luke, speaks to the Christian community today.

God's self-revelation is thus to be viewed as an ongoing, ever-present event in the formation and continued life of the Christian community. Scripture too retains its central, irreplaceable role in this ongoing life of revelation. For Scripture serves to crystallize, objectify, or capture in the written word the story of God's revelation first to the Jewish people and then to Jesus and his followers. Scripture functions today to make this story of Jesus available to Christians and to the nations in that ongoing act of revelation/faith whereby Jesus is acknowledged to be the Christ, one's Lord and Savior.

The Canon of Scripture

The Scriptures, as we have seen, were composed over a long period of time, more than one thousand years. And there were, of course, many other extant religious writings. We turn now to the process by which the Christian church identified those particular books which would be authoritative for the community. This was a process that also took place slowly over several centuries. The word *canon* refers to that collection of books that are acknowledged to be authoritative in the church. In Greek, a canon meant simply a reed or a measuring stick. The canon sets the limits or boundaries by indicating which books, and only which books are considered to be the church's holy books of Scripture.[6]

How did the canon emerge? The need for establishing the canon of Scripture arose because of heretical tendencies in the community. In the case of the formation of the canon, two particular heresies were significant. On one extreme was Marcion. Around the year 140 he began to teach that the Creator-God of the Old Testament was an inferior deity. Jesus alone revealed the true God, the God of love. Furthermore, Paul's writings rather than the gospels preserved this revelation by Jesus. When Marcion constructed his canon, it consisted of ten letters of Paul and an edited version of the Gospel of Luke, a companion of Paul. In the face of this repudiation of the Old Testament and this narrowing of the story of Jesus to Paul and Luke, the church had to act to safeguard and preserve the importance of the many writings overlooked or denied by Marcion.

On the other extreme was Gnosticism. While this heresy appeared in varying forms, in general its adherents claimed to have an improved or perfect version of the Christian faith. The claimed to possess secret books, special knowledge (*gnosis*), and information on the life and teaching of Jesus. Thus in contrast with Marcion, the Gnostics expanded the canon or list of sacred writings to include works such as the Gospels of Thomas and of Philip or the Apocalypse of James.

The process by which the canon was established is not to be understood as a masterstroke or magical intervention on the part of God. Rather, under the inspiration of the Holy Spirit, it was the growing faith of the church that led the community and its leaders to recognize their own faith in some writings and not others. By what criteria did church leaders determine that a particular writing was canonical, part of the rule of faith? We have no logbook spelling out the process, but in retrospect we can see that the following considerations were primary. First, the particular book must be of apostolic origin (the Old Testament was excepted and was considered part of the canon for other reasons). By this we mean that it must be closely linked to original witnesses of resurrection faith, not that it must be proved to have been written by an apostle. Second, the book must be part of the liturgical usage of the church, a book which could be read and prayed in the worship of the church. Third, the content of the book must be orthodox, in conformity with the written and unwritten tradition coming from the apostles. In other words, it must be in accord with the lived faith of the community.

The canon emerged, therefore, from below. In preaching and practice, in liturgy and catechesis, the church came to realize that this list of books, and no others, had been and would remain the canon or rule of faith. This list would continually guide the church and provide its basic constitution. These books would be considered the classic documents for Christian faith and life.

This process took time, and it was only in the year A.D. 367, in the East, that Athanasius in an Easter letter designated as canonical the twenty-seven books contained in our New Testament today. Various councils and synods of the late fourth century repeated this canon, and the Council of Trent in 1564, in the face of the Reformation, reaffirmed the list.[7]

One problem remains, however. A comparison of the traditional Catholic Bible with a Protestant Bible reveals that the canon is not exactly the same for these two Christian communities. While both agree on the list of books of the New Testament, the Catholic Bible includes forty-six books in the Old Testament, while Protestants accept only thirty-nine. The seven disputed books are: Tobit, Judith, Wisdom, Sirach, Baruch, and 1 and 2 Maccabees. Books common to all groups are called *protocanonical* or first canon; those restricted to the Roman Catholic (and Orthodox) churches are called *deuterocanonical* or second canon; Protestants designate them *apocrypha,* meaning obscure and secret books. The reason for this divergence is that before the coming of Jesus Christ, the Jewish people used two versions of Scripture, depending upon where they lived. Greek-speaking Jews outside Palestine used the seven books in question, while Palestinians did not. When Saint Jerome translated the Bible into Latin, he used the Greek Septuagint version, now called the Alexandrian canon. This became the Roman Catholic canon. When Protestants in the sixteenth century began to make translations, they used the Palestinian canon, comprising only those Old Testament books originally written in Hebrew. It must be noted that the differences between the Protestant and Catholic canons of Scripture are slight; in no way do they constitute grounds for the continued separation of these traditions.

The formation of the canon can be seen, therefore, as a necessary and inevitable step in the ongoing life of the Christian church. It provides definite limits and shape to the faith of the community. While it does mean closure—no new books can be added—we must also note that in contrast to Marcion's reductionism, the canon allows and celebrates diversity. Both Old and New Testaments are included, and within the New Testament we have not one but four gospels, four different accounts of the Christ event. Different writers and styles of writing, varying viewpoints are incorporated into the canon of Scripture. Each book in its own way points to the rich, unfathomable mystery of God's love in Jesus Christ.

Jesus Christ—the Final Revelation

Canonicity means that no new books will be added or subtracted from the list of sacred Scripture. It also points positively to the sufficiency of Scripture. In those books we have adequate, sufficient saving knowledge or revelation from God concerning the nature of God and the meaning and goal of human life.

The sufficiency of Scripture necessarily leads us to Jesus Christ and to affirming him as the fullness of God's self-revelation. The Second Vatican Council states that Jesus Christ "completed and perfected Revelation, and confirmed it with divine guarantees" (Dei Verbum 4). This was achieved through his life, teaching, death and resurrection, and the consequent sending of the Spirit of truth. So complete and perfect is the revelation of God in Jesus Christ that, the council continues, "The Christian economy, therefore, since it is the new and definitive covenant, will never pass away; and no new public revelation is to be expected before the glorious manifestation of our Lord, Jesus Christ" (Dei Verbum 4).

How is this strong claim to be understood? Does it not set human limits on the power and love of God? How can an event of the past be so determinative and constitutive for all human history? The claim is really one with the Christian affirmation concerning the divinity of Jesus Christ. As the early church came to see that Jesus was risen Lord, the unique Son of God, it almost naturally came to the related conclusion that the revelation of God in Jesus Christ was definitive. The church thus affirms that in him we have not simply another in the row of prophets, but the final prophet; not simply another savior figure, but the unique Savior and mediator between God and humanity.[8]

In Jesus Christ God perfectly and fully expresses God's word, will, and love. Because Jesus is the personal presence of God, no one else could come who could reveal more of the inner life and nature of God. Paul tries to highlight this when he writes that if God did not spare the Son, will this God "not also give us all things with him" (Rom 8:32)? Thus, Scripture, the official witness to this revelation of God's love, is closed because in it the fullness of God's love is revealed. It is closure because of full disclosure; that is to say, by disclosing as fully as possible to the human condition the love of God and the significance of that love for human existence, the Scriptures come to be closed and final.

Yet even here we must make a few qualifications. First, as Vatican II states, revelation will be consummated with the final coming of Jesus at the end of time, even if this in one sense is not part of our age or epoch. Second, there will be no new *public* revelation, that is, no new official Scripture for the entire church. This does not disallow the continued history of private revelation to individuals or groups. Third, it does not mean that Christians merely repeat the words of Scripture. Rather there must be the ongoing attempt, under the inspiration of the Spirit, not only to understand the revelation in Scripture but also to interpret and proclaim that revelation in ever-new situations. There is therefore a history of revelation/faith that is itself creative. While there will be no new revelations to equal or overshadow the revelation of God's love in Jesus Christ, we can say that every time the gospel is heard and accepted in faith, there is a new revelation/faith event. The same God who spoke through the prophets and above all through Jesus, speaks today through the Holy Spirit.[9]

The Inspired Word of God

Another way to indicate the unique and irreplaceable role of Scripture in the Christian tradition is to speak of Scripture as the inspired word of God. At the same time that we designate particular books as part of the canon of Scripture, we acknowledge and affirm in faith that each of these books is inspired.

Two problems arise with the concept of inspiration. On the one hand, some object to it because it seems to remove the Bible from ordinary experience and raise it to some magical, mystical realm as a book set apart. On the other hand, if we hold to inspiration, how are we to imagine it in such a way that it does not take away from the human creativity and freedom of the biblical authors? Both problems will be addressed, but we begin with a more general sense of the word *inspiration.*

Inspiration means literally to be "breathed into." The poet, the artist, the philosopher are often said to be inspired. At work or study we speak of a sudden inspiration. This points to some new input not there before, which comes as a gift and deeply affects or guides our way of thinking or acting.

When applied by the church to the Scriptures, inspiration means the belief that certain books were written under the impulse or inspiration of the Holy Spirit so that God can be called the author of that book and the entire Bible can be called the word of God.[10] The most frequently cited text that points to the inspiration of Scripture is 2 Timothy 3:14–17, part of which reads, "All Scripture is inspired by God and profitable for teaching, for reproof, for correction, and for training in righteousness." (v. 16).

The Scriptures are, however, also the words of human persons, human authors, the words of Paul and Luke, for example. Thus Vatican II explains:

> To compose the sacred books, God chose certain men who, all the while he employed them in this task, made full use of their powers and faculties so that,

though God acted in them and by them, it was as true authors that they consigned to writing whatever God wanted written, and no more. (*Dei Verbum* 11)

This perspective, we may note, is sharply different from those views which picture (as some artists did!) God moving the pen of the evangelist. In the latter case, the gospel writer is a passive instrument. God dictates what is to be written to ensure that every word and phrase of the Bible is inspired. This model, to be sure, is inadequate for several reasons. First, by making the gospel writers into passive secretaries for God, it denies for all practical purposes that they were genuine human authors. Second, it does not square with our present way of understanding how the Bible actually came to be written and assembled. We see, for example, that Paul wrote specific letters to address concrete problems in a particular church. We already indicated that Luke had to gather, listen, and labor to edit and finally write his account of the good news. He himself says this in the introduction to his writings (Lk 1:1–4). Belief in inspiration does not diminish human effort and responsibility. Nor should we imagine that inspiration means that the Bible is 50 percent God's work and 50 percent human. Rather, it is both fully God's word and work and truly and fully human word and work.

One way to illuminate this mystery is by comparing it with the mystery of the incarnation; just as Jesus Christ was truly divine and truly human, so the Scripture is God's word and also equally the word of human authors. Thus Vatican II can say:

Indeed the words of God, expressed in the words of human beings, are in every way like human language, just as the Word of the eternal Father, when he took on himself the flesh of human weakness, became like human beings, (*Dei Verbum* 13)

The new model for understanding inspiration branches out from the narrow focus upon the writer with pen in hand in his or her study, and sees that the inspiration of the Spirit was at work in the entire process by which the Scriptures were formed.[11] The preservation of the memory of Jesus through the preaching of the gospel, the gathering of the stories about Jesus and of the early church, the transmission and preservation of these stories and their assemblage into the books of the Bible as we have them now—all this was done under the guidance or inspiration of the Holy Spirit. Thus, for example, the hymn in the letter of Paul to the Philippians (2:5–11) is not inspired simply while Paul writes or includes it in his letter. Rather it is inspired as a hymn reflecting the faith life of the first Christians and then used again by Paul under the guidance of the Spirit. But the process of inspiration continues even further, as we have seen, to include the establishment of the canon of Scripture. And it continues into the present. When the letters of Paul are proclaimed and listened to in faith, we can say that the same Spirit who inspired them in their origin is present now, inspiring faith, hope, and love in those who hear them today.

Trustworthiness of the Bible

Because the Bible is affirmed as the inspired word of God, it is also said to be inerrant. Literally, this means that it is free from error. While inerrancy has been the traditional way to speak of the truthfulness of the Bible, in recent years this term has been used less often, at least in Roman Catholic circles, because it is primarily a negative description and can also easily lead to misunderstandings. Vatican II, for example does not use the term, but states:

> We must acknowledge that the books of Scripture, firmly, faithfully and without error, teach that truth which God, for the sake of our salvation, wished to see confined to the sacred Scriptures. (*Dei Verbum* 11)

Note the careful limitation included here, namely, that the Scriptures teach without error truths "for the sake of our salvation."

This means that not every part of the Bible need be considered true in accord with the norms of science or of secular history. We do find discrepancies in geographical and historical details of the Bible. In light of scientific understandings of evolution, we need not believe literally that the world was created in six days, as the book of Genesis tells us. While the story of Jonah is a marvelous and deeply religious story, we need not believe literally, to be enriched by that book, that Jonah was for three days and nights in the belly of the fish. Even religious truths that are contained in the Bible evolve and must be carefully interpreted. We read in one passage that we should turn our swords into plowshares (Is 2:4). Another passage says that we should turn our plowshares into swords (Joel 3:10). If we take these two passages out of context and place one against the other, they are contradictory and cannot both be true. Yet when placed in their proper settings, they contain and reveal significant religious truths.

The word of God is inerrant and trustworthy, therefore, only when properly understood and interpreted. This means that we must take into account the meaning the author had in mind, the literary form (whether it be a story, a letter, a poem, etc.) in which the thought is expressed, the circumstances of the time and culture in which the text was written, the varied types of speech and narrative employed, as well as the customs and conventions of those times.[12] This is a laborious task, but it is the only way in which one can properly understand and interpret the word of Scripture.

The truthfulness of the Bible can be understood negatively as freedom from error. In this sense the Bible will never deliberately lie or mislead the reader. But inerrancy must also be understood positively. It is the assurance that in the Bible we have a most reliable witness to God's truth and love. God is faithful and can be trusted. So too God's word can be relied upon. Because of this quality the Bible remains the unique source, the basic norm for Christian life.

Could one ever prove that the Bible is inerrant, or for that matter, inspired? Rather than search for such a proof, what the church offers is the history of the Christian community as faithful witness. Not arguments from the texts, not polemics concerning details of Scripture, but the overall witness of lives transformed through the power of the word attest best to the truthfulness and trustworthiness of Scripture. The Bible has perdured through the ages as a solid, reliable base for life, as a reliable, faithful witness to the mystery of God's love and truth.

The Richness of Scripture

From the more technical questions concerning the revelation of God in Scripture, let us turn now to the richness of the word and see how powerfully, persuasively, and beautifully it reveals the compassionate love of God to the human situation.

It might be helpful to think of the Scripture as a classic, or more accurately as *the* classic of the Christian tradition. It is unequaled by other Christian classics such as Augustine's *City of God*, the *Summa* of Thomas Aquinas, *The Institutes of the Christian Religion* of John Calvin, or *The Spiritual Exercises* of Ignatius Loyola. Classics might be understood "as those texts, events, images, persons, rituals and symbols which are assumed to disclose permanent possibilities of meaning and truth."[13] In confronting a classic, our present horizon is stretched and challenged. New possibilities for transformation are offered. As we interpret the classic, we find that our own lives are interpreted by it. A classic receives its status as classic not by the fiat of authority, but only by gradually coming to be experienced and publicly recognized as a work of enduring quality and universal meaning. This, as we have already indicated, parallels how the canon of the Bible came to be recognized.

Thinking of the Bible as a classic encourages one to approach it as we would any great work of literature. Accordingly, one must be open to the full display of literary forms that it includes. The Bible is in reality not one book but a rich library of books that contains prose and poetry, drama and parable, history and narrative, prophecy and myth, letters and gospels. Through this vast array of writings, the Bible roots our faith in the *past* by including stories and myths of the origin of the world, the origin of the Israelite people, and the origin of the Christian community. The Bible points us to the *future* in hope by challenging us to believe that God goes with us in our journey toward new heavens and a new earth. The Bible challenges us to reach out with love to our brothers and sisters in the *present*, for God is there, the God who identifies God's very self with the poor, the weak, the marginated.

In this encounter with the Bible we do not approach it primarily as a catechism or code of law. It is not a series of cold and lifeless truths for our intellects, not a series of commands to be obeyed by our wills. Rather Scripture, like any classic, opens our imagination to new possibilities, new ways of envisioning God and ourselves. Perhaps, in the words of Paul Ricoeur, it is best described as a nonviolent appeal to our imagination.[14]

Yet we must not delude ourselves into thinking that every part and passage of

Scripture, because it is inspired, will immediately be inspiring or even exciting to us. Some parts are dull. Many parts are hard to unravel. Through it all, however, the rich and varied witness to the incomprehensible mystery of God breaks through.

The Christian Church tries to introduce Christians into the richness of Scripture through the daily readings of the liturgy and especially the Sunday cycle of readings used for Sunday worship. But this is only a beginning. In his or her own way, each Christian must befriend the Scripture, becoming familiar with its classic treasure so that it may truly become God's revealed and revealing word for today.

Because the Bible is so rich and pluriform, particular communities and individuals in different periods and circumstances find themselves drawn to different parts of the Scripture as particularly comforting or challenging to their situation. Thus Luther was drawn to the letters of Paul. Liberation theology challenges us to hear again the cry of the prophets and Psalms that the Lord is on the side of the poor. Women today remind us that in Matthew and John the first witnesses and preachers of the resurrection of Jesus were women. Some speak therefore of key biblical books or passages as a "canon within the canon." Even the official church speaks this way to some extent when it states:

> It is common knowledge that among all the inspired writings, even among those of the New Testament, the Gospels have a special place, and rightly so, because they are our principal source for the life and teaching of the Incarnate Word, our Savior. (Dei Verbum 18)

Within the story of Jesus, the parables of the good Samaritan, the prodigal son, the woman caught in adultery are powerful, indeed revelatory, even for those who do not share Christian faith. The stories of Abraham and Joseph, of Moses and David, of Jonah and Amos, of Ruth and Rebecca are classic stories that continue to give life. The Twenty-third Psalm—"the Lord is my shepherd"— speaks to universal human hopes. The critic, George Steiner, wrote recently that "there is nothing else in world literature, perhaps in world thinking, of the stature of Job."[15] In the encounter with stories and poems such as these, the word of God becomes spoken again, addressed to all who have ears to hear. As we let the richness of Scripture unfold before us and confront us, we become like the two disciples on the road to Emmaus (Lk 24:13–35). The imagination is touched, the heart is challenged, and God's word gives us renewed strength and courage, a new sense of direction for the journey ahead.

Conclusion

At the end we come full circle. We have attempted to move between the two extremes of fundamentalism and secularism, to see the central, yet relative significance of Scripture for Christian life. We emphasized that the Bible must be read, studied, and prayed in close relationship with life. While we have tried to show that the Bible is the most important book, we also emphasized that it is not the only important book. The revelation of God in the Bible (sometimes referred to as Revelation with a capital R) must help us to discover and respond to the revelation of God in our everyday life, revelation with a small r.

We continue on the journey with the powerful presence and guidance of God's word. Armed with that word, we steer a path between the two extremes. We are not like the secularists who do not believe that they need the vision, the spectacles of Scripture to illumine the way. Nor are we like the fundamentalists who may be so caught up in the Bible that they fail to see the joy and hope, the grief and anguish of the men and women of our time.

Scripture is indeed the wisdom that leads to salvation. Thus in the struggles with tragedy and oppression we Christians turn to Job and to Moses to see how they found strength and light amid difficulties. In our joy we think of the woman who finds the lost coin, the father who welcomes back the prodigal son. When we are weak and tempted we think of David or Peter, and return to God with them. When our spirit is troubled, we recall how the Holy Spirit brought new life and hope to the apostles at Pentecost. Above all, the Christian turns to Jesus Christ, the faithful witness. The mystery of his life, teaching, death and resurrection illuminates our own journey from God to God. In this way there is a continual interaction between the Bible and life, life and the Bible. The Bible becomes again the revelation of God's love.

With the guidance of the Bible as a faithful witness to the love of God in Jesus Christ, with the strength of Jesus Christ the faithful witness, the final result should be that the individual Christian and the Christian community in turn become a faithful and living witness to God's love in the world today, a world that desperately needs signs and witnesses to that love. As the Word of God personally took flesh in Jesus of Nazareth, so too, led and empowered by the Spirit, God's Word may again share our flesh in Christian lives today. The fifth Gospel is born, the faithful witness of the Christian community.

Recommended Reading

Three standard reference works contain essays that intersect with this chapter. The essays on Bible, canon of Scripture, inerrancy, inspiration, revelation, Scripture and tradition in *Sacramentum Mundi* treat these issues from the viewpoint of systematic theology. The essays on inspiration and canonicity in the *Jerome Biblical Commentary* emphasize the biblical material and perspective. More recent are essays on canon of Scripture, inerrancy, inspiration, and revelation in *The New Dictionary of Theology*.

Achtemeier, Paul J. *The Inspiration of Scripture*. Philadelphia: Fortress, 1980. Shows how one's theory of inspiration is dependent upon views of how the Scriptures were formed. He writes from the Protestant perspective.
Brown, Raymond E. *The Critical Meaning of the Bible*. New York: Paulist, 1981. Here the

S E V E N | The Church: Context for Theology

T. Howland Sanks

Receive the Gospel of Christ, whose herald you now are. Believe what you read, teach what you believe, and practice what you teach.

Rite of Ordination to Diaconate

The Integrity of the Church

In the previous chapter we have seen that the formation of the canonical Scriptures took place over a long period of time and involved several factors such as apostolic origin, use in the community's prayer and liturgy, and conformity with the written and unwritten beliefs of the community. Scripture was born and bred in the community we call church. The church was the milieu for the composition and recognition of Scripture and remains the milieu for understanding and interpreting it. Chronologically, the formation of the community antedates the formation of Scripture. The Scriptures are the earliest example of the community's self-understanding. The Scriptures are the church's book. Hence, if the Scriptures are to be believable, the community must be believable.

In this chapter we will discuss the fundamental or foundational issues concerning the church. The challenges to the believability of the church have been posed differently in different times and places. Prior to Vatican II, the foundational questions concerning the church were those posed by the growth of historical consciousness in the nineteenth and early twentieth centuries: Did Christ intend to found a church? Did he establish some form of hierarchical order among his followers? Did he confer some kind of primacy and special power on Peter? And, did such authority pass on to the subsequent leaders in the church?

Biblical scholars and historians from a wide range of confessional backgrounds have developed a broad consensus on these questions of the historical origins of Christian community (summarized below). While they must still be addressed, the basic issues about the church which vex thoughtful and inquiring people today stem rather from the "masters of suspicion" of the nineteenth century, Karl Marx, Sigmund Freud, and Friedrich Nietzsche. These new questions concern

99

the relationship between the church's proclamation and its praxis. In short, the foundational issues about the church today center not so much on the verifiability of its historical claims as on the credibility of its religious claims. We are in search not of the "true church" but of a "believable church," a church whose witness is credible in principle.

The masters of suspicion have made us all too aware of the unconscious or subconscious motivations for action, of hidden agendas, of power struggles masked as spiritual battles, of the dialectical relationship between theory (read theology) and its social base, of the ideological content of all thought, and of the necessary connection between proclamation and action in the world. Further, in reaction to the overly individualistic interpretation of post-Enlightenment Christianity, we are more concerned than ever with the life and activity of the church *qua community*, and with its effect in and on our collective social history. I agree with Francis Schüssler Fiorenza when he says:

> It becomes necessary to examine how the Church in its present reality and praxis mediates to the present the concretizations of the relation between Jesus and the Church displayed in the Gospels. . . . For such a question is not simply an issue of social ethics, but rather a fundamental theological issue: how does the Church's mission display its religious identity and thereby show its truth?[1]

This fundamental question of the religious identity and truth of the church is framed for us today amidst the awareness of the alternatives offered by the other great religious traditions of the world. Foundational theology is no longer addressing simply the atheist, agnostic, or pagan unbeliever but also the firm believer in another tradition, and the abiding awareness of these other possibilities within the Christian believer him/herself. The context of this wider pluralism is addressed in chapter 10, but it must be kept in mind when reflecting on the purpose and function of the Christian community.

In this chapter, then, we will discuss first, the historical origins of the church; then, the emergence of theology in the church; the functions and ingredients of theology; the challenges to this communal self-understanding, especially the contemporary challenges; how some self-understandings become authoritative or normative for the community; and finally, the current situation.

Origins of the Christian Community

Although the historical origins of the church may not pose the most vexing question at present, nonetheless the relationship between Jesus of Nazareth and the community called church must still be addressed. The issue can be stated succinctly in the oft-quoted (though truncated) phrase of Alfred Loisy: "Jesus preached the kingdom of God, and what came was the church."[2] Although Loisy was writing to refute the claim of Adolf Harnack that there was little if any relationship between the preaching and expectations of Jesus and the church as it had developed through the ages, his lapidary formula captures the tenor of the issue as it was posed in the late nineteenth and early twentieth centuries. Our current understanding of how movements and social groups develop historically does not allow us to postulate or expect either a clear-cut continuity or discontinuity, or to seek a line of simple direct causality between the will and actions of Jesus and the community of disciples which formed around him and which remained after his death/resurrection/ascension.

It is true that Jesus came to preach the kingdom and not to start an ecclesiastical organization. He did not form anything like the institutional models available in Jewish society at that time, such as a rabbinical school or a closed community like that of Qumran. Nevertheless, there is sufficient basis to assert some continuity between the preaching and activity of the earthly Jesus of Nazareth and the community which came to be called the "church." Daniel Harrington argues that there were continuities in belief, personnel, and practice:

> By accepting the *teaching of Jesus* these disciples were already different from other Jews of their time. Instead of abandoning these teachings after Jesus' death, the disciples treasured and proclaimed them. Also, there was a continuity in *personnel* between Jesus' disciples before his death and those who bore witness to him after the resurrection. In both cases the Twelve and the women were the central characters. There were even continuities in *practice*. The church's common meals commemorating Jesus' death and resurrection surely had their origin in his sharing of meals with tax collectors and sinners. The church's free attitude toward the Law and the Pharisaic tradition can be traced back to Jesus' own example. Even baptism "in the name of Jesus" surely had its root in the eschatological ritual of moral purification practiced by John the Baptist.[3]

These continuities of belief, personnel, and practice are the basis for discerning a direct continuity between Jesus and the gradually developed institutional structure we call the church.

This gradual development of the sociological group with organizational structures can be understood with the help of Max Weber's categories, such as the "routinization of charisma." This is the process whereby the teaching and/or preaching of a charismatic prophetic figure (Jesus in this case) is preserved and carried on by a group of followers who have recognized and received him and his message as being of transcendent significance. While this concept is useful in helping us understand the transition from the preaching of the earthly Jesus to the institutional church, we must remember that Christian theology uses the term *charism* in a specific sense as "gift of the Holy Spirit" rather than in Weber's more generic meaning. Further, institutionalization does not necessarily imply the disappearance of the charismatic element altogether. Both remain in tension in the church through the ages. Avery Dulles summarizes these contrasting aspects of the church: "Charism is spontaneous, personal, temporary, and fluid. Institution is prescribed, typical, stable, and clearly defined."[4]

This shift from the charismatic movement to an incipient institution depended on how the disciples understood and received Jesus and his preaching.

Such developing understanding usually occurs with the help of the symbolic deposit or tradition available to the group at the time. In the case of Jesus of Nazareth and his followers this was the Jewish tradition; the symbolic deposit was basically contained in what is now referred to as the "Old Testament." The "New Testament" records the manner in which this symbolic deposit was "transvalorized," to borrow Eliade's language—building upon the multilayered depth of the symbol, enlarging it and transforming the whole in the process so that there is even more surplus of meaning than before. The disciples used the symbols of the Old Testament to understand who *he* was (Who do men say that I am? What do you say?) and to understand who *they* were. So, they recognized and received him as the Son of man, the Son of God, the Anointed One, the One they were expecting, the Messiah.

Not everyone who heard or saw him, however, received and recognized him. Those who did, although still Jews, gradually began to differentiate themselves from "the Jews" who did not. They became, in effect, a sect within Judaism. Again, they appealed to the symbolic deposit for self-understanding as a *group*, they became the *New* Israel, the *New* Chosen People, the *New* Covenant, the *true* Remnant, etc.

This gradual growth of self-consciousness as a distinct community was aided and abetted if not, indeed, forced upon them by events external to the life of the group and over which they had no direct control. The destruction of the temple in Jerusalem in A.D. 70, for example, caused a major crisis within Judaism itself. In the turmoil which followed, the Jewish disciples of Jesus were eventually expelled from the synagogues (c. A.D. 85), as is reflected in the New Testament, e.g., in the Book of Signs in John's gospel.[5] The nascent Christian community was forced by such events to greater distinction from its Jewish parentage and to greater clarity of self-understanding.

One other factor contributing to the development of the distinct sociological community we have come to call the church was the gradual realization that, although Jesus had proclaimed that the reign of God was at hand, it did not come as fully or as finally as had been expected, and that this movement, this new "Way," was going to continue somewhat longer before Jesus would come again in glory. The shift in the eschatological expectation made it necessary to provide for continuity in preaching and teaching even after the first disciples/apostles died. How various local churches developed in this subapostolic period has been detailed elsewhere.[6]

In summary, then, the historical line of development from the preaching and actions of Jesus of Nazareth to distinctively Christian communities called churches is generally not seen today as historically problematic nor as much of an apologetic concern as had been the case in the latter part of the nineteenth and first half of the twentieth centuries. It is understood as a normal sociological and historical development, and although there may be differences in the interpretation of specifics, scholars of diverse denominational backgrounds would generally agree that the church did indeed naturally and legitimately emerge from the words and deeds of the earthly Jesus of Nazareth.

Emergence of Theology

The self-understanding of a group, or a community, is analogous to the self-understanding of an individual. We (individually or as groups) come to a consciousness of who we are by (1) distinguishing ourselves over against others, e.g., we know what it means to be Roman Catholic in part by comparing and contrasting ourselves with Protestants, Jews, etc.; (2) by retelling the stories of our ancestors, our history, e.g., "A wandering Aramean was my father; and he went down into Egypt and sojourned there." (Dt 26:5); and (3) by a determining vision of the future which moves us to try to fulfill our destiny, e.g., "To make the world safe for democracy," or "Manifest Destiny" in American self-understanding.

We have seen that the earliest Christian communities were forced by circumstances to do just that: (1) to distinguish themselves from their Jewish contemporaries; (2) to employ their own Jewish stories, their own Jewish history to understand who Jesus was and who they were (e.g., Philip and the Ethiopian, Acts 8:26 ff.); and (3) to understand themselves in terms of an imminent eschatological expectation which only gradually had to be redefined (1 Thes 4:11). Thus, *mutatis mutandis*, the self understanding of the early Christian communities developed along lines similar to the self-understanding of an individual. This reflective self-understanding of the community we have come to call *theology*. Hence, we speak of Pauline theology, the theology of the Johannine community, etc.

It is important to note two characteristics of this developing communal self-understanding. First, it was and continues to be precisely the self-understanding of a *community*. This reflection is always done *in, by* and *for* the community called church. The church is the *context* for theology no matter what form or genre it may take. Second, this self-understanding is broadly conceived to include not only questions of meaning or definition (creed) but also the implications for action and the behavior of the members of the community. The experience of Jesus of Nazareth was fundamentally an experience of a new "Way," a new "Way" of living with ramifications for all aspects of the lives of his followers (code and cult). How this new "Way" was to be worked out in the practical details of daily living was also included in the communal reflective awareness. What later came to be distinguished into moral theology, spirituality, and liturgical theology were included in the emerging theology.

Functions and Ingredients of Theology

For several reasons, the Christian community could not help but engage in this self-reflection. It was entailed by their effort to understand who Jesus was vis-à-vis their Jewish history and tradition. At the same time they knew that they were, willy-nilly, differentiating themselves from this tradition. Hence, their reflections had several functions: (1) to explain their own experience of this man Jesus to themselves; (2) to explain their experience to their contemporaries, first to fellow Jews and subsequently to Gentiles; and (3) to justify or legitimate their practices and actions as a community.

These same basic needs have persisted throughout the life of the community as it has developed since apostolic times. Yet all subsequent critical reflection is necessarily mediated by the recorded experience of the first disciples. Hence, there is a further function—(4) that of constructive historical retrieval and interpretation of this mediating experience, whether recorded in canonical writings (Scripture) or in other historical sources (tradition). This latter function has assumed much greater importance with the growth of historical consciousness and the refinement of the historico-critical methods.

These four *functions* also serve to highlight what we might call the ingredients or "raw materials" or theology. Traditionally, the sources or *loci* of theology have been listed as Scripture, tradition, reason, and experience (see chapter 2). Different theologians have prioritized these sources in various ways and some (Paul Tillich, for example) have made a point of saying that experience is not a "source" but a "medium" for our theological reflection.

In light of my description of the process the community's self-understanding, I would like to recast the discussion by talking about the "raw materials" of theology.

1. *Experience*—The experience of the earliest communities and (in some cases like Paul's) of individuals has been recorded in writing and, when recognized by the community as an authentic expression of its faith, has been accorded normative status in the form of Scripture. These canonical writings are the record of communal experiences. To say this is not to deny that they are "revelation" or "inspired by God" (chapter 6), but it is to recall that the experience of Jesus is the basis and root of Scripture.

It is equally true to say that tradition is the record of the experiences of other communities and of particularly gifted individuals. Thus, the writings of the fathers of the church, the decrees of councils and synods, the work of the great theologians are all records of somebody's experience—usually of a community's experience. Robert Schreiter rightly describes tradition as a series of "local theologies."[7] Hence, I would list both Scripture and tradition under the rubric of "experience."

In addition, the term experience also includes the experience of the contemporary communities. Vatican II urges us to "read the signs of the times" (GS 4), meaning that we should be attentive to contemporary experience, not only specifically "religious" experience, but all facets of human life. Contemporary theologians are especially responsive to the social, cultural, economic, and political experiences of the communities in which they live. I would suggest that this was always the case, though perhaps implicitly and unconsciously.

2. *Symbolic deposit*—As mentioned above, the experience of the first disciples and all of us is thematized with the aid of the symbolic tradition available to the community at the time. Scripture and tradition also form part of this symbolic deposit for the contemporary Christian community. The symbolic deposit is not confined to the overtly or specifically religious symbolic deposit but includes natural and cultural symbol systems also.

3. *Conceptual Categories*—The multivalent or polysemic quality of symbols calls for further clarification and specificity for which the interpreters of the community appeal to conceptual categories taken traditionally and most frequently from philosophy, but also from the social and natural sciences or other areas of human thought. Such conceptual categories have greater clarity and definiteness but less depth than symbol systems (See chapter 5). This is the ingredient generally intended by the term "reason" as a source for theology. Since reason can have so many meanings, however, I prefer to speak of "conceptual categories."

How these ingredients are put together, in what proportions, with more emphasis on one or the other, will depend on the needs of the community in various times and places. If the community's self-understanding is under attack from the surrounding culture as in the time of the Enlightenment, then there may be more stress on conceptual categories that will enable the Christian community to explain itself to this world. If the problematic is internal to the community as in the time of the Reformation, there may be greater need to reinterpret the symbolic deposit of the community's own tradition. In any case, the communal self-understanding (theology) has taken many forms and genres throughout its history, and we should not be quick to confine the designation "theology" to the form which dominated in only one time or place, whether that be Antioch, Alexandria, Paris, or Lima.

I want to suggest that, at present, the community's self-understanding is challenged by the apparent dissonance between its proclamation of the good news and its praxis *qua* community. Hence, it is not surprising that greater emphasis is being placed on the contemporary experience of the community or, more accurately, the experience of various local and regional communities, and that some attempt is being made to reestablish the relationship between this lived experience and the symbolic deposit. For this reason there is increased concern for analysis of the community's experience and a corresponding emphasis on social and cultural analysis in theology, as exemplified in liberation theology.

In this rather simplified description of the emergence, development, functions, and raw materials of the community's self-understanding that we call theology, I have referred to the earliest community of disciples grappling with the basic questions of "Who do men say that I am?" and "Who are we who have experienced this man Jesus?" But it is important to realize that this is an ongoing process in the life of the Christian community. Each generation of disciples must respond to these questions for itself in its time and place. No definitive, once-

and-for-all answers are given, and yet each subsequent generation depends upon and must stand in continuity with its forbears. This description is exemplified by all the great theologians, the great interpreters of the Christian experience: Ignatius of Antioch, Cyprian, Jerome, Augustine, Bonaventure, Aquinas, Luther, Calvin, and so on. The cumulative self-understanding of previous generations of Christians we call *Tradition*.[8]

As we have seen, the community called church is the *context* in which this continuing process of reflective self-awareness takes place. But it would also be true to say that those who share this common self-understanding, this common symbol system, *constitute* the community called church. Despite external similarity of practice, those who do not appropriate the shared story of a group cannot be said really to belong to that group. Conversely, those who do understand themselves in terms of the shared symbol system of a group are in fact members of that community, even if they do not always pay their taxes on time.

Challenges to Communal Self-Understanding

The emergence and growth of the community called church and its concomitant self-understanding and reflective awareness were not simple, uniform, or homogeneous. Diversity and pluralism were characteristic of the originating experience of the first disciples. Just as multiple witnesses to any historical event may be said to have significantly (though not completely) different experiences of the same event (think for example, of the thousands who witnessed the assassination of President John F. Kennedy), so it was also true of those who witnessed the life and preaching of Jesus of Nazareth. Depending on each witness's background, previous experiences, specific concerns, personal characteristics, etc., each has a somewhat different experience. So, Mary Magdalene's experience of Jesus was presumably different from John the Baptist's or Judas Iscariot's. This diversity of experience is only compounded by time and distance. Hence, it should not surprise us that records of these originating experiences, written down after some years by redactors (editors) on behalf not of an individual but of a community with its own concerns, life situation, and sociocultural context, should also be diverse. Hence, we have four gospels (we could have had more) and a variety of other literary forms in our "canon" (see chapter 6).

Further, there is no such thing as "raw" or uninterpreted experience. The very act of articulating or thematizing experience is itself already an interpretation of that experience (see chapter 8). Consequently, since there has been (and continues to be) more than one record of the community's experience, there is necessarily more than one interpretation of that experience. Pluralism of experience and interpretation is endemic to the community called church and poses a challenge to the unity of its self-understanding.

A second challenge arises from the very nature of symbols. As mentioned above, symbols are polysemic or multivalent, i.e., bearers of many layers of meaning; therein lies the richness and value of symbolic mediation.[9] The truth communicated in symbolic mediation is not very definite, however; it often lacks precision and clarity. This poses problems for a shared self-understanding in a community such as the church.

This lack of clarity and precision leads to the employment of conceptual categories, as I have indicated. But these, too, pose a third challenge to the ongoing nature of the community's self-understanding, because such categories are always historically and culturally bound. Since language is living and fluid, even technical philosophical terms depend for their clarity and precision on the context in which they arise and in which they are used. Their meaning is not easily maintained if used in a different historical or cultural context. Thus, terms like *logos*, *person*, or *nature* no longer have the clarity and precision they did at the time of the councils of Nicaea or Chalcedon and may convey different meanings now than originally intended.

These three challenges—the plurality of experiences and interpretations, the polysemic character of symbolic communication, and the historical and cultural relativity of conceptual categories—together produce a fourth challenge, which Paul Ricoeur has termed a "conflict of interpretations." There must be some way of adjudicating or reconciling conflicting claims to meaning and truth. These four challenges to the self-understanding of the church have existed from the beginning, and the church has responded to them through a variety of strategies, with more or less success. We cannot detail that history here but do want to discuss how these challenges pose foundational questions in the church at present.

Challenges Today

Vatican II reminded us that pluralism (of experience and interpretation) has been with us from the beginning:

> However, the heritage handed down by the apostles was received in different forms and ways, so that from the very beginnings of the Church it has had a varied development in various places, thanks to a similar variety of natural gifts and conditions of life.[10]

The council was referring to a pluralism of traditions *within* the Christian communion, not only a plurality of *individual* experiences but also a plurality of *communal* experiences and developing traditions. Although this is not new, Yves Congar suggests that what *is* new is "the degree to which people are aware of it and the urgency, extent and depth of their recognition of it . . ." And further:

> What is relatively new is the recognition of the *other* as such. For centuries people have attempted to make others conform to them. The other person has been loved, esteemed, as a step towards his or her taking the same direction as ourselves. The new development is marked by an interest in the other precisely where he or she differs.[11]

Here Congar is referring not only to pluralism within the Christian tradition but to cultural and ethnic pluralism as well.

This greater awareness of cultural and ethnic diversity was encouraged by the recovery and renewed emphasis on the local church in Vatican II. The council recognized that the one and only Catholic Church comes into being "in and from such individual churches," that the variety of local churches is by "divine Providence," and that the local churches "enjoy their own discipline, their own liturgical usage, and their own theological and spiritual heritage" (LG 23). The "Church of Christ is truly present in all legitimate local congregations of the faithful." (LG 26). Such affirmations fostered the emergence of local self-awareness and its concomitant theological expression and development in the churches of Latin America, Africa, and Asia. This is frequently dealt with under the rubric of "inculturation," but the full consequences of this form of pluralism have not yet been realized.[12]

The other form of pluralism with which we are only beginning to come to terms is the increased awareness of other world religious traditions. It is no longer possible for the average person to ignore or not to take seriously the religious claims and achievements of Judaism, Hinduism, Buddhism, or Islam. This is a new aspect of the challenge of pluralism for the church today.[13]

There are various levels of pluralism, then—pluralism on the level of experience, both individual and communal; on the level of interpretation of experience, both within the Christian community and outside of it; on the level of culture and ethnicity both diachronically and synchronically; and on the level of worldwide religious symbol systems. This is a fact and a condition of the situation in which we live and pursue our theological reflection, but it poses a challenge because pluralism is not just the affirmation of differences on these various levels, but also assumes something in common, some point or basis of unity, something we share with one another. As fellow Christians we share the experience of Jesus as the Christ; as members of a particular nationality or region we share a cultural heritage and a language; as fellow human beings we share common human experience and common questions about our existence. (I realize anthropologists and sociologists raise serious caveats about assuming that very much is common and their warnings must be taken seriously.)

For the community called church today, the challenge is to maintain some form of unity in belief, practice, and behavior while at the same time fostering a legitimate emphasis on the different local churches, local customs, languages, and cultural backgrounds. No longer can unity be equated with uniformity of doctrinal formulation, liturgical practice, or moral behavior. Nor can the cultural experience and history of Western Europe be the criterion of global unity. How the church has responded and is responding to this challenge we will discuss after considering the other three challenges mentioned above.

Chapter 5 of this volume has discussed the symbolic structure of religious faith and revelation. Here I only want to mention the particular challenge that the nature of symbolic communication poses for our communal self-understanding.

It arises from the polysemic or multivalent character of symbols. It is precisely because symbols are the bearers of multiple layers of meaning, of a surplus of meaning, that they are able to "introduce us into realms of awareness not normally accessible to discursive thought." But at the same time "the meaning of the symbol . . . cannot be precisely nailed down in terms of categorical thought and language."[14] Our residual Cartesian drive for clarity and distinctness does not let us rest, however, and as Ricoeur has put it, "the symbol gives rise to thought." The difficulty is that it gives rise to *many* thoughts, and a great variety of clear and distinct ideas and categories are used to specify the symbolic tradition.

The next moment in this process of moving from image to symbol to thought poses its own challenge, however. For whatever conceptual categories we adopt to clarify and pin down symbolic knowledge are historically and culturally conditioned. Early Christian theologians found Neoplatonic categories useful, Aquinas made wonderful use of Aristotelian categories, and contemporary theologians are finding Marxist or process or European transcendentalist categories more or less helpful. But Marxist categories, to take one example, were developed in an analysis of nineteenth century industrial capitalism in Western Europe. Can these categories of thought travel to a non-Western, agrarian, or preindustrial society in the late twentieth or early twenty-first century? Or, if they do, will they have the same clarity of content which they did for Marx?

I said earlier that these three challenges together give rise to the most basic challenge to a community's self-understanding, a "conflict of interpretations." The various mechanisms or strategies for dealing with such conflict within the community called church is the subject of the last section of this chapter.

Authoritative Norms in Community

Any community must develop some means to resolve internal conflicts, preserve its unity, and maintain its identity. It must draw some boundaries beyond the pale of which membership ceases. As we have seen, shared self-understanding constitutes a community, but the self-understanding also includes modes of behavior and practices implied in that shared consciousness. Just as the shared self-understanding develops only gradually, so too do the boundaries of that awareness develop mainly in the face of challenges to it or conflicts about it.

For the community called church, clarity about those practices, beliefs, and norms which it held in common and which held it together came only gradually and in the face of conflict. Commonly held beliefs are usually called doctrines, dogmas, or authoritative teachings, sometimes even infallible teachings. Much of the discussion about such authoritative teaching in recent times, especially prior to Vatican II, was couched in very juridical and legalistic terms. Avery Dulles, in his discussion of these issues, sketched the postconciliar attempts to transcend this "non-historical and juridical type of thinking" and there is no need to repeat that here.[15] But I do want to outline the factors involved in arriving at authoritative and normative positions for the Christian community. Let us retrieve the early church's experience of conflict resolution, prescinding for the moment from the language of juridical rights and obligations, of assent, dissent, of the quantitative weight of propositional statements, or infallible and noninfallible magisterium in which so much of the recent discussion has taken place.[16] Let us go back to the beginning.

Acts records the early conflict among the first disciples about the need to impose the Mosaic law concerning circumcision and dietary regulations on gentile converts to Christianity (Acts 15). According to that account, the apostles and presbyters convened and, after much discussion and listening to the arguments put forth by both sides, they resolved, in agreement with the whole church, to send representatives with a letter to the church at Antioch which began: "It is the decision of the Holy Spirit, and ours too, not to lay on you any burden beyond that which is strictly necessary."

This (and the parallel account in Gal 2) is the earliest record we have of resolving a conflict of interpretations in the Christian community. It contains all the elements for adjudicating a conflict and making authoritative decisions—convening the leaders of the community, hearing all sides, extensive discussion, and agreement of the whole community—and most importantly of all for the Christian community, the Holy Spirit. For, from the beginning, the Christian community recognized that the exercise of authority among its members was to be distinct from other human groups. Authority in the Christian community should not be exercised in the manner of the "Gentiles," but rather as befits "one who serves" (Lk 22:24–27) and in imitation of the master who washes the feet of his disciples (Jn 13:1–17). Decision-making in the early Christian community was understood to be more than a mere sociological necessity; it was a manifestation of the Spirit of the Lord.

This Spirit-based authority was manifested in a variety of gifts and a variety of forms of service—apostles, prophets, teachers, workers of miracles, healers, helpers, administrators, speakers of tongues (1 Cor 12:4–31; Eph 4:11; Rom 12:6–8). Charismatic gifts, then, along with proximity to the originating event (experience of the earthly Jesus and witness to the risen Lord) as well as recognition and reception by the whole community were the criteria for authoritative decision-making in the community called church. The ultimate criterion for what was normative for the community was, of course, the life and preaching of Jesus; but Jesus did not speak on each specific issue the community faced, so their judgment had to be by inference or implication, as in the case of not imposing the Mosaic law on gentile converts. This was a decision about behavior, but soon disputes about belief and formulation of belief arose (e.g., Gnosticism). Clarity about the latter was more difficult to come by, as the early christological controversies show.

The point here is, of course, not to retell the history of theology, but to describe and explain how the "conflict of interpretations" has been and is resolved and how some forms of communal self-understanding become normative (doctrine) and binding on the church (dogma). We have already indicated the factors involved—the Holy Spirit manifested in charismatic gifts, apostolicity, recognition and reception by the whole community. These criteria are rather vague and fluid and have come to be specified practically in a variety of ways. Where and how does the community find the promised Spirit of the Lord who would teach us all things? How could we tell that the apostolic teaching was to be found here and not there? And what constitutes recognition and reception by the whole church?

As indicated in the account in Acts 15, the *Spirit* was to be found when the leaders of the community assembled together, discussed and heard all sides. So the Spirit is to be found in synods, regional and ecumenical councils, in representative gatherings of the various churches. The Spirit is also manifested in particular individuals with obvious gifts (charisms) such as speaking in tongues or prophesying, as well as less dramatic gifts such as teaching, administration, healing, etc. And as these gifts became structured offices in the community, the Spirit was understood to be with the officeholders entrusted with the care of the community (2 Tim 1:7, 14). Finally, the Spirit is manifested in the canonical Scriptures considered to be "inspired" (see chapter 6).

Apostolicity was also specifically located and locatable. First of all, apostolicity referred to the teaching of the apostles, the apostolic tradition that was contained in the Scriptures but also in the canon of truth or the *regula fidei* that was a summary of the faith accepted in widely diverse geographical areas by the second century and summarized by Irenaeus in *Adversus Haereses* I.x.1 (c. A.D. 180). Congar rightly points out, however, that this "rule of faith" was first of all lived out in the life of the church before it was actually formulated.[17] For Irenaeus also, apostolicity was located in those who are the official guardians and teachers of this canon of truth, the bishops who succeeded the apostles in their sees in an unbroken line of succession and who handed on (*tradere*) this teaching from one to the other.[18] Gradually, these official teachers, rather than the content, became the chief criterion for apostolicity, with the Church of Rome assuming an ever-increasing role as the ultimate touchstone.

The nature of *reception* by the whole church has also taken a variety of concrete forms. In general, reception

> can be described as a process by which one ecclesiastical body adopts as its own a spiritual good which originates in another and acknowledges and appropriates it as applicable to its own life of faith. This process may include a formal juridical act of reception on the part of church officials. Correspondingly, there may also be a response on the part of the other members of the community to the authoritative act in which obedience to formal juridical authority has a place, but the spiritual reception by the whole community includes a degree of consent and possibly judgment as to whether what is being received serves the common good.[19]

I am not using the term here in the narrow juridical or legalistic sense, but in the more general meaning of the acknowledgment by all levels of the community that this spiritual good is indeed an expression of their faith. We saw that this general sense of reception of Jesus' life and teaching was the very beginning of the church, but reception was also involved in the formation of the canon of Scripture and in the practice of baptism and the eucharistic meal. When reception is lacking, even official decisions do not hold in practice, as exemplified in the failure of the Orthodox Church to receive the decision of the Council of Florence in 1439 that *officially* ended the schism between East and West, but *in practice* did not. The widespread nonreception of *Humanae Vitae* since 1968 has been cited as a more modern example of the need of this ingredient for a decision to be normative in practice. Whether reception occurs as a formal decision by a synod or council, or by an official representative of the church such as the pope or a bishop, or by the actual practice of the faithful, reception in the broadest sense is required for theological opinion (*doxa*) to become a normative ecclesial doctrine. At present, much attention is focused on the notion of reception as a necessary ingredient in the ecumenical dialogues between various Christian denominational bodies. It has become apparent that consensus among theologians cannot move the churches further along the path of unity without a more widespread reception of their consensus among the faithful.[20]

In summary then, normative beliefs (doctrines and dogmas), cultic practices (liturgical regulations), and moral behavior (moral law) are arrived at in councils, either ecumenical or regional, with the aid of gifted theologians and leaders in the community such as the fathers, doctors and popes, always in keeping with the canonical Scriptures, and with some manifestation of reception by the community as a whole.

We have been describing how the community called church arrives at normative beliefs, practices, and behavior in a very general way that applies to the various forms of Christianity—Orthodox, Protestant, and Roman Catholic. But for the Roman Catholic form of Christianity the locus of the Spirit, of apostolic tradition, and of reception on behalf of the whole has become specified, indeed even concentrated in the papacy.

Without detailing the growth of the papacy historically, we can say that the great popes of the Middle Ages such as Leo I, Gelasius, and Gregory the Great enhanced the papal claims to supremacy and fullness of power over the universal church. It was really the Gregorian reform of the eleventh century, Congar argues, which in its attempt to free the church from its identification with the political society and domination by local rulers, gave rise to a more centralized and juridical notion of authority in the church.[21] Although this was the dominant trend from the eleventh to the sixteenth centuries, there were countercurrents such as the movement known as conciliarism, which argued for the supremacy of council over pope and kept alive the alternative loci of decision-making in the church. In protest against this centralizing and juridicizing of normativity in the Christian community, the Reformers raised the cry of *sola scriptura*, denying that ultimate authority in the Christian community could be located in structured offices, especially the papacy, and affirming Scripture as the *norma normans non normata*. The Roman Catholic response at the Council of Trent and thereafter was to reemphasize the unwritten traditions handed down from the apostles as complementing the canonical Scriptures. Subsequently, as Congar argues, official Roman Catholic theology concentrated not on the content of this apostolic tradition, the *quod*, but on the transmitting organism, the *quo*, or the magisterium,[22] and this in turn became concentrated (at least in the ultramontane and dominant view) in the teaching authority of the pope.

This movement reached its high-water mark in the definition of papal infallibility in 1870 at the First Vatican Council. Since that council was unable to complete its work, it was not until the Second Vatican Council that the Roman Catholic form of Christianity was able to recover the importance and necessity of Scripture, of all bishops, and of the body of the faithful in arriving at normative decisions for the community called church. Papal infallibility, therefore, should be located in this larger historical development of decision-making and resolving conflicts of interpretation. The specific historical context and exegesis of the 1870 definition of papal infallibility has been the object of much attention in the recent ecumenical dialogues, and a more nuanced and sophisticated understanding of it has been offered by such Roman Catholic theologians as Avery Dulles.[23]

In summary, then, the activity of the Spirit, apostolic tradition, and reception by the community have been the constant factors in arriving at authoritative norms for the Christian community. These factors have been variously located in Scripture, in charismatic individuals, in institutionalized offices, in councils, in the sense of the faithful, in learned fathers and doctors of the church, and in the papacy. Dulles pointed out some time ago that in the history of the church, emphasis has been given to one or other of these "secondary authorities," but "when any one authority is absolutized at the expense of others, it weakens itself and loses credibility." He also points out that in periods of transition, such as the post-Vatican II church, when particular forms of authority of the recent past are (being) criticized as no longer satisfactory, "it may seem that authority itself is being contested and undermined; but on reflection, and in a wider perspective, it becomes apparent that authority is merely changing its forms."[24] It is precisely this wider perspective that this chapter attempts to provide.

Current Situation

I have framed this discussion of doctrine, dogma, and theology in the church in terms of the resolution of a conflict of interpretations within the experience of the community. Stressing that such questions arise from an original unavoidable pluralism of experience and interpretation, I have tried to put the question of authoritative decision-making in the church in a more neutral, less polemical fashion than has been the case recently. With a similar intent, but from a rather different perspective, George Lindbeck has offered a proposal to understand doctrine on the model of "rule theory." He argues that doctrine functions like the rules of grammar in a language, regulating what can or cannot be expressed in that language. Indeed, religious language determines not only what can be *expressed* but even what can be *experienced.* Instead of the symbol system enabling us to understand and express our experience, the experience is derived from the religious language.[25] The *only* function of doctrines as communally authoritative teachings is *regulative.* Lindbeck argues that they do not express and illuminate the community experience, as I have argued, nor are they truth claims, as in the "traditionalist-propositionalist" position.[26]

Since Lindbeck does concede that the relationship between religion or religious expression and experience is dialectical and that the causality between the two is reciprocal, I think he overstates his case to make a point.[27] What is certainly valid in his claim is the recognition that language *does* limit the possibilities of understanding or of thematizing experience. What is not valid is his claim that language *gives rise to* or is the *source* of the experience. When Jesus asked his disciples, "Who do people say that I am? They replied, Some, John the Baptizer; others, Elijah; and still others, one of the prophets" (Mk 8:27–28), they were calling upon the symbolic deposit available to them at that time and place. They could not have replied, "A new manifestation of the Lord Krishna" or "A reincarnation of Joseph Smith!" They groped among the symbols in their tradition to express their experience of Jesus, and Peter finally said, "You are the Messiah," thus expressing the most adequate understanding of the community at that time. It was not the language that gave rise to Peter's experience of Jesus. It was an experience not derived from his understanding of the Messiah, but an experience which transformed that understanding and caused him no end of problems in doing so!

The relationship between experience and the religious language which becomes authoritative for a community is dialectical. The authoritative formulation (dogma) certainly *regulates* what is acceptable (or more accurately *unacceptable*) in the community—what is unthinkable or prohibited in moral behavior or liturgical practice. But that is not its *only* function, as Lindbeck would contend. It does express truth on the symbolic level, and with as much clarity as the conceptual categories, given their limitations, permit. As Dulles argued in his *Models of Revelation,* dogmas themselves are symbolic and "communicate more than can be contained in clear concepts . . . The propositionalism of the rationalistic age lost sight of the dynamic aspect of dogma, treating it rather as a picture or scale model that could be substituted for the reality to which it referred. Dogmas should never be allowed to become objects in which the understanding comes to rest. They must function disclosively."[28] Dogmatic formulations are always tending toward the transcendent truth and point the community beyond themselves. In that sense, they provide guidance for the church in keeping with the belief that the church as a whole cannot err in matters of belief (LG 12).

We have seen that there has been a plurality of experiences, of interpretations, of symbols, of conceptual categories, of communal self-understandings, of theologies, in the life of the community called church. It has devised various strategies and structures for dealing with the resultant conflicts. These strategies have always involved at least three basic (or essential) elements: the Spirit manifested in a variety of ways; apostolicity; and reception by the whole community. When this pluralism is not recognized and accepted, when the procedures for resolving conflicts of interpretation are truncated and do not involve all the segments of the community, or when justice and fairness are lacking, the church becomes quite literally incredible, unbelievable, implausible.

I suggested at the beginning of this chapter that such a lack of credibility is *the foundational* problem for the church today. But it is not a problem that can be resolved by greater theological sophistication or new conceptual categories. Rather, it is a matter of the praxis of the community called church. How the church operates in fact, both internally and with regard to the rest of the world, is perceived by many both within and without her community to be at variance with the good news she proclaims.

A believable church will have to be bold and courageous in adopting and fostering the aspirations of the marginalized and oppressed peoples of the world, aspirations voiced by the variety of liberation theologies coming from Latin America, Asia, and Africa and by blacks and women on all continents. A believable church will have to be an example in its own internal structure and praxis of the justice and equality which have come to be expected in the post-Enlightenment world. A believable church will have to embrace and embody both individually and as a community the simplicity and poverty of the gospel. A believable church will have to be modest in its own claims to truth and sincerely respectful of the claims of other traditions to truth. In short, the church today must bring its praxis into line with its proclamation or it will remain *unbelievable*.

Recommended Readings

Congar, O. P., Yves. *Diversity and Communion.* Mystic, CT: Twenty-Third Publications, 1985. The master ecclesiologist's recent essays on pluralism and unity among the churches, with insights on many of the topics touched on in this chapter.

Dulles, S. J., Avery. *A Church to Believe In: Discipleship and the Dynamics of Freedom.* New York: Crossroad, 1982. These essays deal with the problem of the credibility of the church, with special attention to the issues of the magisterium and a contemporary understanding of infallibility.

Granfield, Patrick. *The Limits of the Papacy: Authority and Autonomy in the Church.* New York: Crossroad, 1987 Although focused on the papacy, this excellent historical study explores the other loci of decision-making in the church.

Harrington, S. J., Daniel J. *God's People in Christ: New Testament Perspectives on The*

E
I   Scripture in Theology
G   Pheme Perkins
H
T

Major themes in Father Dulles's work such as ecclesiology, revelation, the
nature of doctrine, and the prospects for ecumenism, have been enriched by the
flowering of biblical studies among Roman Catholics. No one has been more
appreciative of the efforts of biblical scholars than Avery Dulles. When he was
Gasson Professor at Boston College, it was not uncommon for a very polite mid-
afternoon knock on my office door to signal the arrival of a few more pages to be
checked for their suitability in the light of New Testament scholarship. Reading
that material was never a chore because there was so rarely anything to be added
or revised.

One might wish that such "inhouse" ecumenism occurred between the various
theological specialties more frequently. But one usually finds a wary hostility
between systematic theologians and exegetes. Many theologians continue to use
Scripture to "prooftext" conclusions reached on other grounds. Many exegetes,
wary of the misuse of their carefully nuanced conclusions by theologians, do not
attempt to draw theological implications from their work. Despite this "communication gap" between exegesis and systematic theology, exegetical work
today does suggest ways in which dialogue between the two theological specialties ought to occur. This essay examines three major areas of concern: (1) an
understanding of "hermeneutics" that enables us to recognize the historical
character of human understanding without accepting an historicist relativism
that robs the tradition of any meaningful claims to mediate truth to the present;
(2) developing models for recovering the significance of Scripture for theology
and ethics that are sensitive to the historical and social contexts of biblical
material; (3) moving from the genuine pluralism of the canon to new understandings of unity in pluralism that contribute to the problems of unity and
ecumenism today both within the Christian family and between Christians and
Jews. Each section seeks to point out major directions and ongoing problems in
relating Scripture to theology.

117

Hermeneutics as Foundation of Exegesis and Theology

The intellectual world of the twentieth century has been marked by the perception of the radically historical character of human social, cultural, and political achievements on the one hand, and the mechanistic manipulation of the world and persons understood as "dead matter," on the other. An alliance between our culture's historicism and the technocrat's positivist mentality produces a view of language as mere instrument or as a collection of signs that can be manipulated at will since they are without meaning in themselves.[1] Since exegetical work seeks to situate the biblical traditions in concrete historical circumstances and often presents explanations for the text through a reconstruction of its history, exegesis is frequently accused of historical positivism. Its methods require that the Bible be analyzed like other books; that the meaning of its words be tested against the words of other writers of the time, and that the history of the peoples who shaped and preserved the biblical tradition be reconstructed using the tools and methods appropriate to writing the history of any ancient people. Can any religious authority remain for Scripture when it has suffered such dissection?[2]

Exegetes and theologians have answered such charges by appropriating philosophical analyses of understanding that describe the complex interaction between the world and the *pre-understanding* of the subject matter that each interpreter brings to the task of understanding a text, a work of art or a historical period. Rudolf Bultmann's famous essay "Is Exegesis without Presuppositions Possible?"[3] finds in hermeneutics the answer to Nietzsche's charge that historical analysis will destroy the "life-giving" illusions of a past that should be constantly reshaped by the artistic imagination. Bultmann insists that it is the pre-understanding of the subject matter which initiates our life-giving relationship to it. Pre-understanding is not "prejudice," since we allow our understanding to be corrected and reshaped by the text. However, for a text to have this "life-giving" character it must be of vital interest to us. By learning to know our history, we come to know ourselves.[4]

A philosophical hermeneutics may explain how we continue to find "truth" in great works that have shaped human cultures, but it does not address the special position of the Bible as canonical Scripture. The biblical text is not just any "classic work" which might engage our attention and existential concern. It represents the "testimony" of the believing community that points to a particular, individual, historical moment as the manifestation of the ultimate reality in which all human life is grounded and toward which it moves.[5]

We cannot adopt a naive literalism that expects the Bible to convey its message of salvation without the intervening efforts of human interpreters. An interpretive "distance" between believers and the kerygma was created as soon as the gospel was put in writing. The immediacy of oral testimony and personal witness typical of the earliest days of Christianity gave way to the text that now grounds what is experienced as Christian tradition.[6]

For much of Christian history, the Bible has been understood as the authoritative grounding for doctrines. Christians even distinguished themselves from others by their position on particular doctrinal questions. Biblical theology meant discovering concepts in the Bible that provided the basis for the key elements of theological syntheses.

Meeting the "History-of-Religions" Challenge

Emergence of the "history-of-religions" approach to studying the Bible challenged that view of Scripture. The Bible came to be seen as recital or narrative rather than as the product of theological reflection. It presents the reader with the "saving events" in the language of poetic symbolism, myths, and other images.[7] This language was often borrowed from the poetry and myth of surrounding cultures. Such borrowings confirmed a fundamental postulate of the history-of-religions approach: religion is fundamentally syncretistic. Myth, cult, mysticism, and magic anchor religions in human life—not doctrinal syntheses constructed by some of its adherents.[8]

Though he contributed much to a history-of-religions understanding of the New Testament, Rudolf Bultmann maintained reservations about its appropriateness to the "subject matter" of the New Testament. These reservations were grounded in a theological understanding of the New Testament as the decisive word of salvation. When the history-of-religions approach is taken to its logical conclusion, Christianity becomes nothing more than a cult piety centered upon the figure of Christ. Bultmann insisted that the faith response called for by the kerygma, submission to the claim of God and the neighbor, presupposed a distinctiveness in the history of Jesus. It had to be unlike that of any other human person.[9]

Bultmann's students have often adopted the history-of-religions methods without Bultmann's theological caution. To understand Christianity, lines of influence must be drawn that connect non-Christian groups and sources to what we find in the New Testament. Christian religious expressions are then measured by their closeness to or distance from what is found in the Jewish or Greco-Roman environment.[10] Helmut Koester, for example, insists that the christology of the divine Son in the Fourth Gospel reflects a gnosticizing redeemer myth. The myth was created from fragments of older Greek myths to justify the cultic actions of cultic groups. One should not make the mistake of thinking that such myths were created independently of the cultic practices they were invoked to explain.[11]

The threat that Christianity might be dissolved into an expression of Greco-Roman religious syncretism could be met in two ways. One might emphasize the persistent critique of the religious and cultic practices of nonbelievers in both Hebrew Scriptures and the New Testament. Or one might insist upon the critique of social structures and their religious legitimations that appears in the prophets and the teaching of Jesus. Both approaches seek to show that a historical-critical reading of the biblical evidence can differentiate its understanding of faith from "religion" as a mythic system of cultural legitimation. From a theological perspective, neo-orthodoxy insisted that the word of God in the Bible stands in judgment of all human culture, all human efforts to create security apart from the free gift of God. Religious syncretism represents such a human effort. Bultmann agreed that an unredeemed humanity would use both its science and its religious "myths" to secure its place in the world.[12] He insisted that faith is a nontheoretical understanding of oneself. The way in which one acts and lives in the world is determined by the gospel. When a person discovers a love of God that accepts persons as they truly are, then the old way of living in the world comes to an end.[13]

Bultmann's existentialist approach to expressing the unique claim on human life mediated by the New Testament witness insisted that theology is founded on anthropology. Liberation theologians have transformed the existentialist description of anthropology with its emphasis on the individual believer into a sociopolitical description which focuses on human communities. Juan Luis Segundo can agree that theology is based on the New Testament's anthropology. He can agree that central categories in Pauline thought include human bondage to sinful structures which can only be overcome by the free grace of God in Jesus Christ. But when the liberation theologian comes to read Romans 1: 16–32, he or she finds the imprisoning powers of sin in dehumanized relationships with other human beings.[14]

Both existentialist interpretation and its liberationist offspring accept the view that theology and exegesis cannot be sheltered from the developments of the world in which we live. They belong to the global experience of technological, social, and cultural development which must become part of our understanding of the word of God. Otherwise the religious tradition will become an artifact unable to shape the developing consciousness of humanity.[15] Scripture is not simply a historical artifact or a work of literary art. As a narrative of the "saving acts" of God, it seeks to transform the lives of individuals and communities.[16]

Scripture as "Classic" Narrative

Both the existentialist and liberationist hermeneutics employ systems of understanding human persons and communities formulated apart from dialogue with biblical material by philosophers and social scientists. Seeking an approach that is more directly focused on the text of the Bible, theologians and exegetes often turn to the hermeneutics of "classic texts" or other strategies of literary criticism to explain how Scripture functions as an authoritative text. For example, Jesus' parables are said to create an authoritative vision of the world that demands that the hearer pass judgment on the "world" of everyday experience.[17]

David Tracy has made a case for understanding the role of Scripture as analogous to that of other "classic" texts. Such texts have formed a culture. They will always contain an "excess of meaning" that can engender new readings and

will challenge any attempt to pin them down to univocal, single interpretations.[18] While exegetical analysis attempts to recover the New Testament by
reconstructing the tradition history of the text, Tracy prefers to proceed from the
pluralism of memories of Jesus that have been preserved in the tradition.[19]

Within exegetical circles this shift is represented in the turn toward narrative
theology. Biblical narrative renders the Christian picture of God as agent. Jesus
enacts God's will before all people and thus serves as the "exegetical key" to
meanings hidden in the parables.[20] This approach challenges the usual exegetical treatments of New Testament christology, which describes the titles
used of Jesus (Messiah, Son of Man, Lord, etc.), their Jewish or Greco-Roman
background, and then draws conclusions about what the titles meant for claims
about Jesus' person. Instead, the narrative approach argues that each gospel
creates a memory of Jesus by projecting an autonomous story which itself
explains how Jesus is to be understood.[21]

Narrative and the Questions of History

Even when pursued within the larger framework of an existentialist or liberationist hermeneutic, historical-critical exegesis advances hypotheses about the
intended meanings and probable motivations of persons in particular circumstances. Such claims always remain probable reconstructions, and they are
always open to challenge. For narrative theology, the historical accuracy of
particular details about Jesus is unimportant. Stewart Sutherland argues, for
example, that the critical fact about Jesus is that his self-giving defines a way of
life that is possible for humans to pursue. We will never be able to demonstrate
that Jesus as a historical person possessed the goodness which the tradition
attributes to him. But we can acknowledge that his life demonstrates the
possibility of living in a self-giving way.[22]

Edward Schillebeeckx has questioned the theological adequacy of a purely
literary approach to christology. He admits that a "story" may bring us closer to
the deepest intentions of Jesus than painstaking historical analyses ever could.[23]
But a figure who is simply a literary model would never have created a movement
that took steps to enact the liberation of persons and to carry forward into
history the religious values that it traces to Jesus.[24]

The hermeneutics of Scripture as narrative may avoid the difficulties of
reconstructing histories of the emergence of Christian belief and questions about
the intentions of Jesus and the New Testament writers. But this shift cannot
evade them altogether. Critical analysis indebted to Nietzsche, Freud, and Marx
has raised questions about the ideology behind appeals to "classic texts." Such
critics ask whether a text can claim to carry a message about human self-
transcendence when it originated in a context, in which human communication
was fundamentally distorted by sociocultural biases of class, economic oppression, and sexism.[25]

The critical philosophers see the more traditional forms of hermeneutics as based on a model of disclosure that presumes both the possibility of significant analogies between the world of the text and our own and that is blind to the structural distortions operative in both contexts. A church that bases its life on Scripture as the founding classic of the tradition will not be challenged to reject the distorted communication found in its Scripture. They insist that the only appropriate pre-understanding to bring to reading the Bible is that developed in a church "engaged" on the side of the oppressed in their struggle for liberation. The "truth" of an interpretation of Scripture can only be measured by the praxis which it supports.[26]

A logical consequence of this view is that a thoroughgoing commitment to praxis could lead the theologian to reject any normative status for biblical tradition. The Bible represents a reservoir of metaphor and symbol to which theologians may appeal when appropriate. But much of the Bible may even be rejected as no longer appropriate or even counter to the liberating praxis in which the church must engage. Sallie McFague's appeal for a new metaphorical theology in which God is mother, lover, and friend—not father, creator and king—is grounded in the conviction that images shaped by the hierarchical and patriarchal power structures of the past will no longer work. The need for a theology that can respond to the nuclear crisis, can evoke concern for the ecological welfare of the planet, and unite the badly divided peoples around the globe cannot be met by religious symbols that are so deeply embedded in creating the problems that we face.[27]

A hermeneutical approach to exegesis and theology insists that the Bible expresses a vision of human reality which has permanent validity. It remains capable of challenging persons to faith and action in historical and social circumstances quite unlike those of the millenia in which its traditions were shaped. This approach recognizes that we cannot understand without interpreting, and we cannot interpret without bringing the text into dialogue with situations, categories, methods of analysis, and visions of the world that are external to the text itself. Exegetical, theological, and practical concerns have led to vigorous debates over which methods and dialogue partners are most appropriate to explicating the message of Scripture.

Scripture for Theology and Praxis

Most theologians and exegetes agree that the Bible does not live in the believing community simply as a great work of literature or the source of theoretical systems of doctrine. Understanding what the Bible means does have to include the dimensions of personal and community life.

David Tracy's response to the challenge posed by critical theory has been to insist that theology must seek a middle ground between a hermeneutics of "retrieval" and one of "suspicion." Truth cannot be dichotomized into transformation (hermeneutics of praxis) or disclosure (hermeneutics of classic works) models.[28] Christian tradition takes as its paradigmatic religious experience the power of the word spoken from God to an ambiguous human self.[29] The event and person of Jesus Christ are the focus of Christian understanding of persons, history, and society. But that event is appropriated in very different ways in different contexts. Jesus represents the saving presence of a gracious God. Jesus on the cross also represents the negativity and brokenness of a sinful world.[30]

Exegetes have responded to the challenge to "recover" a liberating Christian past in Scripture by asking questions about the development of the tradition. The descriptions resulting from their investigations often take one of three forms: (1) an attempt to characterize the ethos of early Christian communities using anthropological or sociological categories; (2) an attempt to describe the development of a particular theological topos (e.g., christology, ecclesiology, eschatology) as a dialogue between available traditions and changing circumstances within the community; (3) an attempt to discover the liberating imperative at the origins of the tradition before that tradition was distorted by the presuppositions of the larger culture.

The Ethos of Early Christianity

Attempts to describe the ethos of early Christian communities frequently adopt categories from the social sciences. Most analysis has focused on the community of Jesus and his disciples and on the Pauline churches. The argument over whether the Jesus movement was a renewal or liberation movement depends upon the sociological models employed by a given exegete.[31] However, many exegetes agree that Jesus' message about the kingdom or rule of God did not refer to some future, heavenly destiny. It called persons to a reshaping of their lives and relationships in the present.[32]

Richard Horsley describes the Jesus movement as one whose renewal sprang from the power of basic themes of Exodus and liberation under a Davidic leader raised up from the people by God. This renewal sprang from the religious tradition as it existed among the populace, not from the official forms of the tradition that had been shaped by scribal and priestly movements at the time. Jesus catalyzes a renewal among the people in which we see diverse groups drawn into a pattern of egalitarian social relationships. Jesus' meals with tax collectors and sinners exemplify the open character of the community which his mission calls into being.[33]

The "house church" communities of the Pauline mission faced the challenge of incarnating Christianity in a completely different, urban environment. But they too created a new form of association, not exactly modeled on any ancient counterpart, in which personal, egalitarian relationships prevailed. Informal modes of persuasion, face-to-face communication, and mutual exhortation provided the control necessary in the community. These groups were remarkably free of the preoccupations with hierarchy and titular distinctions that marked other ancient associations. Their language is laced with affective terms that reinforced the familial bonds which unified persons of diverse backgrounds in a single "body." Christians also learned to expand their vision beyond the local community to others which were not attached to it by any immediate ties. Paul uses the collection among gentile Christians for the poor Jewish Christians at Jerusalem to represent the global character of Christian unity.[34]

Reconstructions of the social world of the earliest Christian communities recognize that communities are formed by rituals, by small details of personal interaction, by confessional uses of language, by the special circumstances of their interactions with the larger social environment. While one may describe the "ethos" of those communities, with its relation to the figure of Jesus and claims about salvation, it is difficult to derive formal imperatives for doctrine or practice in today's churches from such studies. One approach simply takes the view that what remains significant is the emergence of reflective, conceptual understandings of God, Christ, church, and the like, whatever their communal origins and implications may have been. An antithetical approach argues that enduring norms are provided by the founding intentions discernible in the Jesus movement and the earliest Pauline churches.

Tradition as Developing Insight

Developmental views of the relationship between the New Testament and later Christian theology presume that it is possible to sketch patterns of emergence by which later doctrine makes explicit what is implied or only partially expressed in the New Testament. One may argue that the impulse toward theological articulation of Christian truth is found in the New Testament itself. It lies behind the formulaic hymns and creeds. It is more explicit when Paul, in response to opposing claims about the gospel, articulates his own understanding of the gospel of Christ crucified (as in 1 Cor).[35] The need for subsequent reformulations of Christian faith lies in the limitations of human language. The linguistic and cultural modes of expression available to humans at any one time are limited. What can be conveyed only partially in one context may receive a much fuller expression in another.[36]

Raymond Brown rightly insists that two principles must guide the relationship between exegesis and doctrine. First, the emergence of doctrines not attested in Scripture does not create a new "literal meaning" for the text to prove such doctrines. Rather, they are to be understood as consistent with the basic understandings of salvation that we derive from Scripture. Second, exegetical difficulties in ambiguous texts should not be resolved in a way that is prejudicial to later doctrine.[37] Brian Hebblethwaite has insisted that two explicit features of New Testament language form the foundation for the later emergence of a trinitarian understanding of God: (a) the persistent use of personal relations in speaking about God; (b) the early community's worship of the risen Christ.[38]

C. F. D. Moule is even willing to argue for an implicit move away from functional christology toward an ontological way of describing Jesus' identity with God. He admits that the New Testament does not use philosophical terms like "Word of God" or "firstborn" or "image" in the technical sense of Middle Platonic philosophy. But the juxtaposition of such terms with the concrete person of Jesus Christ creates something new which must be explained. John 1: 14 acknowledges that to make that link implies that Jesus is the unique, only revelation of God. But given the monotheistic confession that Christianity retained from Judaism (e.g., 1 Thess 1: 9), an ontological explanation of Christ's relationship to God will be required.[39] Doctrinal development spurred by Christianity's dialogue with changing circumstances must result in a pluralism of theological expression. Theologians should see in such pluralism the unity of faith which claims that in Jesus God brings about redemption for the world.[40]

Founding Intentions Critique the Tradition

In contrast to such positive accounts of development, other exegetes and theologians critique the tradition from the perspective of modern religious or social imperatives. They argue that even doctrines clearly expressed in the New Testament (like the death of Jesus as atonement for sin) do not "translate" well into a modern context that needs to transform the world and not to be rescued from it.[41] Classic disputes between Catholic and Protestant exegetes about the appropriateness of the transition from eschatological expectation to salvation history enacted through the church or the emergence of a structured church such as one finds in the Pastoral epistles have reemerged in the modern discussion. All sides may agree that one finds in the New Testament both an apocalyptic eschatology of imminent destruction of this world, its powers and structures, and an understanding of God continuing to work through the history of the community of faith—a community that stands in continuity with God's saving activities in the story of Israel. All sides may agree that the emergence of hierarchy, church office, and structural authority took place at different times in different churches and cannot simply be said to be a late, postapostolic development.

Yet agreement on such historical details of the development of New Testament community does not lead to common normative judgments about the status to be accorded particular developments today. One might argue both that the founding of a church as an ordered, enduring sociopolitical community runs counter to the model of a gathering of disciples around Jesus and that ordered forms of church polity are necessary as well as appropriate. But others may insist that any form of institutionalized church departs from the founding vision of a "new humanity" realized among the earliest disciples.

The discipleship model is oriented toward the eschatological expectation of a rule of God which is to break into human history and reverse its values and structures.[42] It can never be comfortably incarnated in established cultural patterns and norms. A community of disciples gathered around Jesus is not equivalent to what emerges with the institutionalization of "church." Feminist exegetes have protested the demotion of women and the loss of their initiative that occurred when sociopolitical pressures transformed the community of equal disciples into the sociological entity recognized as "church."[43] Feminist theologians deny that the facticity of "what happened" in the development of "orthodox" Christianity creates an authoritative claim to being a divinely ordained plan. Instead, they insist, the modern imperative of liberation requires the invention of new models of church inspired but not constrained by the New Testament images of discipleship.

Feminist criticism demonstrates that combining a hermeneutics of retrieval and one of suspicion does not resolve the problem of how normative claims are grounded in Scripture. The quest for founding intentions is pursued by analyzing a text that is already the product of distorted communication and repression of critical elements in the initiating message. The developmental approach, on the other hand, must presume that whatever "corrections" might be introduced by a hermeneutics of suspicion will affect the externals and not the fundamental structure of Christian life and faith as it has emerged from its New Testament origins. Analysis of the ethos of early Christian communities may be pressed into service on either side of the dispute. Its results in advancing theological proposals for ecclesiology and ethics may look quite different depending on whether one thinks that the tradition has developed those initial insights in constructive dialogue with changing circumstances or whether one argues that today's church must break with the capitulation to distorting social and cultural models of the past. The methods of exegetical analysis may be employed to correct particular claims about the Jesus movement, Pauline communities, and Greco-Roman society; but they cannot adjudicate the fundamental disagreement between the hermeneutics of suspicion and that of retrieval.

Scripture and Christian Unity

One clear result of contemporary exegesis has been an appreciation for the variety and pluralism within Scripture. This diversity cannot be reduced to abstract, logically and metaphorically coherent syntheses. Consequently, we should not expect Christian theologies grounded in Scripture to produce identical systematic results either. Early Christian communities were diverse. The ethos of Pauline communities was not necessarily that of the Jewish Christians in Jerusalem or even of other churches of gentile converts like those which produced the Johannine writings. Any monolithic reconstruction of New Testament Christianity, whether grounded in a hermeneutics of suspicion or of retrieval, will fail the scrutiny of exegetical investigation.

Unity and Pluralism in the Canon

Since theology does not begin with the reconstructed history of particular Christian communities or traditions but with the group of writings collected in the canon, exegetes have begun to emphasize the necessity of situating the individual writings within the larger context. Collection of diverse perspectives in individual books and then incorporation of the individual books into a single witness to Christian faith challenges exegetes and theologians to describe the unity of which the various members are a part.

According to this view, the task of interpretation is not finished when the social and historical context of a particular book and the development of its tradition has been described. Since the individual books are now incorporated into a canon, they must also be interpreted in relationship to other writings which comprise the canon.

One way of characterizing the "unity" in the canon is to focus upon its pointing toward a single God whose perspective and ability to act in and for a sinful humanity dominate the whole collection. Liberation theology has developed a powerful version of this proposal that the unity of the canon lies in its vision of God's acts in relationship to a sinful humanity. The "option for the poor" as a fundamental ethical norm is grounded in a picture of God developed throughout the canon."[44] God is the redeemer of a weak and oppressed people.

Another approach to the unity of the New Testament canon has been found in its concern for a universal proclamation of the gospel. Wayne Meeks has argued that the emphasis on universalism evident in the Pauline letters is quite unlike claims to universal significance by any other ancient religious group, even the Diaspora synagogue. Its foundation must be a combination of the monotheistic confession of Israel with the Christian sense of bearing God's definitive message of salvation for all of humanity.[45] Paul's reflections on the universality of human sinfulness in Romans 1:16–3:20 provide the basis for claiming that the gospel is also to be addressed to all peoples.[46] This universalism points toward a rethinking of what is meant by humanity. In relationship to God's salvation the boundaries of class, culture, and gender become meaningless (Gal 3:26–28).

The Struggle for Unity in New Testament Churches

New Testament visions of unity should not be confused with the realities of life in New Testament communities. Attempts to trace the story of "local churches" in the New Testament show us that "unity" was more of a regulative ideal than a reality. One finds conflicting perceptions of church unity separating the apostle Paul from his addressees in Corinth and Galatia, for example. A single city like Antioch had a wide diversity in its Christian communities. Some were Christians of Jewish background, who continued their ancestral traditions. Other groups may have been largely Gentile in background but also included Jewish Christian members. More radical gentile Christian groups probably challenged the appropriateness of any links with Christianity's Jewish past. Johannine Christians appear to have been somewhat isolated from other Christian groups. They did not trace their founding to Paul or to one of the Twelve. They had been expelled from the synagogue and would not have welcomed or been welcomed by Jewish Christians.[47]

Paul Achtemeier's reconstruction of the events surrounding the "Jerusalem

Council," Paul's dispute with the Jerusalem authorities over the place of Gentiles in the church, and his separation from the Antioch community in which he had worked, suggest bitter divisions that were never healed. Yet Luke creates in Acts quite a different "memory" of Paul. There we find a Paul who will compromise his view of the relationship between the law and faithfulness to the gospel to preserve the unity of faith. Luke presumes that a compromise was reached that left no animosity between Jewish and gentile Christians, though both Galatians and Romans 9–15 show us that Paul's mission continued to be dogged by those who rejected his understanding of the gospel.[48] Luke's narrative provides a framework in which the "unity" which these early communities understood as the goal of their efforts is an actual reality, one which the later church is to reflect on in its own life.

Working Toward an Ecumenical Theology

Two elements of the conflict that plagued Paul's mission remain an urgent part of today's ecumenical task: (a) the quest for a genuinely ecumenical theology that unites rather than divides Christians; (b) the problem of Christianity's relationship to Judaism and Israel's ongoing place as "God's elect." Both issues need to be addressed within a theological framework that unequivocally asserts the possibility of irreducibly distinct ways of articulating Christian faith. Indeed, as Avery Dulles has pointed out, our modern experience of global communication has increased rather than lessened the diversity between persons and cultures.[49] Creed, church structure, forms of worship, and ethics are all practical problems for Christian unity. The Letter to the Galatians shows that all of these elements played a role in the conflict over whether or not gentile converts should adopt Jewish practices. Paul sees such a requirement as a denial of the gospel message that all persons are saved through Jesus. Yet the experience in Galatians shows that a resolution must emerge from the community's response to the apostle's persuasive appeal to their Christian experience and their understanding of the gospel. No top-down solution can be imposed in these areas of lived Christian life.[50]

The imperative for working toward ecumenical theologies can be derived from the relationship between evangelization and unity in the New Testament tradition. As Romans 1:19–21 implies, God's word to Israel was also spoken to all humanity. Humanity as a whole rejected the Creator and stands under God's demand for justice. The "good news" is likewise addressed to all humanity, not some isolated group of persons.[51] If the message is for all humanity, then its theological elaboration should also strive to be inclusive rather than particularistic or sectarian.

Theologians like Dulles have been exploring the basis for doctrinal agreement among Christian churches.[52] Scripture lies at the heart of any such agreement, since all Christians can recognize that its testimony to Jesus as Lord and Savior of humanity is antecedent to any particular "Christian" community of faith. The witness of the first generations of believers found in the New Testament must be the basis for the life and mission of any church.[53] We can learn from the struggles of the New Testament communities that Christian "communion" can and does extend beyond juridical boundaries; that incorporation into Christ through baptism, acknowledgment of a common Scripture, and basic creedal affirmations are sufficient for persons to be accepted as Christian sisters and brothers.[54]

Just as exegetes have come to recognize that there are irreducibly different theological affirmations within the New Testament, so the explicit doctrinal formulations of various Christian communions are not necessarily equivalent or interchangeable.[55] But the same methods of historical contextualization used in exegesis apply to the doctrinal affirmations of different communions. In some cases differing views are equivalent though shaped by a different context. Ecumenical theology should also take us beyond mutual toleration. Hearing the objections and insights of different traditions may also open up the possibility of new formulations of creed and doctrine that remove some of those objections.[56]

Theology and the Problem of Israel

Though both exegetes and official church teachings have often acknowledged the necessity of a renewed, positive understanding of Judaism, the magnitude of the task has hardly been recognized. The entrenched pattern of a salvation history in which Jesus is fulfilment of the Law and the prophets (Mt 5:17) taught Christians that after Jesus nothing remained for an unrepentant Israel. Matthew's warnings against a hypocritical Pharisaism—directed at the danger of such developments in his own community (Mt 23:2-13)—was taken to be a historically accurate description of the role of the Law in Jewish life and adequate reason for Israel's alleged loss of the promises of salvation. Though exegetes have long challenged the established construal of such passages, the characterizations of Judaism involved in such readings are in fact reinforced by ways in which Christians translate the New Testament.[57] The abstract term *Judaism* and the euphemism *Judeo-Christian tradition* often shelter Christians from thinking concretely about their relationship to the Jewish people. Yet they constitute the "Israel" of Romans 11:1-36. They are the ones for whom there still remains a place in the "mystery" of God's plan of salvation.[58]

The reifying and dogmatizing of "Judaism" by exegetes and theologians alike contribute to the inability of Christians to take any real responsibility for the Holocaust. This blindness can also be reinforced by "well-meaning" presentations of Jesus among exegetes and theologians. One of the most common criteria for arguing that gospel material is characteristic of the "historical Jesus," its divergence from the commonplaces of Jewish expression and from early Christian developments, becomes a covert argument for the "uniqueness" (i.e., "divinity") of Jesus. It also separates Jesus from the experiences of his people. The stories of conflict between Jesus and other Jewish teachers become reasons for the rejection of Israel rather than evidence of Jesus' own efforts to restore the wholeness of Israel as God's beloved children.[59]

More serious attention to the question of Israel will raise problems with central formulations of Christian teaching. Has trinitarian theology really preserved the monotheism of Abraham, Isaac, Jacob, and Jesus? Or must any christology that would retain that monotheistic impulse (also expressed in Jesus' Abba prayer) be "subordinationist" and functionally oriented?[60] If the latter, then those atonement theologies in the New Testament that are "theopractic," that is, see God as the author of atonement acting through Jesus, would be more appropriate than those that present Christ as the one who wins and mediates salvation. The latter already show a concern to link the "nature" of Christ with his function (e.g., Col 1:15; 2:9; Eph 3:19).[61] Further, the focus on redemption as achieved "in the cross" destroys the distinction between Jesus and the "one to come" (e.g., Mk 14:62). Yet, as the "one-to-come" Jesus' messianic role may still be unfinished. Jew and Gentile are not "reconciled" so long as the Jewish people still have to fear what they may suffer from the gentile nations.[62]

The ecclesial consequences of the theory of cosmic atonement on the cross such as that in Colossians/Ephesians make it difficult to imagine a history of salvation that is not finished with Jesus' death and heavenly exaltation. For Colossians/Ephesians the reign of the exalted Christ is expressed through the church. In such an ecclesiology there are no genuine initiatives for salvation left except those which may be offered through the mediation of the church. If Christians enter into dialogue with Judaism from that perspective, then the presumption remains that the "place" of Judaism is determined from the Christian side. Jews are not allowed to tell us about God's saving power or their messianic election in suffering. They are not allowed to tell us that we have been wicked tenants in the vineyard, more than willing to kill God's beloved children.

Concluding Reflections

Both exegetes and theologians struggle with the problems of expressing the significance of Christian revelation in a pluralistic and complex world that shares few of the assumptions on which earlier scholars could rely. Positivistic historicism and naive fundamentalism even work together to make the task of expounding a revelation presented in metaphoric, pluralistic, and even discordant voices extremely difficult. We cannot escape the various pre-understandings of the subject matter of theology and the appropriate praxis for Christian churches today that we bring to the theological task. The presuppositions of our various methods require an ongoing process of exploration and dialogue.

Scripture, church as the community of faith, and theology as the systematic articulation of faith can never be "rent asunder." Contemporary exegesis invests much of its energy attempting to understand the origins and development of the biblical communities of faith and their relationships with other groups. It insists that however one reads the tradition—whether through the lens of a hermeneutics of suspicion or one of retrieval—the Bible is first and foremost the reflection of a believing community. It is not the product of isolated artistic genius or theoretical speculation.

The process of interpretation requires understanding both the biblical wit-nesses and ourselves in such a way that both can be adequately represented in theological reflection. Both the complexity of the subject matter and that of the world in which we live suggest that the dialectic of interpretation must always reach outside the comfortable boundaries of our specialties, our individual churches, and our favored traditions. It must even include those whose voices have never "been heard in the land." No one has set us a better example of intellectual honesty, integrity in appropriating the tradition, and willingness to search out all the "still, small voices" of truth than Avery Dulles. And we look forward to what we have yet to learn from him.

Recommended Readings

Brown, Raymond E. *Biblical Exegesis and Church Doctrine*. Mahwah, NJ Paulist, 1985. Treats the relationship between exegesis and doctrine from the perspective of an exegete who accepts the view that doctrines not explicitly taught in Scripture may nevertheless be consistent with biblical revelation.

Dunn, James D. G. *Christology in the Making: A New Testament Inquiry into the Origins of the Doctrine of the Incarnation*. Philadelphia: Westminster, 1980. A detailed, exegetical investigation of christological material in the New Testament, which seeks to discover how affirmation of the preexistence and incarnation of Christ emerged in the earliest period.

Kelsey, David H. *The Uses of Scripture in Recent Theology*. Philadelphia: Fortress, 1975. A groundbreaking study of the understandings of the nature of Scripture and its use in twentieth-century Protestant theology.

Meeks, Wayne A. *The Moral World of the First Christians*. Philadelphia: Westminster, 1986. Reconstructs the "ethos" of various groups in the social world of the New Testament churches and the "ethos" of communities and traditions within the New Testament.

Von der Osten-Sacken, Peter. *Christian-Jewish Dialogue: Theological Foundations*. Phila-delphia: Fortress, 1986. A strong statement, from a German exegete, of the need for Christians to reassess the theological place of Israel in light of an exegesis that is sensitive to issues raised by Jewish-Christian dialogue.

Schüssler Fiorenza, Elisabeth. *In Memory of Her: A Feminist Theological Reconstruction of Christian Origins*. New York: Crossroad, 1983. A groundbreaking statement of the methods of feminist theology and exegesis as well as a feminist construction of New Testament evidence for Christian origins.

N
I
N
E

Christian Doctrine in a Historically Conscious World

John P. Langan

I am writing this chapter on 7 December 1987. It is the day that Mikhail Gorbachev, the general secretary of the Communist party of the Soviet Union, arrives in Washington to meet with President Ronald Reagan of the United States. At the summit meeting the two men propose to sign a treaty requiring the elimination of intermediate-range nuclear forces from their national arsenals. There is intense speculation about what the long-term effects of the meeting and the INF treaty will be on relationships between the superpowers and on the prospects for further nuclear disarmament. There is anticipation that this is an event that will continue a story of progressive disarmament and of a relaxation of tensions between the Soviet Union and the United States; but the considerable uncertainty whether this will be the pattern of the future is one source of disagreement about the meaning and importance of the event.

Forty-six years ago today naval and air forces of Japan attacked the forces of the United States and the United Kingdom throughout the Far East and the Pacific. The day the Japanese attacked Pearl Harbor, 7 December 1941, was called by President Franklin Roosevelt "a day that will live in infamy." It was one of those days on which everyone above a certain age remembers what he or she was doing when the news came. I was not old enough to be aware of what had happened, but years later I met a fellow student who told me about hiding under a table while the bombs were falling. He was three years old at the time, and his father was serving at Hickam Field, the army air base near Pearl Harbor. He remembered the day vividly.

The events of the attack on Pearl Harbor happened to a relatively small number of people, probably under one hundred thousand, but they became part of the shared public memory of many millions. The interpretation of the events became highly controversial, especially after it became clear that parts of the American government could or should have known what would occur. But everyone could see that the events marked the beginning of an important development in international affairs. Cultures and states that had previously been remote from each other were now actively engaged in hostilities. Young men from Kansas and Kyoto would die in the mountains of New Guinea and on

132

the beaches of Tarawa and Okinawa. The war begun on 7 December would end with drastically altered power relationships around the world and with a decisive technological transformation of warfare when the first atomic bombs were dropped by American planes on the cities of Hiroshima and Nagasaki.

The beginning of the war in the Pacific stands by general consent as a historic event of major importance. At the same time, while Pearl Harbor provided an exceptionally dramatic beginning for hostilities between the United States and Japan, it brought these states into a war that had already been going on for some time and in which Germany, Italy, France, the British Empire, and the Soviet Union were active participants, a war related in exceptionally close and complex ways to the earlier war involving these same powers between 1914 and 1918. The event, while exceptionally important, was not an absolute beginning, and it became a part of complex stories that would be told differently in Washington and Tokyo, in London and Berlin, in China and Indonesia, by Pacific islanders and Western traders, by diplomats and warriors. These stories would reflect various points of view and different ways of experiencing the events, different sets of values and different beliefs. Considered together, the stories would overlap, supporting and contradicting each other on certain details. But all the participants and politicians and diplomats, the analysts and historians agree that planes of the Imperial Japanese Navy did attack the ships and bases of the United States in Hawaii on the morning of Sunday, 7 December 1941.

"Anno Domini"

The date itself deserves reflection because it refers indirectly to a time long ago, a time to which we can refer only by adopting a certain set of cultural conventions. These conventions, as it happens, are themselves laden with theological content. For, as we all know, the Western world has for many centuries dated events *Anno Domini*, "in the year of the Lord." It has taken as its central reference point the birth of Jesus, an event that (somewhat awkwardly), is not datable with historical precision.[1] Though it was not regarded as a history-shaping event at the time and passed unobserved by the multitudes, Jesus' birth was to serve as the central reference point for the entire scheme of historical events in the West and later throughout the world, once the culture of the West came to link diverse cultures together.

We can contrast this method of dating events with the practice prevalent at the time of Jesus himself and throughout most of the ancient Mediterranean world. Chapter 3 of Luke's gospel, for example, relates the beginning of the ministry of John the Baptist "in the fifteenth year of the reign of Tiberius Caesar, Pontius Pilate being governor of Judea, and Herod being tetrarch of Galilee and his brother Philip tetrarch of the region of Ituraea and Trachonitis, and Lysanias tetrarch of Abilene, in the high priesthood of Annas and Caiaphas." In Egypt, Greece, and Rome, events were dated by reference to the tenure of various civic and religious dignitaries, particularly the king or the emperor or the consuls (in the case of Rome). The Greeks added references to the games celebrated every four years at Olympia, and the Romans took as a general starting point the founding of the city of Rome.

The Western scheme of dating was adopted well after the Christian community came to confess the lordship of Jesus Christ and even after Christianity became the dominant religion of the Mediterranean world. It has also come to be used by societies that have little or no sympathy with Christian theology. Even from a secular standpoint, it has the great advantages of simplicity and uniformity. It serves as a fundamental means of orientation as we sort out the memories of our various cultures and as we record new events and experiences.

But from a theological standpoint this method of dating events reminds us that for the Christian community the coming of Jesus is the central event of the ages, the beginning of a new order of relations between God and human creatures, an order which is definitive and not to be surpassed. As Christians we both share in the new covenant and inherit what God has done for Israel. Because of the fundamental importance Christianity accords to the life, passion, death, and resurrection of Jesus, and because of the way in which it situates these events within the narrative of God's dealings with Israel, Christianity has always had a significant narrative dimension. Saint Augustine (354–430) gave the classic synthetic presentation of this approach in The City of God, tracing the story of the two cities of God and of sinful humanity, from Genesis to their end in heaven and hell. His synthesis brought together biblical and nonbiblical elements that have important differences in literary character, historical worth, and theological value. But it made a lasting imprint on the historical imagination of the West and provided a general theological framework for interpreting secular history and anticipating further religiously significant events.

While Christianity has treated its basic narratives as conveying truths of fundamental religious importance, it has not (for the most part) been a religion that looked backward or in upon itself. It looks outward to a world whose religious destiny it understands better than the world itself does and which it has a divine mandate to evangelize. It looks forward to further manifestations of God's saving power. Christianity has not always kept the narrative element in clear focus and has at times presented itself as a timeless body of metaphysical or ethical truths. It has also been riven by disputes which debated the best way to relate its narrative element to secular ways of understanding history.

Precisely because narrative elements have a central importance in Christianity, the rise of historical consciousness in its modern form was bound to have serious effects on the way we understand Jesus, on the connections that we see between Jesus and human destiny in general, and on the way we understand ourselves as believers and agents and as persons who live in a historical process and articulate a historical understanding of events. But before we examine the impact of modern historical consciousness on our understanding of Christianity, we have to examine more closely what this complex intellectual movement means.

The Origins of Historical Thought

From the beginning of written records, we can see that people have been fascinated by stories, particularly by stories of great events. In the very act of writing there is a manifest desire to preserve a permanent and accessible account that survives the death of the individual storyteller and the memories of those directly affected by the original event. At the beginning of the Western literary tradition, we find the *Iliad* and the *Odyssey*, the great epic poems whose artistic narrative has preserved historical echoes of the great deeds of the Greeks and their adversaries before Troy. At the beginning of the Bible, we find stories of the origin of humanity and of the early Hebrew patriarchs. These stories were not simply interesting for people who lacked electronic forms of entertainment. They were also identity forming; they conveyed to new generations a sense of what being a Greek or an Israelite meant. But interest was focused largely on the deeds of heroic figures from the legendary past.

In the great Greek historians of the fifth century B.C., Herodotus and Thucydides, we find an interest in preserving a lasting account of current events and in showing the causal links between these events and earlier developments. A similar interest in recounting quite recent events is found much earlier in 2 Samuel 9–20, the story of the reign of David.[2] Along with the interest in narrating recent events there naturally came an increased concern for using evidence and argument to establish conclusions about what happened and why it happened. This led to more restricted notions about what kinds of realities can be the causes of events. In the case of Thucydides, these changed concerns yield an austere narrative of the war between Athens and Sparta. Thucydides constructs his narrative without using legendary material and without showing overt partisanship; he displays considerable analytic power in a history almost completely taken up with political and military affairs. He is deeply interested in the moral justifications that people advance for their actions. He articulates these in the speeches he puts into their mouths, but the relationship of his narrative to larger schemes of religious meaning is not manifest.[3] The kind of political and military history that he and most of the other famous historians of the classical world wrote was well suited for provoking reflection on questions of public morality and on the conduct and structure of government. In the *Federalist Papers*, for instance, Alexander Hamilton and James Madison make frequent appeals to politically relevant lessons about human conduct and human nature drawn from ancient history.[4]

Some influence from Greek conceptions of historical writing appears in the New Testament, specifically in Luke-Acts.[5] But the central theological purpose of the New Testament writings, including the gospels, should prevent us from simply equating them with ancient historical writing. They present quite special difficulties of historical assessment and interpretation. However, when Christians became the dominant religious group in the Mediterranean world, they did recognize the importance of recording their own history, and with the pioneering work of Eusebius of Caesarea at the time of Constantine, they began to produce histories of the church.[6]

Even though historical writing was one of the great accomplishments of Greek culture in the fifth century B.C., Plato and Aristotle paid comparatively little attention to historical thinking. Aristotle begins the Metaphysics with a historical review of the opinions of his major predecessors. But he also makes the deprecatory observation that "poetry is something more philosophic and of graver import than history."[7] The source of this disparaging assessment was the view that both Plato and Aristotle had of knowledge, which was primarily knowledge of the universal and necessary rather than of the particular and contingent. This position nourished an attitude in which history was regarded as a source of facts and examples that might show forth some aspects of timeless truth.

This attitude prevailed not merely in ancient philosophy but in early modern philosophy. René Descartes, for instance, made clear his lack of esteem for historical discourse.[8] In both post-Reformation theology and early modern philosophy strong demands were commonly made for absolute certainty; there was also a heavy reliance on mathematical demonstration as the paradigm of knowledge. As a result, historical knowledge was treated as of secondary importance and was often regarded as little better than antiquarian lore. The aspiration of the Enlightenment was to obtain secure possession of the timeless truths of mathematics and physics, of metaphysics and morals. Even in a thinker such as Gotthold Lessing, who lays out a panoramic view of the religious and intellectual development of humanity, the decisive point is the affirmation of timeless moral truths such as the fatherhood of God and the brotherhood of men.[9] Compared with certain and evident moral and metaphysical knowledge and the absoluteness of faith as well, historical knowledge seemed comparatively petty and highly fallible to many philosophers and theologians.

Modern Historical Consciousness

During the Enlightenment, four important developments helped to shape modern historical consciousness and its impact on religion. The first of these was the early attempt at historical criticism of the Bible, particularly in the work of the Jewish philosopher Baruch Spinoza and the French priest Richard Simon.[10] Scholars began to apply some of the critical methods used by philologists on classical texts since the time of the Renaissance; they proceeded to point out some of the inconsistencies in the biblical narratives. Second, writers from Pierre Bayle through Voltaire and the Encyclopedists turned with great zest to the critical scrutiny of religious legends and to the rational reconstruction of our beliefs about the past on a nonmiraculous and antisupernatural basis.[11] Third, Gottfried Leibniz, one of the major rationalist thinkers, developed a philosophical system that stressed the logical uniqueness of the individual, who was considered as inherently dynamic and self-actualizing rather than passive, under divine or metaphysical agency.[12]

Fourth, the Italian philosopher and jurist, Giambattista Vico (1668–1744) working in the comparative obscurity of Naples, wrote his *New Science*, which was a theologically inspired interpretation of history. For Vico, societies went through cycles of development in which social structures, states of consciousness, types of art and literature, dominant virtues and values were systemically linked. He reacted strongly against Cartesian rationalism and proclaimed that we know the social world of human action better than we can ever hope to know the world of nature, precisely because it is a world we have made.[13] Vico's idea of the social construction of the human world would gain further plausibility and depth when set within the perspective of Immanuel Kant, for whom our understanding of nature itself was the product of an active human intelligence rather than the passive reception of ideas and forms. Vico held that the ideas, cultural products, and social structures of a given period are linked together in ways that are not captured either by the universality of logical or natural necessity or by simple juxtaposition of independent facts. This view was to prove enormously fruitful as a heuristic device for thinking about human society and culture. While the cyclical character of Vico's scheme presented obvious problems for the progressive interpretation of history that Christianity offered, it also challenged the classic ideal of timeless stability and affirmed a plurality of modes for understanding and evaluating the works of human beings in their social world. Human achievements were not measured by their approach to or decline from an atemporal standard of perfection, but by their appropriateness to their age and its problems.

In addition to these comparatively specialized philosophical and theological contributions to the rise of modern historical consciousness, five broader currents moving through European culture helped to make modern historical consciousness a major factor in Western civilization in the nineteenth and twentieth centuries. The first of these, which had been taking shape since the Renaissance, was the development of critical historical scholarship and its instruments. Classical scholars, students of ancient inscriptions and manuscripts, editors of texts elaborated methods for determining the authenticity and the dating of ancient documents. They probed behind the classical texts that had enjoyed enormous cultural prestige and questioned the written accounts of early Greek and Roman history which included many legendary elements. They also distinguished documents on the basis of literary form, an approach that would later have profound importance for the study of Scripture. On a more popular level the educated European public began to read more and more works of history, of which the most famous was probably Edward Gibbon's *Decline and Fall of the Roman Empire*.

Second, European culture in the early modern period was marked by what could be called a strong "over the shoulder" habit, that is, a habit of looking back to two historically remote but normatively weighty periods. These two periods were the apostolic church, which had special normative status in religious and theological matters, and classical antiquity, which presented models of heroic action and artistic accomplishment. This retrospective habit was inculcated by both religious authorities and the educational establishment. Over time, it was bound to produce reflections about differences between then and now and also to stimulate questions about the normative bounds set in these earlier periods. This normative reliance on earlier periods depended on two contradictory assumptions and carried one hope that could not be realized. The contradictory assumptions were (1) that historical time was fundamentally homogeneous, so that these earlier periods continued to be normatively relevant, and (2) that historical time was not homogeneous, so that the earlier periods were decisively important and unsurpassable. The unrealizable hope was that the normative tensions between these two different periods and the different cultures of Athens and Jerusalem could be suppressed or reconciled on a permanent basis. One sees how these normative tensions appeared before and after the rise of historical consciousness if one contrasts, for example, Saint Thomas Aquinas's careful harmonization of classical and Christian values in his interpretation of Aristotle[14] with Matthew Arnold's emphasis on continuing tensions resisting synthesis in his treatment of Hebraism and Hellenism in *Culture and Anarchy*.

In the late eighteenth century, a third major factor begins to shape modern historical consciousness, namely, the romantic movement in literature and the arts. The romantics did not by any means reject classical art or the civilization of Greece, but they did reject the imposition of neoclassical canons of taste and proportion on their own work and on their appreciation of previous ages. They became enthusiastic proponents of Romanesque and Gothic art, of Shakespeare and medieval romances. Many of them were drawn to an imaginative representation of Christianity, in which doctrine and moral teaching were less important than the nourishment of feeling and imagination. In most European cultures romanticism in turn led to realism, which found material for high art both in urban bourgeois pleasures and in the strivings of proletarian or peasant life. It led also to nationalism, which celebrated the historic roots of local, non-cosmopolitan cultures. Ways of thought and feeling and norms for action came to be understood in these movements as elements in a long-term narrative and as responses to a changing social situation.

A still more fundamental change in the way in which history was understood in the West was produced by the development of modern science in the seventeenth and eighteenth centuries. During the long period of European exploration and expansion from 1450 to 1650, the scientific revolution scored its first major public successes in physics and astronomy. It then went on to fundamental discoveries in chemistry, biology, and physiology. By resolving old scientific questions that had baffled the Greeks and by discovering a vast new range of phenomena, European science showed clearly that it had moved beyond the limits of Greco-Roman culture.

In the period of the Enlightenment, the philosophical expositors of the new knowledge were able to mount searching questions about many traditional religious conceptions and to aspire to a new scientific interpretation of human beings. The materialism of such thinkers as de la Mettrie, Helvétius, and d'Holbach was inadequate to the complexity of human cultural development. It was repellent to the romantic temperament as well as incompatible with Christianity. But it was to be the forerunner of many attempts to discredit the Christian understanding of human nature and destiny by an appeal to modern science. More broadly, the breakthrough of modern science and the subsequent development of new forms of technology (a process which continues to be active and fruitful and disruptive in our own time), combined to form a foundation for progressivist interpretations of human history that were also heavily Eurocentric. In one sense, they could be seen as secular expressions or parallels for progressive elements in the general Christian narrative. But as new and unforeseen features in humanity's social and intellectual life, they underlined the incompleteness of the theological narrative and indicated ranges of unsuspected possibilities.

The scientific and industrial revolutions are probably the greatest and most perduring factors that have sustained a general sense of progress, of change beyond the limits of previous cycles, of questioning existing limits and regarding previous forms of social experience and organization as obsolescent. While such a sense is widespread, particularly in the United States, its bearing on Christianity is not easy to discern. Few theologians today would think that it necessarily leads in the direction of Rudolf Bultmann's remark that "It is impossible to use electric light and the wireless and to avail ourselves of modern medical and surgical discoveries, and at the same time to believe in the New Testament world of daemons and spirits."[15] Few would think now that changes produced by increased reliance on science and technology are universally beneficent. But that reaction has grown in strength only since 1945 and the beginning of the nuclear age.

More specific than the general sense of progressive historical change powered by the engines of science and technology has been the development of biology since the publication of Darwin's *Origin of Species*. Darwin situated human development within a vast evolutionary perspective in which eons of change brought the universe to its present condition with the emergence of an enormous variety of life forms. Scientific work in geology, paleontology, biology, and anthropology first sketched out a greatly extended prehistory and then filled it in with a mass of supporting detail. The evolutionary view of prehistory seemed to require a progressive materialist understanding of time past. (Most earlier forms of materialism had been static and mechanistic.) On the one hand, it folded human history as a coda into the great cosmic process. On the other hand, this evolutionary materialism relied in a central way on the distinctiveness of the human knower. Looking to the future, it also relied on the human agent's sense of responsibility for preserving the ecological balance of the evolutionary environment.[16]

A fifth major element in the rise of modern historical consciousness was the experience of profound political change that marked the North Atlantic world from 1775 to 1815 and then spread through the Spanish colonies in America.[17] One may think of this political transformation primarily in terms of revolution-aries overthrowing the Old Regime in France or of Founding Fathers establishing a new order for the ages (novus ordo seclorum) in the United States. But the changes of this period were profoundly important, even where they were system-atically rejected—as in Britain, Spain, and Germany. The revolutionary up-heavals showed that it was possible not merely to redraw boundary lines between states but also to refashion the basic institutional structure of society. Subse-quent historical scholarship has taught us to see the continuities between prerevolutionary and postimperial France, between 1789 and 1815.[18] But it should also be noted that when the revolutionaries set up their new republic in 1792, they proclaimed it to be the year 1 of the new calendar; that is, an event superseding in importance the coming of Jesus Christ.[19]

Diverse Interpretations

Cultural developments of such breadth and complexity could not fail to find expression in both philosophy and theology. But they found their fullest and most influential expression in philosophy, particularly in the metaphysical sys-tem of G. W. F. Hegel (1770–1831) and in the revolutionary, materialistic synthesis of Hegelian dialectic and British political economy hammered to-gether by Karl Marx (1818–1883). For Hegel, the French Revolution marked the point at which humanity became fully conscious of itself as the shaper of its social life and institutions; there the veils of divine legitimation were cast aside, and the Spirit became fully conscious of itself in its historical working.[20] Hegel was able to present the cultural and intellectual history of humanity, especially of the West, as the progressive and dialectical self-realization of Spirit. He could claim to have made even metaphysics itself—the study of being and its timeless categories—a historical enterprise. To the unfolding of his system Hegel brought a richness of cultural reference, an opaqueness of style, and an inexhaustible supply of suggestive ambiguities. His speculative ambition and his shrewd con-servatism drew on his head the withering criticism of Søren Kierkegaard and Marx, but he still became the dominant intellectual figure of nineteenth-century Europe precisely because he articulated on the grandest scale the understanding of our social and intellectual lives in historical terms. His system transformed many of the assertions of traditional Christianity even while it kept the general pattern of the progressive and dialectical interpretation that Christianity had given to the human story.

Karl Marx took this same pattern and put it in the service of a revolutionary transformation of society. He offered a comprehensive interpretation of social, political, and intellectual history in terms of class struggle and the development of the economic forces of production. He laid claim to a scientific grasp of the historical process which would enable his followers to predict the necessary direction of social development and to bring about a utopia in which the struggles and divisions of ordinary history would be definitively overcome. Marx's program stimulated an enormous amount of historical research from both disciples and critics. It also turned a new focus on historical movements among "the lower orders" and helped to make social and economic history comparable in importance and appeal with political and intellectual history. But it had even broader effects because it provided a historical orientation for the most enduring and wide-ranging political movement of the twentieth century.

As the examples of Hegel and Marx show, historical consciousness was not one undifferentiated reality, nor was it unopposed. Over the last hundred years it has been criticized not merely by conservatives who were disturbed by its relativizing implications and its disturbing effect on the (often recently) established order, but also by various new forms of historical rationalism such as phenomenology and analytic philosophy. A major shift to quantitative research and model building in the social sciences also called it in question. In Central Europe and Britain during the first half of this century the defining ambition of the positivists and empiricists who drew up their programs for the rational reconstruction of our cognitive world was to achieve a logically ordered reduction of our ontology to elements knowable by physical observation and a parallel reordering of our language. Not merely the beliefs of traditional Christianity but also the meaningfulness of religious language and the cognitive standing of ethical discourse were called into question.[21] The grandiose historical systems of Hegel and Marx were dismissed because they failed to meet cognitive tests of verifiability and meaning and because they were regarded as ideological supports for totalitarian tyranny.[22]

History, both as the account of our previous speculations and as an indispensable part of the matrix within which we carry on our investigations, was put on the sidelines. The history of science was presented along simple progressivist lines; more careful observation and increased mathematical rigor were to replace religious myths and metaphysical confusions. Partly in reaction to earlier manifestations of positivism in the nineteenth century, the German philosopher and cultural historian, Wilhelm Dilthey, stressed the distinctiveness of historical understanding, *Verstehen*, and held that it was not reducible to the kind of knowing that we have in the physical sciences.[23] But the positivists of the twentieth century were reluctant to accept this.

But in the late 1960s, a significant reaction took place against the positivist interpretation of the history of science. The new approach was heavily historicist and it emphasized the dependence of observation on theory rather than presenting observation as the neutral test of theory. The new approach was not progressivist in the way that both Hegelians and positivists had been, and it shied away from appraisals of previous work in terms of its similarity to current views. The most widely read book in this new approach, *The Structure of Scientific Revolutions* by Thomas Kuhn, has had considerable impact well beyond the limits of the history and philosophy of science. The recent widespread rejection of foundationalism or the search for absolute first principles of knowledge has not been accompanied by abandonment of the modes of argument and the cognitive demands that were widely used to discredit traditional and customary beliefs.[24] The contemporary result is a widely diffused skepticism, in which historical considerations play an important part and in which pragmatic appeals are decisive. Given the inadequacy of schemes of rational reconstruction on new foundations and the profound dissatisfaction that many intellectuals and religious thinkers experience when they reflect on the individualism and the apparently irreconcilable divisions of contemporary life, it is not surprising that there is a search for historical guideposts that may point us to the future and a readiness to think about issues in broadly historical terms.[25]

Types of Historical Consciousness

Even this thumbnail sketch of very diverse thinkers and movements should alert readers to recognize that modern historical consciousness is not a simple reality. It has been shaped by many different causes, it has been linked to different intellectual movements, and it has meant very different things.

Precisely because there are so many different forms of historical awareness which affect different and important aspects of our thinking, we run the risk of becoming confused. It may be helpful, then, to distinguish three types of historical consciousness. A first type (Type 1), direct historical consciousness, is a comparatively sober and straightforward matter. It begins with our awareness of the occurrence of events in time and with the practice of leaving records of what are taken to be the most significant or recordable events. This form of historical consciousness is present in many cultures and provides much of the source material for the construction of complex historical narratives. It is often accompanied by a comparative neglect of subtler changes in society and in patterns of thought, especially when the historical focus is on high politics or military achievements. But it can still have a sharp critical focus manifested in questions about the authenticity of documents, the establishment of correct texts, the precise record of events. It is a mistake to think that modernity alone has aspired to provide an accurate account of the way things actually happened, *wie es eigentlich gewesen*, as Leopold von Ranke (1795–1886), the great German historian put it.

Relativizing historical consciousness (Type 2) is struck by the differences that occur in things over time. Careful critical examination of materials provided by Type 1 will reveal in a fair number of cases that things are not what they appear to be at first blush. This leads to complex comparisons of various sorts: sources and authors of different periods appear not to mean the same thing by the same term; different cultures interpret the same action in different ways; social institutions and forms of life are not essentially the same in all cultures, with only accidental or trivial modifications. This sort of historical consciousness can affect biblical studies, cultural anthropology, the comparative study of legal systems, the history of science, and the history of dogma. It can also be present in some of the ordinary judgments about what we can expect in other cultures in other places at other times. It draws not merely on historical research but on the life experience of millions of people in an interdependent world where older social patterns are challenged and often replaced. I suggest that the repeated experience of social transformation, particularly as this is interpreted for contemporary awareness by the media in the West, has a strong, relativizing impact. But that impact is not correlated with any disciplined and self-critical grasp of historical method or of historical data.

Historical consciousness of Type 2 can thus be found in both sophisticated and popular forms. The central characteristic differentiating it from Type 1 is the denial of the homogeneity of key aspects of our social experience over time. Type 2 need not be committed to denying the possibility of some higher viewpoint for ordering the historical heterogeneity of experience, but it does confront a dilemma at this point. If it allows such a higher viewpoint, then the question is bound to arise whether and in what ways this higher viewpoint is historically conditioned. If, on the other hand, it disallows such a higher viewpoint, then it shares with other relativistic positions the difficulty of stating its case in a way that will not be self-defeating and that will not destroy the possibility of understanding the evidence it marshalls in order to make its case.

The third type of historical consciousness (Type 3) attempts to integrate into a unified narrative or system the diverse events and social transformations recognized in Types 1 and 2. The integrating structure may be cyclical or progressive, metaphysical, economic, or religious. But the key requirement is to provide a general structure for interpreting the course of events; its scope often includes the future as well as the past, and so it commonly extends beyond the bounds of historical verification. At the least it is bound to introduce tensions with historical consciousness of Types 1 and 2, which may offer evidence against the integration ambitioned by Type 3. Yet, as the examples of Hegelianism and Marxism show, proposals of Type 3 can have considerable heuristic value. The grand integrating schemes of Vico and Hegel, Auguste Comte and Arnold Toynbee are both attractive and vulnerable.

Here we may recall the examples with which we began. The choice of the birth of Jesus as a central point of reference for dating historical events expresses a judgment coming from the third or integrating type of historical consciousness. The Japanese attack on Pearl Harbor and Gorbachev's visit to Washington are events that can be ascertained within Type 1. At the same time, when they are included in longer narratives that may be constructed from different points of view, they are subject to different interpretations and evaluation in Type 2. Still there has to be some agreement not merely on brute facts but also on some basic interpretations of them; otherwise, we could not be sure that we are talking about the same events. Stories in which the British or the Germans bomb Pearl Harbor or in which the Japanese attack as a means of establishing an alliance with the United States do not count as different interpretations of the events of 7 December 1941.

The example of Gorbachev's visit underlines the difficulty of obtaining all the relevant information we need to answer the straightforward questions that arise within the first type of historical consciousness. It also makes evident the extent to which our interpretation of events in the recent past is dependent on events in the near future which, when they occur, may help us to answer questions that arise in both the first and third types of historical consciousness. For instance, Gorbachev's actions over the next few years will help us to answer questions that we currently have about his intentions and about the ways in which Soviet political processes work (Type 1). They will also provide evidence for various proposals about how the long struggle between capitalism and communism will be resolved and what its relative importance in the development of humanity will be (Type 3).

Challenges to Theology

When we reflect on these different types of historical consciousness, it is clear that they do not challenge Christian theology in the same way. The first type raises questions about what really happened and about the evidence for our answers to these questions; its challenge arises primarily within the study of Scripture and those areas of church history in which doctrinally or ecclesiologically significant issues are raised. Such questions were particularly troubling for some forms of theology, such as the historicist apologetics for the divinity of Jesus. Briefly, this kind of apologetics held that strict historical method can show that the gospels are reliable historical sources written by eyewitnesses, that Jesus claimed to be Messiah and Son of God, and that he proved this claim by his prophecies and miracles. However, modern biblical scholarship agrees that this approach fails to recognize the actual literary character of the gospels and their confessional intention of making, in Avery Dulles's words, "an urgent call for faith."[26]

At the same time, the limitations of historical investigation in answering fundamental religious questions about God and Jesus have to be recognized. Dulles puts the matter thus:

> Pure historical method, conceived according to the norms of the historico-critical school, is not fully competent to reconstruct the life and doctrine of Jesus on the phenomenal plane: it cannot by itself establish any solid and indisputable version of the words and works of the real Jesus. Still less is scientific history capable of settling the question of religious interpretation. Such interpretation lies within the competence of a man committed, or at least open, to religious values.[27]

Dulles does not want to make religious commitment a matter of blind or arbitrary preference. But he commends an apologetic that focuses on "the intrinsic qualities of the Christian message" and especially on what he calls "the greatest marvel of all," namely "the portrait of Jesus which we find deeply embedded in all the four Gospels" and which Dulles acclaims as an example of "spendthrift charity" appropriate to God incarnate.[28] This approach does not make historical considerations irrelevant, but it does set them secondary to the contemporary response of the whole person to the call of the gospels of faith.

The second type of historical consciousness, which is particularly important at the present time, emphasizes the extent and importance of historical change. It implies that on many topics the question the church's teaching was originally intended to answer is no longer the question being asked today. Many harmonizations and identifications that church tradition took for granted are dissolved under critical scrutiny. Arguments that seemed to work in patriarchal or pre-capitalist social conditions are seen as insufficient or outmoded. Teleological claims that seemed evident before relevant scientific facts were known or before technological interventions were possible now seem highly questionable. In the contemporary situation, the challenge of the relativizing type of historical consciousness primarily affects the church's moral teaching and its internal discipline, particularly its exercise of authority and its sacramental practice.

In focusing on the relativizing challenge to the church's moral teaching, I do not wish to minimize the importance of the questions posed for systematic theology by the realization of the diversity and historically conditioned character of the conceptual schemes that have shaped traditional Christian theology.

But three points seem relevant to this observer. First, in systematic theology we are more familiar with the distinction between a faith affirmation and the historically conditioned formulation and explication of that affirmation. Second, since the moral life inherently demands decisions, there is a continuing pressure for definite approval or disapproval of at least general courses of action. Living the moral life within a community of rational persons does not require the prior resolution of all theoretical difficulties; but it does not allow for the indefinite bracketing of practical issues. Third, a truly radical relativism can dissolve not merely traditional religious beliefs, but also the critiques of these beliefs. It can present not only Isaiah and Luke but also Ludwig Feuerbach and Joseph-Ernest Renan as historically bound theological thinkers.

To preach the gospel in any form, twenty centuries after the events to which it refers, we need some account of how an interpretation of these events can speak to our deepest dilemmas and to our sense of the meaning of our lives. In both the moral and the systematic fields, Christian theology must respond to the array of factual conclusions and questions raised by the critical historical consciousness of Type 1. It must recognize that an unopposed exercise of the relativizing type of historical consciousness will undermine its general position and continuing relevance. In both cases it needs a theory of development. This theory has to be sufficiently flexible to do justice to the undeniable evidence of historical change in many areas of Christian life and doctrine. It must be stabilizing enough to preserve essential elements of continuity with the Christian tradition and fidelity to the gospel, to the word that we have received. At least since the time of the Tübingen school of Catholic theology in the nineteenth century and John Henry Newman's pioneering *An Essay on The Development of Doctrine* (1845), this has been a major concern for fundamental and systematic theologians.

The extent and legitimacy of doctrinal development have been debated ever since the Reformation began to rely on Scripture alone as a norm for the criticism of Catholic doctrine and practice. But within Roman Catholicism today the problem of development is particularly acute because the correctness of previous changes (for instance, Vatican II's affirmation of religious liberty) has to be affirmed in a way that assures the authoritative hierarchical teachers of the community that continuity is being preserved. Since Newman's time the problem of development has also been generalized and intensified because historical factors have been recognized as affecting our most fundamental and familiar notions, and not merely specific points of theological controversy. The human subject in both its knowing and its practical activity has come to be understood as itself a social and historical product, not simply as a thinking substance (Descartes) or a passive reporter of impressions. This sense of the individual subject emerges comparatively late in the historical process and should not be assumed throughout that process.[29]

More specifically, in the period since Vatican Council II (1962–1965) Roman Catholicism has had to work out an understanding of itself as a religious community subject to historic change. It has had to deal with the theoretical problems this creates for earlier ways of understanding Christian doctrine and the teaching authority of the church. Pastorally, it has also struggled to meet the needs and expectations of both those who regarded the church as immune to historical change on all issues that really matter and those who want the church to accommodate with almost uncritical approval to recent social and intellectual changes in different parts of the world.

Dulles's writings over the last two decades show a major concern to provide a theological orientation for those who must deal with these problems. He has sought to do this by remaining faithful to the Catholic tradition in its essentials and yet honestly recognizing the complexities and difficulties that a scholarly view of that tradition uncovers. He has pointed out the ironic origins of the current crisis of historical consciousness within Catholicism. In *The Survival of Dogma* (1971) he observes that the "great concern on the part of Catholics to rise above historical relativities and to articulate the faith in timeless formulas"[30] is relatively recent; and he recalls the variety of patterns of thought in the New Testament and in early Christianity. He goes on to indicate the source of the current Catholic problem in this area:

> The modern concern to find concepts and terms that could be imposed on all the faithful is itself paradoxically conditioned by a particular historical crisis. In the nineteenth century, when historical consciousness broke through in the secular disciplines, exposing the radical historicity of human thought, the Church made itself the defender of some of the most cherished theses of eighteenth century

rationalism. Theologians took the view that the truths of revelation, at least, were indubitable, universal, and immutable.[31]

In contrast to this static view of Christian doctrine, Dulles holds that the terms in dogmatic formulations are not immutable and that we should look for a position that "affirms the doctrinal infallibility of the church while allowing for reformulation in terminology and concept."[32] He argues for accepting "a paradoxical combination of the absolute and the relative" in human knowledge, such that true, circumscribed, and nonreversible statements are made within a larger whole that is never fully expressed, within a mystery that is prior to and surpasses human understanding. At the same time, he affirms the power of the human mind to transcend particular intellectual frameworks and given social and cultural conditions; it is this transcendence that enables the human person to grasp worlds of ideas and systems of thought quite alien to his or her own.

The third or integrating type of historical consciousness may be thought of as Christianity's home turf, since Christianity has accustomed us to think of human history as the unfolding of a single story of salvation affecting all peoples. Presented in more or less secularized forms as well, the effort to provide a single comprehensive story takes us well beyond the limits of critical history and requires a suprahistorical setting, whether metaphysical or mythical. Mythical versions of this setting are narrative and so may be taken for historical. But a moment's reflection should make it clear that narratives of the beginning and the end of the world cannot be anything other than myths. This is not to deny their religious importance or even in some sense their truth.

The search for a comprehensive vision of history, for a suitable setting for the entire human story may indeed be a category mistake, a confusion of facts and dreams, of particular stories and ontological assertions. But it seems clear that whether cast in the religious terms provided by Christianity and apocalyptic Judaism and Islam or else in the secular philosophical terms of Comte and Marx, or in some mixture of the two, such a vision appeals to enormous numbers of people from many different cultures. A speculative philosophy or theology of history has vital attraction because it can provide a sense of orientation regarding past and future and some ranking of the priority of various goods. Marxism, for instance, clearly values economic production more than religious activities, and it constructs its account of the stages of human development in terms of which group shapes and controls the forces of production.

Speculative philosophy or theology of history can also serve as a theodicy or a justification for "the ways of God to man" in history. For history, in Hegel's famous observation, is "the slaughter-bench" of the peoples.[33] There is a pressing intellectual and spiritual need to understand history in such a way as to affirm that the enormous sufferings of humanity are necessary for or contributory to attaining goals of transcendent worth. Such an interpretation, as the history of totalitarian and terrorist movements over the last two hundred years makes plain, may also encourage strategies for treating people as means to revolutionary ends. It can offer an extensive set of often specious justifications for doing all manner of terrible things. But more positively, it enables a person to shape a plan for his or her life along lines that will be understood as leading to success or vindication or salvation. This plan will not be merely the arbitrary choice of an isolated individual freedom but will have an inherently social character. If the plan is based on the correct reading of the human story, it can be in accordance with "the march of history" or "the will of God."

Conclusion

Christianity may reasonably be regarded as the major carrier of this desire for a comprehensive integration of history. More recently, it has also had to compete with interpretations of history attempting to displace it. It must also respond to philosophies and views of life that regard larger metaphysical or religious settings for human action as unnecessary, illusory, or even pernicious. It seems clear to nearly all that to adopt a Christian grand narrative of the sort proposed by Saint Augustine in *The City of God* as an integrating framework for one's life is to take a step well beyond ordinary historical thinking. It is also to follow one path within the Christian community, a path that is neither mandatory nor universally accepted, even if it is correct to count most intellectual Christians in the West from the fourth to the nineteenth centuries as followers of this path. Clearly believers may put large questions of social destiny to one side and interpret their way of living the life of faith as personal discipleship or fellowship with Jesus. The demand for a larger sense to life, for a meaning that integrates the entire historical process, and for access to a higher point of view that makes this meaning evident is sometimes offered as evidence of the unsatisfactory nature of atheistic or positivistic conceptions of human nature and destiny. But it can also be regarded as evidence of our unwillingness to accept our creaturely limitations and to come to terms with the inescapably historical character of all of our thinking and acting.

The problem of justifying a particular integrative understanding of world history seems to be insoluble. Two sources of this difficulty are apparent if we think back to the examples with which this paper began. The consequences of the 1987 Washington summit, the conclusions of the story into which this event fits are not yet known. The unknown and even more the unsuspected aspects of the future undermine our earnest efforts to interpret history as a whole. But also, as both examples suggest, there is no unique viewpoint from which the interpretation is to be given. Rather, as in the case of Japan's attack on Pearl Harbor, there is a diversity of interested and affected parties. One may uncritically assume or consciously adopt the viewpoint of one party or group of parties, e.g., the U.S. government or the American military forces or an idealized ordinary citizen of the United States. But this does not provide rational grounding for making that viewpoint decisive and for subordinating to it the viewpoints of, say, the Japanese government or Japanese sailors and soldiers. In conflict situations many observers, even professional historians, tend to adopt the viewpoint of the winning side or the side that seems closest to contemporary values. The adoption of a viewpoint is both a necessary presupposition for the historian's work and a matter for critical assessment. It clearly influences the historian's selection of relevant evidence and significant issues, as well as judgments on causality and moral responsibility. Many of the complaints made by black and feminist historians and by scholars from various marginal groups about standard versions of U.S. history arise from disagreements about the appropriate viewpoint and from resentment over the unself-critical way in which the majority imposes its viewpoint. This consideration applies even more strongly when we are assessing the interpretations of an integrative understanding of world history, one that is to apply to the ancient civilizations of India and China with their own religious traditions, to the militant world of Islam, to the economic activism of East Asia and the Pacific Rim, and to the divided societies of Latin America.

At the beginning of this century Ernst Troeltsch argued that "it is impossible to construct a theory of Christianity as the absolute religion on the basis of a historical way of thinking or by the use of historical means."[34] Arriving at an affirmation of the absolute character of the Christian religion requires faith, as Thomas Aquinas and Avery Dulles would insist. Faith offers the prospect of an ultimate integration in our understanding of the historical process. But this prospect is presented to us in symbolic form, imaging the progress of humanity and its world from creation, through fall and redemption, to judgment and ultimate fulfillment. Christ stands as the midpoint of this history but also as its Alpha and Omega. The confident Christian affirmation of these articles of faith does not yield anything more than a most general framework for understanding history, even while it underscores the enduring importance of what human beings do and become in the course of the ages of history. Christian faith is neither the deductive offspring of historical investigation nor its jealous rival and supplanter; rather, when properly understood, it is the generous and encouraging parent.

Recommended Readings

Butterfield, Herbert. *Writings on Christianity and History.* Edited by C. T. McIntire. New York: Oxford University Press, 1979. A British Methodist and a practicing historian, Sir Herbert Butterfield showed an uncommonly acute eye for both moral and epistemological issues.

Harvey, Van. *The Historian and the Believer: The Morality of Historical Knowledge and Christian Belief.* New York: Macmillan, 1966. A recent exploration of the fundamental tensions between Christian belief and historical consciousness.

Kuhn, Thomas. *The Structure of Scientific Revolutions.* Chicago: University of Chicago Press, 1970. The work that shaped the turn away from progressivist and positivist interpretations of the history of science.

T
E   Expanding Horizons:
N   A World of Religions
    and Jesus Christ

Thomas F. O'Meara

I

My father grew up on a farm in Eastern Iowa, where his parents had moved from the banks of the Mississippi shortly before the end of the nineteenth century. Earlier his grandfather had fled the famines of Ireland and had bought fifty acres from the newly opened state of Iowa. A businessman in Des Moines, my father during his lifetime never traveled further west or south than Tulsa, Oklahoma, or further east than Detroit; he had been to Canada once. Gregarious and outgoing, he was, nevertheless, not very interested in life outside the Midwest and could not be coaxed onto an airplane. Yet before his death in 1963, one of his children was an airline employee, another was in the military in Asia, and the third was about to depart for Europe to study.

One of the important questions in Christian theology today—perhaps the most important one—is the presence of grace outside Christianity. Is there salvation for people who do not believe in Christ? Is there God's favor outside of what we might call the "3 Bs"—belonging (to a church), baptism, and belief? In terms of the past, the length of human history implies a large population living before and outside of European history. In terms of today, we live in a world unified by media and travel. More and more people would find it incredible that one form of religion (the Christian religion) practiced somewhere in Europe or in the United States should assert that streams of peoples struggling between life and death are damned because birth placed them far from Christianity. Every Christian and every church not wishing to be reduced to a shrill believer or sect that claims to possess the only truth must ask how salvation exists outside of Christian church faith and baptism.

But then, how does this wider presence of God support the central role in religion and history the Bible claims for Jesus Christ?

Exploration expands not only maps but minds. When human beings leave behind their own world views and enter those of new countries and new peoples, some of their limited ideas are challenged. So it has been with our issue; exploration around the globe queries the extent of God's plan: Is there salvation on earth outside of the Judeo-Christian record of salvation? When we meet the wider world, when we actually see self-sacrificing and loving people who do not belong to our church or faith, we must ask about the presence of the kingdom of God. Was it intended by Jesus for Europe or for an entire planet? If we think deeply and look carefully at the human race, we will find amid a world of religions a world of grace.

As the third century began, the size of the Christian population in the Roman empire was reaching a notable size. Christians were no longer drawn largely from the lower classes. The church with its leaders and theologians had to ask about the relationship of the gospel of God's salvation in Christ to Hellenistic culture: to schools of philosophy, to pagan religions, to other religious movements. Great figures such as Justin Martyr in Rome and Clement and Origen in Alexandria showed that the Christian faith did not necessarily imply that all those living before or beyond the message of Christ were cut off from God's light.[1] These Christian thinkers appreciated the riches of Greece, saw philosophers striving for the truth about God, and may have talked with some who had traveled so far east that they had met Buddhists and Hindus. Both Jewish and Christian Scriptures give incidents of God's grace working in "outsiders": in Syrian men and women, in Roman soldiers. They are praised for their faith, but this faith cannot mean a knowledge of the details of Christianity. It describes, rather, the orientation of their lives to the kingdom of God. The theological writers of third century explained that while the divine Word was present in Christ in a special and personal way, clearly and vocally, its "words" (bestowed by the same divine Word) could also be present in other creeds and religious movements. They too strove for God's light and help and for an avoidance of evil and error.

Almost a thousand years later the Crusades turned the Middle Ages into a time of discovery. There is considerable discussion between Muslims and Christians over God and human reason. But there is little discussion by Christians of how salvation and grace are present or absent in Islam. It is not that other religions are judged harshly but that their existence is left unconfronted or ignored. This may be due to the constant warfare between the two religious worlds as the needs of war obscured the issue of grace.

In 1492 with the discovery of Asian and American worlds, the geography of continents and so of religions expanded for Europeans. Within fifty years, Spanish theologians and bishops in the Americas were faced in a painful way with the issue of God's salvation apart from faith and baptism. Some Indian nations responded enthusiastically to the gospel but others did not. The officials of the Spanish Empire, however, viewed the continuing adherence of the American Indians to their own religions as an excuse for enslavement. After all, if their not being baptized meant eternal damnation, why should that not be preceded by a few years of enslavement in the mines of New Spain? Bishops in the new world, particularly the extraordinary Bartolomé de las Casas, enlisted the aid of theologians at the Spanish universities to attack the government's policies and its theology. They argued that God's saving grace was not limited to explicit faith in Jesus or to baptism. Salvation could come through a personal relationship of a man or a woman who accepted conscientiously the glimpsed belief and morality of contact with God.

Again in our times, exploration makes the power of grace outside of Christianity an important issue. We meet the cultures of the world. With the arrival of jet travel and electronic transistor, we do not just learn vaguely that there are Hindus. Like enormous bees, heavy laden jet aircraft arrive at the hundred or more international airports of the world, hourly disgorging streams of passengers who will experience human and religious worlds different from their own. At home, the nightly news brings us the elections, the wars, the stock markets of the globe. Business or tourism may take us to India where we are brought face to face with millions of men and women who consider their religions to be normal. The faces, colors, and shapes of their views of God, not ours, fill their minds. Their religions have the same issues of sin and grace, of the transcendent and of a mediator.

There are not a few cities like Malacca in Malaysia where on the "Street of Harmony" one can hear (the result of six hundred years of racial and religious meetings) the call of the muezzin of Islam above the chant of Buddhist monks while crowds enter the Catholic cathedral. Meeting a man or woman from another religion, seeing briefly thousands of people seeking meaning and salvation—these were rare for Americans until thirty years ago. Once the trip to the state university was momentous; now the college student spends her or his junior year in Florence or Tokyo.

II

Those who sat behind the carved and ink-stained wooden desks of Catholic parochial grade schools in the first half of this century learned answers about the religious condition of non-Christians from a small catechism. Briefly, there were three ways in which people were saved: baptism by blood, baptism by water, baptism by desire. The young students had been baptized by water, and because of their confirmation they knew of martyrs who had died for Christ before receiving baptism. "Baptism of desire" was an exception made by a generous God for distant peoples, peoples few and far away.

Jesus' preaching and Paul's theology announced the good news of an invitation for all to enter the kingdom of God. This reign had arrived with a new intensity. God's grace was powerful and would crown the faith of each man and woman by the Spirit of the risen Jesus. Nevertheless, as Christianity became less a popular movement and more the official religion of the Roman Empire, another teaching arose. Looking at a multiplication of small churches and Christian sects, Cyprian in the middle of the third century expressed the view: "No salvation outside of the church." Augustine, almost two centuries later, drawing on his own personal experience of evil and looking at history from within a large worldwide church in chaotic times, saw human nature as deserving of damnation. Salvation for some (an increasing percentage of Europe) came through faith in Christ and sacramental baptism, but all others were to exist outside of God's saving love. (And yet Augustine saw that grace and true religion had existed from the very beginning of humanity and found all worthy of it.)[2] For the subsequent millennium and a half, theologies influenced by Augustine could give Christians a negative view of other religions. As Europe from the fifth to the fifteenth centuries passed through times of introversion without the experience of exploration, it lacked both conviction and theory concerning a positive relationship of Christianity with other religions. When isolation was shattered through explorations occurring in each of the centuries after the 1490s, questions arose again about the extent of the human race and the extent of God's love.

Millions of people lived before Christ. Recently it was thought that human beings appeared on earth 250,000 years ago: now almost a million years has been added to that figure. Computers estimate that in 10,000 B.C. there were ten million people alive. In Chinese and Indian cultures, with populations beyond seven hundred million, vast numbers of men and women have lived out their human lives in rich religious traditions with no opportunity to hear of Christ.

Many people would never hear of Jesus Christ and would never be baptized; martyrdom was rare. "Baptism by desire" offered a way of understanding the kingdom of God being widely present. For Catholics, this phrase gave the normal answer to our puzzling topic as it was viewed from 1850 to 1950. Baptism by desire did not mean that millions of Hindus desire in their minds the Christian sacrament of baptism. "Desire" meant an orientation, a drive, a movement toward God and God's love for each of us on earth.

But people outside Europe who had not heard of Jesus and his Gospel did not really "desire" baptism. Rather, aided by God's grace, they desired and concretely strove for the love of God as they and their religion portrayed it. Some church leaders tried to explain this desire as a way of belonging to the Catholic Church (since "outside of the church there is no salvation"). But such theologies were always metaphorical and limping. In fact, members of Islam do not belong to a Christian Church, and Catholicism has always argued for the visible recognizability of the church as contrasted with the kingdom of God. This desire emerged not in a vague longing for baptism or church, which were unknown to most or unpersuasive to members of other religions, but through a life faithful to an understanding of God and morality as individual conscience viewed both. So, while a real desire for living in God's presence and grace had the benefit of not condemning millions and was itself open to exploration, the theology was flawed in that the salvation of so many depended upon general philosophical ideas and ethical actions. The impression was given that God's grace was marginal, hardly necessary or operative outside of Christianity. It furthered the idea that other religions were not a means but a hindrance. It was general ideas about God which saved, not God's grace.

Today we would say they that people of other religions desire not so much church or baptism (which they do not know) but the kingdom of God they may know—and live amid—in their own way. Nonetheless, "baptism by desire" sustained the broader, mysterious worlds in which God and peoples spoke with each other about the meaning and contours of our life and implied that salvation came not by the right religious words but by the full orientation of an individual life.

Catholics received in the past a double message. On the one hand, they were taught that Catholicism was the true church and Christianity was the true world religion. On the other hand, they had received (through "baptism of desire") suggestions that the issue was not that simple. Whatever power or presence saved people seemed to exist also in the provinces of Celtic and Ibo religion. Catholics gave the impression that people outside of the Catholic Church—even Protestant Christians—were in a questionable condition. At the same time, if they reflected, Catholics could see that their Christian faith did not imply such a negative view of other people.

Previously church leaders and theologians sought to find words or ideas that different religions had in common, e.g., one supreme God. So, at best, Islam or Shintoism appeared as a vague, harmless philosophy caught within a religious panoply of idols and creeds which were bizarre if not evil. From God's point of view, even if the religions of the Hopis, Yorubas, or Fon were to be utterly avoided, many religions had preserved a few seeds of truth about God. Inquiring into the lists of individual beliefs—the existence of one God or many, life after death—did not alone describe salvation. The presence of grace, the evil of sin become visible and tangible in the forms of a religion.

But grace is more than religious ideas. Salvation is the active acceptance of God's active power in me. I am not saved simply by knowing phrases, although these can be important; not just religious faith is important in salvation, but the orientation of a person's life. A life, whether in Sri Lanka or Chad, is lived within issues of sin and charity, mercy and hope.

To study the presence of God's word and kingdom on earth is to ponder not simply people's religious ideas but the religions themselves, and particularly the orientation of a person's entire life. As Jesus observed more than once, it is not religious doctrines that save but a person's inner orientation. Faith is not ideas but orientation, new life, hope for a future. To address Christ and the world religions with their billions, Christians must become analyzers of grace—diagnosticians of God's presence loose in the world.

III

When the tourist or the business representative checks through customs in Asia or Africa, the next step is to take a bus into the heart of the city whether that is Calcutta, Lagos, or Kyoto. This drive through a new culture gives us experiences few human beings previously had. It offers direct, existential contact with other men and women in their own worlds. If we could follow them to their mosques, temples, and schools, or hear their conversations, we would see religious lives similar to ours: in Hinduism, the concern about grace, sanctity, and God's activity in the world; in Islam, the schools of spiritual life.

For the last forty years theologians like Jean Daniélou, Karl Rahner, Hans Küng, Pierre Teilhard de Chardin, Paul Tillich, and W. C. Smith have labored on our topic, creating theologies of the religious world prior to and outside of explicit Christianity. As we can see, the Catholic theologians are not offering sensational ideas or easy salvation. They are trying to explain a well-hidden Roman Catholic theological position—grace outside of formal Christianity. At the same time, the easy solution that no revelatory faith can claim to be central, and that religions are, within one developmental framework, different but equal is not accepted. Such a quick solution is today proposed mainly by journalists or thinkers outside of church life.

The new approach to the relationship of Christianity to the world religions focuses not upon comparative dogmas or rituals but upon the deeper divine presence. It sees religion or salvation to be concerned with a personal and active presence in life rather than only or mainly with ideas and institutions.

The ecumenical council, Vatican II, was important not because it began or deepened the present multifaceted dialogue with the world religions but because, as a church event, it encouraged this theological exploration. It taught that the religions of the world are not philosophies but attempts, over centuries, to respond to the mysteries of the human condition. The beliefs and practices of Hinduism, Buddhism, Islam can contain what is not only true (in an intellectual, metaphysical sense) but holy (the realm of grace). "The Catholic Church rejects nothing of what is true and holy in these religions. It has a high regard for the manner of life and conduct, the precepts and doctrines which, although differing in many ways from its own teaching, nevertheless often reflect a ray of that truth which enlightens all people."[3] The council exhorts Christians "while witnessing to their own faith and way of life acknowledge, preserve and encourage the spiritual and moral truths found among non-Christians, also their social life and culture."[4] Looking at the Christian commitment to spread the gospel of Christ, it observes the seeds of what is good in the rites and cultures of peoples, and asks that "whatever good is found sown in the minds and hearts of men or in the rites and customs of people" should not disappear but be raised up, purified where necessary, completed.[5]

Vatican II's statements were important, for while Protestant and Catholic theologians were struggling after 1900 with the positive meaning of the world religions, a Christian fundamentalism was also making itself felt. After World War I, more enlightened European thinkers and missionaries were often replaced in the mission fields of Africa and Asia by Anglo-Saxon fundamentalists and provincial Catholics. In their theology, everything outside of Bible or church was evil. This shift in attitude is reflected in movies of the 1940s where Africa was portrayed as a "dark continent" filled with witch doctors in masks and Asia as a land whose temples are populated by malicious, grotesque statues. In short, the black and white images on the screen suggested that other religions were demonic.

Without diminishing the approaches of Friedrich Schelling, Ernst Troeltsch and Paul Tillich, or Henri de Lubac and Teilhard de Chardin, a particularly coherent and influential interpretation of grace in the religions of humankind was fashioned by Karl Rahner. Beginning in the early 1960s he argued that while Christianity understands itself as destined for all human beings in a unique way, the world religions should not be viewed as something alien or distant but as true bearers, communities, and realizations of that presence and life of God which, in the faith of Christians, finds past and future fulfillment in Jesus Christ, the New Adam.[6]

Karl Rahner pointed out that a truly divine and credible God is not a God who is failing to save most men and women in history but a God whose will to bring human beings into deeper relationship with divine life is powerful enough to do this. God's universal salvation is the being-of-God-toward-us. Second, God's love for us (which is what grace and salvation are) is not abstract and general but personal. Its goal passes beyond (but through) earthly religion to eternal life in what Jesus called the kingdom of God. Its voice and influence in us are personal, suited to our historical, cultural, and hence religious conditions. Grace is not a commodity moved through one church or religion; it is the presence of God to people.

We easily forget that for Christianity there is no neutral world. There are no assemblies of human beings preserved from the human condition we call "original sin" but also no world of human beings where God is not present and reigning. Theologically there is one human family existing amid sin and grace. The issue we are investigating cannot be solved by a liberal theology's blandness; the grace which Saint Paul described and Jesus preached must be discovered even where Jesus is not known. In this sense, the severely Augustinian damnation of a large percentage of humanity, which some Christian churches still espouse, is a realistic if harsh solution. But once the temporal and spatial extents of human history are seen, that cruel project (and the small God it presupposes) is incredible.

God's self-communication in grace, the history of salvation, the kingdom of God and its verbalization as revelation—these did not begin two or five thousand years ago. They looked toward Christianity but were not separate from the religions of humanity. Was it not important to realize that, like human history, God's special presence in salvation had a history? World history is coextensive with salvation history. One special segment of salvation history is recorded in the Jewish and Christian Scriptures, but as important and climactic as that special history is, its clarity and power should not imply that God's love only falls upon Christians and Jews.

The grace of God is everywhere. It is coextensive with the human race, as *Genesis* implies. It was active before Jesus and outside of Jesus. Jesus is indeed grace and salvation as a human being, God's clear word for humanity in a person. "At various times in the past and in different ways God spoke to our ancestors through the prophets; but in our own time, the last days, he has spoken to us through his Son, the Son that he has appointed to inherit everything and through whom he made everything there is" (Heb 1:1–2). Christians believe that Jesus is the special word, expression, and power of grace. As the center of religious history, he is a magnetic force (yesterday, today, and tomorrow) for every religion. But the grace that came to climax in Jesus does not war against religion; it draws religion to a fulfillment.

Theologians offer different approaches to our topic; some struggle with the centrality of Christ, others with the being of God. Some are concerned with the role of the church in the world, others with the prevalence of evil and sin. In a way, however, patristic, medieval, and contemporary Catholic theologies have kept a single focus. While discussions of the centrality of Christ *in active conversation with other religions* have been few, so have condemnations of other religions as such. The perduring topic has been the grace of God. Grace outside of Christianity has been pursued precisely when the inner Christian world was opened up by exploration.

IV

Christianity has made a rapid entry into Africa. We are told that 200 million will be Christian and 120 million Catholic by the coming turn of the century. When I taught in Africa, in Nigeria, I asked the son of a polygamous Ibo family who had become a Catholic priest why so many Africans in the past century had accepted Christianity. He explained that the Ibo religion, which affirms a supreme God, a network of spirits, justice and familial loyalty, was not largely false or demonic, but it was sparse. For the great issues of human origins and the next life, for a more explicit depiction of human life from God's point of view, of history amid the swirling clouds of sin and grace, the teachings of Jesus were light.

What of the presence of grace in religion? It is one thing to develop academic theories for similarities between religions, it is something else to perceive God's grace, aided by the teaching of Jesus, in the devotions, temples, and practices of other religions. Karl Rahner wrote:

> The history of religion shows that this historical . . . revelation [of Christ] comes down to us in such a way that various histories of religion arise in different places in the world and at different times in the history of the human race. . . . Nothing really happens in the realm of the categorical [concrete words and forms in Christianity] which does not also happen in the history of every other people.[7]

"Religion" is simply an abstract word for the strivings and images of human life within grace and sin.

The attempt is made in every religion, at least on the part of human beings, to mediate the original, unreflexive, and nonobjective revelation historically, to make it reflexive and to interpret it in propositions. In all religions there are individual moments of such a successful mediation made possible by God's grace.

Why should we imagine sin to be universal and powerful, and not the grace of a living God?

> Just as God has permitted humanity's guilt, and this guilt has its darkening and depraving effect on all of humanity's collective and social dimensions, this is also the case in the history of humanity's objectifying self-interpretation of gracious revelation.[8]

God is love, and God's love for us ("grace") is personal: it is not a distant attitude or an indiscriminate force but a love suited to us as individuals. Love reaches individuals as individuals, and men and women live in their proper religious worlds. There are not two kinds of divine presence: one for Christians, a second for other human beings. God does not arbitrarily preselect part of the human race to be Christian and then reject the rest of the world's population. Nor does the gospel teach that we live in a world in which accidents of birth meet a mercurial divine will bestowing salvation upon very few.

A fresh consideration of the religions of millions led Hans Küng to speak of them as peoples' ordinary way to salvation,[9] and Rahner affirms

> the view of faith concerning the general and serious will of God for salvation vis-à-vis all people. . . . Certainly we know that this belief says nothing with certainty over the *individual* salvation of people as actually achieved. But God wills the salvation of all. And this salvation is the salvation of Christ, of supernatural, divinizing grace . . . conceived for all people . . . in ethnic histories, cultures and epochs of the greatest extent.[10]

It is the individuality of human life that makes the religions of this man or woman significant. Catholicism teaches that all humans are predestined by God and saved by the cross of Jesus, although each must freely accept this power. God's love for us is personal both in terms of the God revealed by Jesus and in terms of our own individuality. The divine universal will is not a blind or an indiscriminate force but is suited to us as individuals as we live in our own religious worlds. Grace is not a deficient commodity or shy spirit but suited—also for non-Christians—to this person in this religion. Every religion lives within the same paradigm—grace, sin, people—and so religions have more in common with each other than they have with sinful rejections of God's grace. The salvation-fashioning plan reaches the individual person according to the will and permission of God in the *concrete* world of religion.

And what is salvation? How are we saved? Not by words or temples, not by statues or observances, but by the hidden conversation of each man and woman affirming the never-heard love of God.

This exploration of God's saving grace in other religions is a dialogue—but a dialogue involves two speakers. The impact of Christianity's move beyond Europe into a world of religions is not only felt in Christians' understanding of other religions but appears in the forms and teachings of Christianity. While the faith of Jesus began as something Jewish and oriental, it has remained largely Greek, Roman, and Germanic, i.e., European, for many centuries. Now it is not just converting other peoples and cultures but attempting to become incarnate among them, not to be a European church addressing them but to be a Malaysian or Senegalese church among them.

The religions of the world can offer new insights about Christianity. Jesus is not originally Greek, Roman, or Germanic. His Jewishness places him at the cross section of East and West. Avery Dulles has described this crisis and opportunity, noting that the church today faces many cultures:

> It is by no means easy to see how the church can adjust to the new technological culture of the West and at the same time implant itself in the ancient, traditional cultures of Asia and Africa. Can a church that simultaneously moves in these contrary directions keep enough internal homogeneity to remain a single social body? Can the church adapt new symbols, languages, structures and behavioral patterns on a massive scale without losing continuity with its own origins and its own past?

As he has for many ecumenical issues, Dulles points a careful but courageous way forward. He notes that the center of Christianity is not a metaphysical principle but Jesus of Nazareth. Jesus enables the presence of God in various cultures because he is truly a divine power and a historical figure who survives history. The church, in turn, must not see diversity and particularity as problematic and divisive. "The biblical and ecclesiastical paradigms can inspire us to new imaginative achievements, faithful to what has been given but not slavishly repeating it. New symbols, rites, words and concepts must be found to actualize the biblical and traditional patrimony in new circumstances."[11]

In the past twenty years a missionary approach that treated cultures as sinful or useless has been relinquished. Now, however, we are only at the edge of further discoveries. Beyond a timid appreciation of music, art, language, and ritual, there are deeper issues. As the incarnation of Christ has been explained by Greek Platonism, so it can be depicted in terms of the African world of diverse spirits, present ancestors, powers, and forces which bridge matter and spirit. In other religions there are mystical, liturgical, rational communal emphases and schools, and there are figures like Origen, Augustine, Eckhart, Catherine of Siena, Ignatius Loyola. Far from approaching an apocalyptic end, the life of Christianity has only just begun.

V

Ten years ago, after teaching in New Zealand, I was able to return to the United States by way of Japan. Reading Thomas Merton introduced me to similarities between

Zen Buddhism and the German Dominican medieval mystic, Meister Eckhart. In Japan I spoke to Buddhist university professors, philosophers educated in Germany and deeply interested in Eckhart. I met the Jesuit Enomiya-LaSalle who had pioneered the dialogue in practice between Zen and Christian spiritualities. He mentioned a retreat center one hundred and fifty miles east of Tokyo conducted by Dominican priests and sisters where one was introduced in austerity and cold to the meditation of Zazen. One February afternoon I took the train into the mountains and reached the center as night fell.

The human race has unity in fallenness and in grace. Called to a perduring love by God, billions of people will not be reached by the self-communication of God while disdaining or remaining apart from religion. People do not live in their religion by abstract ideas developed by academicians but by religion-in-action. Apart from religious forms and practice, God's Spirit cannot reach billions of human beings pondering what for them is sin, identity, and grace. Grace, then, must be present in the particularity and concreteness of world religions. The Holy Spirit is not prudish about religion, for in accepting people it accepts something of their religious existence. Why should words and concepts be neutral while external manifestations of religion (liturgy, mysticism, monasticism) are demonic or primitive? What has been disdained or feared in religion—its visibility and particularity—is now the access for grace.

When entering Christianity, converts from other religious worlds, for example, Tiv, Ibo, Hindu, have generally been expected to give up their own tradition as evil or neutral. Why does one enter Christianity through yet a second religion or worldview, whether that be Greek philosophy or Judaism? Why could men and women in the first century but not in the twentieth enter into faith in Christ through one's religion? Why should evil be explained in terms of Genesis or Job, or the Timaeus, but not the Upanishads? Why could not the first reading at Liturgy come (as Indians have requested) from the Bhagavad Gita? Could not Christians develop a spirituality fully from within the forms and ethos of Japan— which is much more than molding a few insights into forms given by spiritualities that are feudal German, Celtic, or Greek?

In my visit to the *Soan*, the retreat center run by Dominican priests and sisters but conducted in the mode of Japanese Buddhist meditation, I saw the ecumenical effect of religious experience. There people from various Christian churches, Japanese more or less affiliated to Buddhism, and nonbelievers from various countries pursued the rigorous discipline of meditation. The Christian Eucharist and compline were celebrated—but the central discipline was meditation in a wooden chapel heated by twigs burning in a deep iron pot. Instructions were given in the practice and experience of *Zazen*: "sitting," "meditating."

It seemed that this practice, introducing a quiet perspective into busy lives, slowly bestowed a deeper realization of oneself. After more or less time, not logic or Scripture but silent, repeated meditation led to an awareness or a confrontation with the ground of one's being, opening beyond agnosticism to Someone whose being was still mystery. For Christians who came from a tradition of spirituality (the pioneers of this dialogue in Japan had been Jesuits; the directors of this center, Dominicans), meditation became the atmosphere where religions learned from each other. Silence was their dialogue. Christianity and Buddhism could converse because the mysteries of human existence and divine presence spoke in both.

To the extent that the Christian churches today remain European and pre-exploratory, they are sectarian, naive. They do not see the length, periodicization, and organization of human history and religious history.

If salvation history includes a spectrum of religions variously arranged on a long line of history, each of which is to lead explicitly to the kingdom of God, what then is Christianity? Is Christianity one religion replacing and fulfilling a second earlier one? Is it the total replacement of Judaism? Is it another world religion? Is it in competition with Islam and Hinduism? Or, is the preaching of that reality metaphorically expressed in terms such as "leaven," "kingdom," etc., meant to suggest that Christianity's mission is to work within religious histories, not to replace or end them? "Christianity is not an indoctrination into certain conditions or facts or realities which are always the same, but is the proclamation of a history of salvation, of God's salvific and revelatory activity on human beings and with human beings."[12] Faith in Jesus as the special prophet of God's plan of salvation, as the divine Word in a human being, implies the centrality, the uniqueness, of Jesus. But this confession of faith does not say at once how, in a long history, Jesus is central or how his uniqueness may be incarnate in different cultures and religions.

VI

The famous Trappist monk Thomas Merton, was quite faithful to the vow of remaining at his monastery in Kentucky. But in 1968 he received permission to accept an invitation to speak at the conference on Catholic monasteries for women and men in Asia. Before the conference, he took this opportunity to visit Buddhist hermits and monks, particularly in northern India. Passages in his Asian Journal *depict how he was able at once to talk familiarly about life in a monastery, about prayer and mysticism with these monks outside of Christianity.*

We began with exploration and we end with it. There is an outward, geographical exploration reaching beyond the earth's moon, and it extends our topic beyond the world of earth's religions and religious conditions. There is an equally important inner exploration. In my interior conversation (troubled or praying) with the ground and savior of my own existence, I meet God. At a deeper level, the same God is moving through all human beings. The more we are in silent conversation with that God, the more we have in common with what is deepest and most central in every religion.

Theologians tend to focus their attention upon religious teachings, but understanding also comes through the informed experience of prayer and worship. After all, it is there rather than in conceptual analysis that most human beings find religion and God. In the newer and richer dialogue with the world religions, meditation and the spiritual life have been profound sources of appreciation of another religion. Figures such as Charles de Foucauld, Bede Griffiths, Heinrich Dumoulin, and H. M. Enomiya-LaSalle have been pioneers in the contemplative dialogue between Christianity and other religions, while in recent decades Christian monasteries of men and women have drawn upon the monastic and meditative approaches of Asian countries to enhance a Christian life of prayer.

Thomas Merton is a particularly striking example of this dialogue by a Christian with another religion. He had long been interested in Asian religion, particularly Buddhism. Personally acquainted with the early interpreter of Buddhism in America, D. T. Suzuki, the Trappist monk himself became a pioneer of living dialogue with another religion, and by the 1960s was appropriating Zen into his Cistercian spiritual life.

Merton's evolution in appreciating Buddhism is instructive. In 1949, with little reading and no direct contact, he expressed doubts that other religions could have true mystical experience.[13] But he recorded in his famous autobiography, *The Seven Storey Mountain*, "I had turned spontaneously to the east, in reading about mysticism, as if there were little or nothing in the Christian tradition. . . . So now I was told that I ought to turn to the Christian tradition, to St. Augustine and told by a Hindu monk."[14] By the early 1950s he had read widely not only in Christian theologians and mystics but in those of other religions: He wrote that "pages in the works of St. Gregory of Nyssa . . . St. John of the Cross . . . might easily fit into a context of Zen Buddhism or Patanjali's Yoga."[15] As further years' of study passed, Merton came to see that Zen was both a view of reality and a technique of living. Zen can be accepted in a broad sense, not as a religious doctrine but as mode of the spiritual life rooted in Buddhism, much as the teachings of, for instance, the Carmelite mystics on life and prayer do not immediately imply every devotion or dogma. "Zen is consciousness unstructured by particular form or particular system, a trans-cultural, trans-religious, trans-formed consciousness. It is therefore in a sense 'void.' But it can shine through this or that system, religious or irreligious, just as light can shine through glass that is blue or green or red and yellow."[16] Although its roots lie in a great religion, centuries have brought Zen to a state where it need not be religion or philosophy, certainly not a doctrine. It is meditation; it neither affirms nor denies "grace," "salvation," "the will of God," because it must first transcend these words, which can be psychological fetters and burdens, in order to reach the purer atmosphere where everything (including God) can be.

Merton's position was balanced: the Zen approach to meditation could lead the Christian to a deeper conversation with God. But Zen was not a world beyond the human psyche—that was precisely what it did not want. "To put it in grossly oversimplified language, all religions aspire to a union with God in some way or other, and in each case this union is described in terms which have very definite analogies with the contemplative and mystical experiences in the Christian and particularly the Catholic tradition."[17]

Despite the geographical limitations of his monastic life, Merton's explorations were wide: friends and intellectual contacts, an instinct for what was both new and significant, years of reading and meditation, took his inquiring personality to new religions and worlds. When in 1968 the opportunity came for him to travel to Asia, he could contact the Buddhist persons and schools which so interested him. As always he kept a journal, and its pages record his conversations with Asians devoted to a spiritual life. With Tibetan and Indian hermits in the Himalayas, with practitioners of the monastic and solitary life, with the Dalai Lama, Merton recognized that he could discuss with ease the issues and difficulties of a life devoted to prayer and contemplation. "Talking with the various rimpoches [proven spiritual directors] has certainly been helpful, and above all the Dalai Lama himself. I have great confidence in him as a really charismatic person. The Tibetans are all quite impressive and their solidity does a great deal to counteract the bizarre reports about some of their practices. It is all very good experience."

Merton spoke with many: here is how he records the ease with which he discussed the spiritual life with Chatral Rimpoche in the foothills of the Himalayas, "the greatest rimpoche I have met so far and a very impressive person. . . . He said he had meditated in solitude for thirty years or more and had not attained to perfect emptiness and I said I hadn't either."[18]

> We had a fine talk . . . must have talked for two hours or more, covering all sorts of ground, mostly around the idea of dzogchen but also taking in some points of Christian doctrine compared with Buddhist: dharmakaya . . . the Risen Christ, suffering, compassion for all creatures, motives for "helping others"—but all leading back to the ultimate emptiness . . . going "beyond God" to the ultimate perfect emptiness.[19]

Meditation grounded in a concrete faith—Buddhist or Christian—led to a simpler religious contemplation. From there, like climbers on a high ridge looking back at lakes and trails, the deeper meaning and goal of beliefs and liturgies could be glimpsed. Merton does not offer a theory of the relativity of all religions but his own experience in faith of the future terrain where the religious history of grace interprets itself.

> The unspoken or half-spoken message of the talk was our complete understanding of each other as people who were somehow *on the edge* of great realization and knew it and were trying, somehow or other, to go out and get lost in it. And that it was a grace for us to meet one another.[20]

Accepting God's history of grace offers no final solution to the problems of the multiplicity of religions or of the centrality of Christ. Merton's talks with the

Tibetan masters convey not theory but an event born out of a simple conversation. The conversation is possible only because of the similarity of lives.
Evidently, the same Spirit was at work in both during the thirty years of
meditation.

Explorers are, as Thomas Merton put it, "people who were somehow *on the
edge* of great realization and knew it and were trying, somehow or other, to go out
and get lost in it." We have been exploring two vast worlds—human religions
and God's presence. Far from having a complete theology for Jesus Christ in a
world of religion, we have only recently reached a Christian perspective that
permits us to ponder the vastness of the problem. In this new world of worlds, we
do not glimpse the questions, much less their responses. Language fails as life is
contemplated rather than analyzed. The theologians past and present who have
been our guides are not experts in diverse religions but thinkers about the
Christian view of grace. The new perspective we have gained moves away from
the philosophy of religion, from academic dialogue about concepts, away from
salvation by ideas. It looks beneath doctrines and rites even as we gain respect
for those of other religions in their transparency to grace. Religion becomes the
kingdom of God in religions (as well as sin); grace ceases to be a divine but timid
electricity and becomes God's presence guiding religion; religion moves from
being philosophy to being life.

The puzzle remains as to how Christ is central. For Christians, he is central
not because some scriptural passage says so, but because he was seen by his
followers to be God's kingdom in a human being, to be God's image, plan, and
word in an individual. A true incarnation implies the centrality of Christ for all
religions. The New Testament and the early Christians knew that Christ in the
future would be different. This centrality lies in the future: as Raimundo
Panikkar indicated, "the unknown Christ" of Hinduism is, first of all, unknown
to Christians who do not understand how Christ would be incarnate now in
Asia.

Whatever centrality Jesus Christ has in the plan of God for human history, it
is a role that will exist over a long history and in a future always different. Since
we are only beginning to explore this topic, only now leaving the provincialisms
of the later Roman Empire, of the European colonial powers in the eighteenth
and nineteenth centuries, and of Anglo-Saxon fundamentalism in this century,
it is not surprising that we do not quickly find the perfect theory. The Christ of
the future is the Christ of the incarnation. Rather than dismissing the incarnation of the Divine Word in Jesus as myth or metaphysics (Clement of Alexandria
in the third century compared it to a sun appearing after a long dawn), we should
be pondering and experiencing its presence and meaning beyond biblical or
philosophical terms.

Right now we are the destiny of the incarnation. The Spirit of the risen Christ
lives through the ongoing incarnation of grace in men and women almost
without number: incarnations in other languages and cultures, in diverse epochs
and continents, in liturgies and mysticisms. This future, the destiny of Jesus and

his kingdom, is scarcely glimpsed. But we do perceive a long early morning promising a greater but as yet unimagined future of Christ. It works in the church, the sacrament of Jesus' kingdom, but also in a world of religions which in words and stones, in water and incense, are places of God's grace.

Recommended Readings

A popular introduction to faith and grace outside of Christianity is D. L. Carmody, *What Are They Saying about Non-Christian Faith* (New York: Paulist, 1982), while an extensive guide to how Protestant and Catholic theologians have in recent decades viewed salvation outside of Christianity is provided by Paul Knitter: *No Other Name? A Critical Survey of Christian Attitudes Toward the World Religions* (Maryknoll, NY: Orbis, 1985).

The most extensive survey of the history of Christian theologies over nineteen centuries on this topic is found in S. Harent, S. J., "Infidèles (Salut des)," in the *Dictionnaire de théologie catholique*, 7: 2 (Paris: Letouzey et Ane, 1927), 1726–1930. The texts of the theologians of the first century are collected in C. Saldanha, *Divine Pedagogy: A Patristic View of Non-Christian Religions* (Rome: Libreria Ateneo Salesiano, 1984).

For contemporary theologians, see Hans Küng, *Christianity and the World Religions* (New York: Doubleday, 1986); Karl Rahner, essays in *Theological Investigations*, vols. 5 and 8 (Baltimore: Helicon, 1966, 1968) and sections of Leo J. O'Donovan, ed., *A World of Grace* (New York: Seabury, 1980); Paul Tillich, *Christianity and Encounter of the World Religions* (New York: Columbia University Press, 1963); and Avery Dulles, "The Emerging World Church: A Theological Reflection;" Michael J. Scanlon, "Systematic Theology and the World Church;" Wilfred Cantwell Smith, "The World Church and the World History of Religion: The Theological Issue"—all in *Proceedings, Catholic Theological Society of America* 39 (1984) 1ff., 13ff., 52ff.

For an insightful view of Christianity's limitations and challenges in terms of Indian religion, see R. Panikkar, *The Unknown Christ of Hinduism* (Maryknoll, NY: Orbis, 1981) and his *The Trinity and the Religious Experience of Man* (New York: Orbis, 1973), where the author sketches how the different major world religions emphasize different aspects of God. Thomas Merton's ideas are found in a number of his books, e.g., *Zen and the Birds of Appetite* (New York: New Directions, 1968); *Asian Journal* (New York: New Directions, 1973); *Mystics and Zen Masters* (New York: Delta, 1961); *The Way of Chuang-Zu* (New York: New Directions, 1969).

On the relationship in the spiritual life of Asian religions and Christianity see (as well as Merton and Panikkar) the pioneering writings of Bede Griffiths, H. M. Enomiya-Lasalle, Heinrich Dumoulin as well as William Johnston, *The Still Point* (New York: Fordham University Press, 1970), and J. K. Kadowaki, *Zen and the Bible* (Boston: Routledge and Kegan Paul, 1980).

E L E V E N

Fundamental Theology and the Christian Moral Life

David Hollenbach

During the years since the close of the Second Vatican Council in 1965, Roman Catholic thinking about the shape of the Christian moral life has been in a state of rapid development. Concrete questions of personal ethics in the areas of sexual relationships, family life, and care for the sick have been at the center of intense discussion and conflict within the church. Social ethical questions have also increasingly become part of the ongoing discussion on the grass roots level of the church and in theology as well. Analysis of these practical questions must, of course, continue. However, disagreements about how they should be answered are not due simply to the arbitrary preferences of those involved in the debates. The disputes reflect fundamental theological differences about the shape of an authentically Christian life. This essay will outline several of these deeper religious and theological questions and suggest how recent developments in fundamental theology can help to address them.

The essay begins with an overview of the council's teaching on the relation between Christian faith and ethical understanding. Then it outlines the broad issues in the postconciliar theological debates about the distinctiveness of Christian ethics. Next it presents some of the contributions from recent fundamental theology that can help clarify what is at stake in these debates. This is followed by a critical assessment of these contributions. Two concrete issues—the morality of participation in warfare and the ethics of sexual equality—will be briefly analyzed to illustrate the implications of this assessment. All this leads to the conclusion that the task of moral theology is a process of discovering what the gospel demands in light of all sources of Christian wisdom. The task of the moral theologian, therefore, is the intellectual counterpart of the challenge of faithful discipleship.

Perspectives from Vatican II

The initiatives undertaken by the Second Vatican Council to bring about a renewal in the life of the church have forced the underlying theological presup-

167

positions of moral theology to the surface. From the time of the Council of Trent to the eve of Vatican II, most Catholic moral discourse relied on the natural law categories of Scholastic philosophy. Human reason, reflecting on the experience of what it is to be a human being in society, was judged capable of discovering the norms of Christian living. Distinctive Christian perspectives drawn from study of the Bible and reflection on the moral significance of central doctrinal convictions in areas such as christology, soteriology, and eschatology played relatively minor roles in this moral theology.

Vatican II judged this approach not fully adequate to the moral problems of the contemporary world. The council's judgment was heavily influenced by the biblical renaissance spurred on by the issuance of Pius XII's *Divino Afflante Spiritu* in 1943. It was shaped by the historical and doctrinal studies of theologians such as Yves Congar, Marie-Dominique Chenu, Henri de Lubac, and Karl Rahner, all of whom sought to relate Christian tradition and doctrine to contemporary experience in a revitalized way. The ecumenical concerns of the council also gave it greater openness to the more biblical and explicitly theological approaches to the moral life commonly found in the Protestant churches.

Thus the council called for a renewed linkage of religious faith and identity with the moral perspectives and principles that should guide Christian behavior. As *Optatam Totius* (the council's Decree on Priestly Formation) put it:

> theological disciplines should also be renewed by livelier contact with the mystery of Christ and the history of salvation. Special attention needs to be given to the development of moral theology. Its scientific exposition should be more thoroughly nourished by scriptural teaching. It should show the nobility of the Christian vocation of the faithful, and their obligation to bring forth fruit in charity for the life of the world.[1]

It is noteworthy that moral theology was singled out as particularly in need of renewal in this passage.

The council not only *recommended* the development of a theology in which the links between Scripture, the central doctrines of the faith, and the moral life would be made explicit; it sought to *exemplify* such an approach in its own teachings. *Gaudium et Spes* (the Pastoral Constitution on the Church in the Modern World) stated that its goal was that of "scrutinizing the signs of the times and of interpreting them in the light of the gospel."[2] It further argued that an explicitly theological perspective, formed by an understanding of and response to the person of Jesus Christ, is necessary for the attainment of an adequate grasp of the normatively human:

> The truth is that only in the mystery of the incarnate Word does the mystery of the human person take on light. For Adam, the first human, was a figure of Him who was to come, namely, Christ the Lord. Christ, the final Adam, by the revelation of the mystery of the Father and His love, fully reveals human beings to themselves and makes their supreme calling clear.[3]

The council, in other words, argued that an accurate interpretation of the meaning of historical experience ("the signs of the times") and of the full reality of human nature ("the mystery of the human person") are dependent on an appropriation of the gospel and a living relation to Christ. Such a contention challenges the idea that ethical reflection on the Christian moral life can rely exclusively on philosophical reason and natural law.

Nevertheless it would be wrong to conclude that the council rejected the traditional Catholic confidence in the great importance of reasoned reflection on human experience in the development of ethics. For example, *Gaudium et Spes* continued to affirm that both the innate dignity of human beings and their essentially social nature can be known not only by those who believe in Christ but by unbelievers as well.[4] It also rejected the notion that all the questions that arise in personal and social morality can be answered by theology alone, without attending to the resources provided by philosophy and other nontheological ways of understanding the human condition. The sphere of secular thought enjoys a certain autonomy and should not be subjected to a form of theological or religious imperialism.[5] The council repeatedly appealed to reasoned arguments to present its moral analysis of contemporary problems.

For instance, *Dignitatis Humanae* (the Declaration on Religious Freedom) stated that the right to religious freedom is grounded in the "very nature" of the human person.[6] It flows from the freedom and dignity of human beings whether they are Christians or not, and it is in principle knowable by all persons.[7] It is true that the council also presented an explicitly theological argument for religious freedom. This argument was based on a theology of faith as a radically free act, which in turn leads to that fullness of freedom that only Christ can bestow.[8] But the council did not presume that one must affirm this deeper theology of Christian freedom in order to reach the ethical, political, and legal conclusions that every person has a right to freedom from coercion in matters religious. If the council had made such a theology a prerequisite for its argument, it would have ended up in the self-contradictory position of setting religious and theological preconditions for the exercise of the right to religious freedom.

These considerations show that the question of the role that the central religious and theological orientation of the Christian faith should play in the development of ethics is not a simple matter. The council steered a course between the Scylla of a theological or ecclesiastical claim to hegemony over the domain of ethical knowledge and right behavior and the Charybdis of a secularism that would declare faith irrelevant to or even destructive of an adequate morality. Avery Dulles, whom we honor with this volume, has written that "the church must walk a fine line between sectarian withdrawal from the world and secularist absorption in it." Faith and morality are neither fully identical nor fully separate. Their relation to each other is an example of the "unity in difference" that Dulles sees as characteristic of the Catholic understanding of the relation between nature and grace.[9] The council, however, did not attempt to provide a systematic analysis of the nature of this "unity in difference." Thus it left the way open for further theological discussion of the matter in subsequent years.

The Debate on a Distinctively Christian Ethic

Within Roman Catholic discussions since the council there has been a vigorous debate underway about the contribution Christian belief should make to the moral life of Christians and indeed about whether there is a distinctively Christian ethic at all.[10] This debate is enormously complex, and only a few elements of it can be dealt with here. My purpose in noting these elements is to highlight a point of intersection between this debate and issues being raised in contemporary fundamental theology.

On one side of the dispute are those theologians who maintain that the gospel and grace of Christ make a substantive difference in the content of Christian ethical norms. This distinctiveness is derived from the fact that authentic Christian life must be informed by the revelation of God contained in the Scriptures, a revelation that claims our response not only through intellectual assent and confident trust in God but also in action and practice.[11] This revelation is historical and particular; it is not grasped and known from reasoned reflection on human experience alone, but only from an encounter with the Word of God made flesh in Jesus of Nazareth and handed on in the living tradition of the Christian community. Hans Urs von Balthasar, for example, defends the thesis that "Christian ethics must be elaborated in such a way that its starting point is Jesus Christ. . . . [Christ is] the concrete and plenary norm of all moral action."[12] The central point of this thesis is the affirmation that the Christian life is essentially a life of discipleship, founded on faith in Christ and obedience to his call.

The theologians on the other side of this debate point out, however, that the exact meaning of a position such as von Balthasar's is subject to a number of interpretations. What precisely are the concrete implications of saying that Christ is the norm of all moral action? Can the answer to every contemporary moral question be found in the teachings of Christ, or are other sources of understanding necessary? Does the distinctiveness of Christian ethics imply that there is one morality for Christians and another, inferior morality for the rest of humanity, or even that there is no morality at all outside the Christian community? Such an interpretation could lead to a denial of the existence of universal obligations that bind *all* persons and of virtues that *all* persons are called to cultivate. Denial of this element of universality in the moral life subjects moral existence to the acids of a kind of relativism that can destroy the very notion of moral obligation itself. The claim that only Christians can know the real meaning of the moral life must also confront the considerable body of evidence that non-Christians often live lives that are as admirable from an ethical point of view as those of many Christians.[13]

However, it is possible to maintain a universalist element in morality while still acknowledging that Christian faith makes a distinctive contribution to it. Richard McCormick, for example, has argued that the Christian story of God's dealings with the human race, contained in the Bible and systematized in church doctrine and theology, opens up

> surprising and delightful insights about the human condition as such. These insights are not, therefore, eccentric refractions limited in application to a particular historical community. . . . Reasoning about the Christian story makes a bolder claim. It claims to reveal the deeper dimensions of the universally human.[14]

The insight provided by faith thus reveals or "discloses" what is most truly and deeply human. This normative understanding of the human is the basis of more specific moral imperatives and virtues. This line of argument enables McCormick to conclude that anyone who, through reason and experience, attains genuine insight into the universally human can come to the same moral conclusions as do Christians. Both Christians and non-Christians are capable of insight into the ontological constitution of the normatively human, though they may reach this insight from different epistemological starting points.

There remains, nevertheless, an ambiguity in McCormick's approach to this question. For he also states that since Christian insights into the human condition can be shared by others, these Christian insights are "confirmatory rather than originating" sources of moral knowledge.[15] This way of putting the matter suggests that reason and experience, not a faith perspective, lead to the *discovery* of the moral meaning of the human condition. These discoveries are then backed up in a particularist way by the biblical story and the Christian tradition. Thus McCormick states that the Christian story provides "particular warrants" for universally valid ethical claims. This view of the matter "makes it possible for the Christian to share fully in the public forum without annexing non-Christians into a story not their own."[16]

The intent of McCormick's argument is clear. He wants to maintain an important place for the Christian story and for faith in Jesus Christ in his ethics while keeping open avenues of dialogue and rational discourse about public moral problems between Christians and non-Christians. Nevertheless his argument has not achieved total clarity. There is a significant difference between the statement that the Christian story "discloses" the meaning of the normatively human and the statement that this story "confirms" insight into this meaning. McCormick makes both claims.

It is possible, of course, that both statements are true, but that they apply to different levels of moral existence and discourse. Joseph Fuchs, for example, argues that the power of Christian faith operates to disclose an encompassing and imaginative moral vision of the human condition. Fuchs calls this encompassing vision a "Christian intentionality" that pervades all specific choices and actions. Fuchs describes this encompassing intentionality as "the believer's fundamental decision to accept God's love in Christ and to respond to it as one who believes and loves."[17] This decision becomes the background horizon in light of which all particular decisions and actions take on their ultimate significance and value, though it is not identifiable with the individual acts and choices of daily living. Clearly, explicit appropriation of the Christian story is necessary for the forma- tion of such an intentionality as the core of the Christian moral life. And the presence of this intentionality will make the ultimate meaning of Christian ethical existence different from other efforts to live a moral life.

For Fuchs as well as McCormick, however, this background horizon does not eliminate the need for careful analysis of more specific questions that arise in the foreground of daily moral existence. Nor does it provide a fully developed set of detailed moral principles that can serve as action guides for concrete ethical choices. The ultimate horizon does not eliminate the need for careful moral reasoning. It cannot replace efforts to uncover the meaning of norms such as justice or truthtelling. The concrete implications of these norms are not self- evident and can be quite elusive in some areas of personal and social existence. Thus a Christian will seek to be just and truthful as a way of expressing a basic orientation to love of God and neighbor, but the precise meaning of justice and the exact demands of truthfulness can only be determined by reasoned reflection on experience. Christians must rely on the same intellectual resources as non- Christians in determining the meaning of these more concrete norms and virtues.

McCormick's notion of the confirmatory power of the Christian story reenters the picture once moral reasoning has done its work of clarifying the meaning of these more detailed norms. The horizon outlined by Christian vision serves as a kind of check on the distortions and errors to which human experience and reason are always subject. Thus the rightness of the more specific moral princi- ples or concrete decisions reached by moral reasoning will be confirmed or rejected depending on how they fit within the contours of the encompassing horizon. For example, when entering into dialogue with the contemporary philosophical debates about the meaning of justice, the Christian vision of human existence provides confirmation for a communitarian understanding of this basic moral norm.[18] For the Christian story presents us with an ultimate vision of human existence as destined for fulfillment in that community called the kingdom of God and the communion of saints. Negatively, one whose basic intentionality has been formed by the Christian vision will be highly suspicious of libertarian understandings of justice that rest on individualistic presupposi- tions. It will reject any philosophical notion of justice that starts from the claim that persons have no obligations to their neighbors other than avoiding positive harm to them.[19] However, these theological confirmations of disconfirmations do not replace the task of moral reasoning.

Some Contributions from Fundamental Theology

From this sketch it should be clear that the debate about the distinctiveness of Christian ethics raises very basic questions about the relative contributions of several different sources of moral understanding and wisdom. In both Roman

Catholic and Protestant ethics, four sources for ethical knowledge claims have been classically identified: Scripture, tradition, reason, and experience.[20] Because the sources of Christian ethics are multiple it is impossible to avoid the question of which source is primary.

If they are all held to make indispensable contributions, the problem of conflicts among them must be addressed. For example, what is the outcome if moral action guides contained in the Bible or Christian tradition clash with conclusions based on reason and experience? Catholic moral theology has often argued that the four sources will in fact be in harmony with each other when they are properly interpreted. This argument, however, begs the question that has become central in contemporary fundamental theology, namely, the hermeneutical question of *how* the diverse sources of theological knowledge are to be interpreted in light of each other. As other essays in this volume have shown, contemporary fundamental theology has been vigorously exploring the relation of normative religious texts, historical traditions, the meaning of rationality, and the interpretation of experience in theology. Inquiry into the role played by each of these sources is equally important in addressing questions that arise in the sphere of ethics. The discussions of this issue in fundamental theology can shed light on the debate about the distinctiveness of Christian ethics.

The three chief ways of understanding the relation among these diverse sources in recent fundamental theology can be called (1) the experiential-expressive, (2) the cultural-linguistic, and (3) the hermeneutical-political.

The experiential-expressive model grants primacy to the source of experience in interpreting the meaning and assessing the truth of religious traditions and the ways of life they imply. Religion is first an experience in the depths of the self, and only secondarily is it expressed externally in the symbols, doctrines, and ethical norms of a particular religious tradition.[21] This model of religion is identical with what David Tracy calls a "romantic" view of language and symbols as expressive of "some deep, non-linguistic truth inside the self."[22] The experiential-expressive understanding is an attempt to resist the corrosive effect of the modern consciousness of pluralism and historical relativity by seeking to give religion, morality, and metaphysics a firm foundation in the interior subjectivity of human self-consciousness. According to the experiential-expressive understanding of religion, therefore, it is quite possible for persons in different religious communities with different traditions to share a common religious and moral experience even though they express it in different ways.

Richard McCormick on occasion relies on such an experiential-expressive theory of religion when he argues that Christian morality is identical with human morality. He has stated that "Christian ethics is the objectification in Jesus Christ of every person's experience of subjectivity."[23] This assumes that every person's experience is identical, at least on some fundamental level. It also assumes that the symbols and beliefs of the Christian faith express the contours of this inner experience, rather than adding something distinctively new to the inner awareness of what it is to be human. McCormick intends to show that the

Christian story does not contradict this experience; Christian faith is not "strange" or "foreign" to the human condition. Any theology that affirms the reality of the incarnation will agree with this.

But the doctrine of the incarnation also means that human particularity, historicity, and diversity must be taken with equal seriousness. The experiential-expressivist understanding of religion does not sufficiently acknowledge this historicity. It implicitly portrays the experience of human subjectivity as something timeless. The role played by different historical traditions in shaping the inner experience of human beings in diverse ways is not recognized. Thus the role of Christian symbols in Christian ethics is restricted to expressing and confirming what all persons can know about morality independent of their historical and cultural locations. Such an approach runs counter to the importance of history and tradition in shaping experience that is so much stressed by contemporary fundamental theologians.

Because of these inadequacies of experiential expressivism, George Lindbeck has proposed a "cultural-linguisitic" theory of religion as an alternative. This theory compares religion to a language or cultural system. Like language and culture, a religious tradition provides a framework that shapes the way those who have learned it perceive reality, speak about reality, and order their lives in action.[24] Human experience is not an independent source of knowledge untouched by historical and cultural traditions. Tradition is formative of and embedded in experience itself. Experience is never "raw" or uninterpreted. The languages and conceptual frameworks as well as the paradigmatic persons and events of a historical tradition are already present shaping the world of the experiencing subject and thus experience itself.[25]

The power traditions have to shape the experience of what it means to be human is particularly evident if one broadens one's horizons beyond the boundaries of a single culture. For example, the difference between the ethical visions of a Western Christian, an Iranian Shiite Muslim, and an Indian follower of Mohandas Gandhi is not simply that they use different religious languages to interpret an experience that they share in common. Precisely because they inhabit worlds shaped by different linguistic and symbolic traditions their experiences are themselves different.[26] Tradition and experience, therefore, partially codetermine each other. The thought world of a Western Christian is indelibly stamped by the Bible, that of an Iranian Muslim by the Qur'an, that of a disciple of Gandhi by the Bhagavad Gita. These normative religious texts are not, of course, the sole linguistic and conceptual influences on the interpretations of the right way to live produced by such persons. The Western Christian's life world has also been shaped by Greece and Rome, by the thinkers of the eighteenth-century Enlightenment, and by a host of other influences, just as Gandhi's reading of the Gita as a charter for his ethic of nonviolence was shaped both by later Indian traditions and by his exposure to Christianity and the West. Nevertheless, any serious attempt to interpret the meaning of the normatively human must recognize that classic religious texts continue to influence the structure of experience within a culture where these texts are alive. They can also profoundly challenge the domesticated understandings of reality into which both popular and high culture too often slide.[27]

The cultural-linguistic theory of religion also helps explain how symbolic and conceptual traditions have a powerful influence not only on experience but also on the way human beings reason about their lives and their world. The structure of rational argumentation is affected by the historical and cultural traditions available to the reasoner. This is so because there is no uninterpreted, purely given, starting point for rational argument. Any reasoned argument that a particular conviction is true must appeal to other, already existing convictions to justify the argument's conclusion.[28] In physics, for example, the problems an inquirer perceives as in need of research and the intellectual tools used in such research will be different depending on whether the inquirer has been born and educated in an Aristotelian, Newtonian, or Einsteinian period in the history of physics. The language and conceptual framework of physics is itself a historical reality. One cannot do physics at all without being socialized into the community of discourse that bears the tradition of physical inquiry.[29] That tradition, of course, is not closed and finished. It has been radically revised a number of times and will be revised again. But the great discoveries in the history of physics were not created ex nihilo. They emerged as a result of the tensions and anomalies that have periodically come to the fore within the tradition of physical inquiry itself.

Similarly, in our efforts to reason about our own humanness, we necessarily rely on languages and conceptual frameworks that we have not invented but learned. Reasoning, especially reasoning about the ethical, is not an exercise of pure logic leading from timeless starting points to timeless conclusions. Moral reasoning is itself historical and is formed by the plural traditions that history makes available to us.

This is evident in contemporary argument about the meaning and justification of human rights as fundamental criteria of social morality. Human rights are moral norms proposed as rational criteria for the evaluation of human behavior and social institutions. They set forward fundamental standards for protecting the dignity of human beings independently of their religious, social, economic, political, or cultural identifications. Nevertheless it is clear that both the justification of these norms and the interpretation of their concrete implications vary in notable ways from one philosophical, ideological, or religious tradition to another.[30]

For example, the religious traditions of Judaism, Christianity, and Islam have a powerful influence on the way the moral concepts of human rights are understood in the Middle East today. The central place of communal identity and of the land of Israel in Judaism leads to a reading of human rights that emphasizes the right of the Jewish people to national self-determination and to possession of the land of Israel by the Jewish nation. Western Christians understand rights in a way that gives greater emphasis to the rights of individual persons, for the universal mission of Christianity relativizes the importance of national identity. The radical monotheism of Islam leads Shiite Muslims to argue that universal human rights will only be secured in a society submissive to Allah—that is, in an Islamic republic.

The religious beliefs of each of these communities are always in the background of the argument about the justification and content of human rights and influence the outcome of such argument. It would, of course, be possible to claim that religious tradition should not be allowed to have such influence. But such a claim would amount to a demand that the communities of the Middle East be thoroughly secularized. Such elimination of the influence of religion in the name of human rights would be a clearly self-contradictory moral endeavor. Rather, the effort to develop an effective human rights ethic in the face of religious pluralism calls for *both* rational moral argument *and* the development of these religious traditions in new ways that are more compatible with the demands of universal community.[31] The need to find a framework that transcends the differences among various religious communities is nowhere more evident than in the Middle East, but this will not be achieved by ignoring the impact of religious and cultural traditions on moral reasoning.

Considerations such as these have led Lindbeck to argue that the meaning of a religion and the ethical way of life it proposes is *entirely* contained in the normative texts of the religion. In the cultural-linguistic view, efforts to understand a religion or religious ethic depend on a willingness to be schooled in the tradition of that religion, much as an apprentice is schooled by a master craftsman. Indeed, it is just as impossible to learn the meaning of a religion or religious ethic from some standpoint outside the framework of the religion itself as it is to learn the Chinese language by studying English translations of Chinese literature.[32] Such a quest is futile because all meaning is immanent *within* the specific uses of that language. Just as the meanings of individual words are dependent on their place within the total system of the language they are part of, so the meanings of particular religious beliefs and ethical norms are a function of their place within a religion as a total way of life. In Lindbeck's terms, meaning is "intratextual."

Thus the Christian meaning of "God" is determined by examining how the word operates within the Christian story and how it shapes the world and experience of faithful Christians.[33] The meaning of "God" for Christians is not specified by identifying some object to which this word refers and describing that object in a language other than that which tells the Christian story. In the same way, Christian love, Buddhist compassion, and the *fraternité* of the French revolution are not diverse expressions that refer to an attitude and form of behavior common to Jesus, Buddha, and Robespierre. These three religious/ moral orientations do not mean the same thing but "are radically (i.e. from the root) distinct ways of experiencing and being oriented toward self, neighbor, and cosmos."[34] Living in accordance with each of them will lead to a distinctive way of life in actual practice.

Lindbeck therefore recommends abandoning the attempt to translate Scripture into extrascriptural categories in the hope of discovering a common human morality. The proper task for the Christian moral theologian it that of describing reality within the scriptural framework and discovering the behavioral implications of this description in the contemporary context. The task for Christians is to "allow their cultural conditions and highly diverse affections to be molded by the set of biblical stories that stretches from creation to eschaton and culminates in Jesus' passion and resurrection."[35] In this regard he remains faithful to Luther's *sola scriptura* principle. The text of the Bible—taken in its entirety— has primacy among the sources of theology and ethics. "Intratextual theology redescribes reality within the scriptural framework rather than translating Scripture into extrascriptural categories. It is the text, so to speak, which absorbs the world, rather than the world the text."[36]

Lindbeck's fundamental cultural-linguistic approach to these questions takes pluralism in deadly earnest. It views pluralism, however, not as a challenge to develop universal ethical perspectives but rather as a call for faithfulness to the particularity of Christian norms. It stresses the distinctive, intratextual meaning of Christian morality as the unsurpassable contribution Christians can make to a divided world.[37] To make this contribution to a pluralistic, increasingly secularized society, Christians should band together to form "communal enclaves that socialize their members into highly particular outlooks supportive of concern for others."[38] The attempt to find common ground with non-Christians threatens to weaken the strength of such communities and their power to contribute to the larger, pluralistic society.

Assessing the Methodological Options

Is the cultural-linguistic solution to the problems raised by pluralism and historicity any more satisfactory than that offered by an experiential-expressive approach to the religious basis of ethics? There are two reasons why I think it is not.

First, David Tracy has commented that it needs to pay considerably more attention than it does to the question of the truth claims of Christianity if it is to avoid the charges of "relativism," "confessionalism," and "fideism."[39] The cultural-linguistic model has little to say about the *truth* of the Christian story and why anyone should turn to Christ as the key to the meaning of existence and to the right way to live.

Lindbeck is clearly convinced of the truth of Christianity. However, his intratextual understanding of the nature of meaning indicates that the only avenue that appears to be open in the effort to persuade others of this truth is that of "socializing" them into a Christian linguistic enclave and its corresponding form of life. This comes uncomfortably close to viewing the proclamation of the gospel as a form of indoctrination. It also rests on a peculiarly passive view of religious understanding and of faith. The process of coming to believe is a more active one than is learning a language. Believing is an act of judgment and commitment.

Avery Dulles has written eloquently about the analogy that exists between the genesis of religious faith and the processes of scientific or artistic discovery. Religious faith is not simply learned; it is discovered through active engagement with the most fundamental human and cosmic questions. In Dulles's words,

> The religious quest, like the scientific, begins with passionate questioning. Persons sensitive to the dimension of ultimacy in human experience, unwilling to rest in the merely proximate explanations that might satisfy more superficial minds, persistently ask whether life and the world, in the final analysis, issue into a meaningless void, or whether the proximate meanings disclosed in everyday experience point to an ultimate and abiding significance.[40]

To understand a religious text or tradition, one must be able to grasp the point of such questions. To believe in Christ one must be grasped by these questions as matters of overriding personal importance and find responses to them in the story of Jesus of Nazareth. The believer cannot discover meaning in Christianity or come to a decision about its truth without actively entering into this quest for ultimate meaning. The process by which Christian identity is formed is not only one of receptivity to the texts that tell the Christian story; it is also one of pursuit of ultimate meaning through questioning and, ultimately, decision. Human experience and reason are actively engaged from the start in coming to understand and believe any religion, Christianity included. This is true not only for someone who converts to Christianity but also for someone who is moving from immature to mature faith. If this active engagement of the self does not occur religious belief will not be faith at all but rather a mere piece of cultural baggage. Lindbeck's model of religion is curiously silent about this active process of coming to believe. And Lindbeck's "communal enclaves" will have to have very high walls indeed if they are to survive in our pluralistic culture.

In other words, there is a greater relationship of reciprocal conditioning between Scripture and tradition on the one hand and experience and reason on the other than either the experiential-expressive or the cultural-linguistic model acknowledges. Lindbeck is quite right in criticizing any theology or Christian ethic that fails to attend to the powerful impact that linguistic and cultural traditions have on the way persons interpret their world. However, in David Tracy's words, "this crucial insight does not mean that we should, in effect, abandon half the dialectic" by maintaining that the meaning and truth of Christianity as a way of life can be apprehended by a process of simple retrieval from Scripture and tradition.[41] Tracy insists, rightly I believe, that a judgment that Christianity is true and worthy of belief calls for "*mutually critical* correlations" between an interpretation of the meaning and truth of Scripture and tradition on the one hand and an interpretation of the contemporary situation on the other. An experiential-expressivist model for theology neglects the former pole of this dialectic; a cultural-linguistic model neglects the latter pole.

Tracy calls this mutually critical relationship among the four sources of theology a hermeneutical-political one.

Two Examples from Contemporary Ethics

The implications of this hermeneutical-political model of mutually critical correlation for Christian ethics can be illustrated by considering the question of Christian participation in warfare and the issue of the equality of men and women.

The debate about whether Christians should adopt an ethic of nonviolence and refuse to take up arms in all circumstances is very much alive in the church today. If one turns to the long tradition of Christian reflection on this topic one finds that this question has been answered both positively and negatively. In Lindbeck's view this diversity arises because the prohibition against participation in war is not an "unconditionally necessary" norm of the Christian life like the "law of love." Rather it is "conditionally necessary." That is, it applied under some conditions (such as those that prevailed in the first centuries of Christian history); it did not apply through most of subsequent Christian history, and it may now apply again in the nuclear age.[42] The ethical question of pacifism versus just war, in other words, rests on an argument about how to "apply" to changing "circumstances" a rule of behavior contained in the Christian story.

The status of the norm of nonviolence within the Christian story, however, is itself hotly controverted. Pacifists such as John Howard Yoder argue that the emergence of the just war theory within the Christian tradition was not an application of the gospel called for by new circumstances but a rejection of "the norm of the cross and the life of Jesus Christ as the way of dealing with conflict."[43] Paul Ramsey, to the contrary, maintains that Christian participation in war can, under stringently defined circumstances, be a way of loving one's neighbor if force is the only way to defend an innocent neighbor against an unjust aggressor.[44] The dispute between Yoder and Ramsey is a fundamental disagreement about the ethical meaning of the Christian story itself. This story clearly contains a profound call to a nonviolent approach to social conflict. It also contains an imperative to seek justice for one's neighbors, as the witness of the Old Testament prophets makes clear. The biblical texts are not self-interpreting when they are examined for guidance on the pacifism/just war question. The interpreter of these texts is actively involved in the process of discovering the meaning of these texts by asking questions of the texts and by the theological reasoning through which answers are sought. The normative texts of the Christian tradition, including the Bible, do not present us with a unified block of meaning that can be simply applied. Rather these texts are ethically polyvalent and call us to pursue a number of fundamental values, such as nonviolence and justice. These diverse values can sometimes conflict with each other. When faced with these tensions within the Christian story itself, we have no alternative but to risk an interpretation of its most fundamental meaning.

This calls for a receptive attention to the texts themselves and a ruthlessly honest effort to retrieve their full meaning, even at the cost of allowing deeply ingrained cultural biases to be shattered. But it also calls for rigorous reasoning about the relation between the diverse values, how they are interconnected with each other, and how the texts taken as a single story respond to the ultimate questions that are at the heart of the religious and ethical quest. The hermeneutical task is therefore one of reconstructing the meaning of the Christian story as well as retrieving this meaning from historically given texts and traditions. Retrieval and reconstruction are in fact two moments within one process of historical understanding. Neither can occur without the other.

Such efforts at critical correlation of the diverse sources are leading to significant developments in both pacifist and just war thinking today. Pacifist thinkers appeal to the central events of the biblical story—the life, death, and resurrection of Jesus—to argue for the norm of nonviolence. But the task of correlating these events with the problems of contemporary political existence leads many pacifist thinkers to reject the sectarian withdrawal from political responsibility that has sometimes marked this tradition in the past. In a somewhat similar way, just war thinkers are being led both by their renewed encounter with the Scriptures and by their reflection on the horrors of modern war to an effort to purge the just war tradition of its tendency to legitimate violence on a far wider scale than the original just war Christian thinkers ever envisioned.

The moral reasoning of each of these Christian subtraditions is made more rigorous by critical encounter with both the Scriptures and with the questions that arise in the exercise of political responsibility today. Both sides in this debate are applying a hermeneutic of suspicion to their historical traditions. And both sides are also applying what Thomas Ogletree has called a hermeneutic of hospitality to insights that come from outside their distinctive traditions as well. By this Ogletree means that they are willing to "welcome strange and unfamiliar meanings" into their ethical thinking, "perhaps to be shaken by them, but in no case to be left unchanged."[45] Though the pacifist and just war stances remain diverse interpretations of the content of Christian ethics, the critical correlation of the sources of Christian morality has begun to bridge some of the gaps that separate them. This is not simply the result of discovering the need for a new application of each subtradition in new circumstances. It involves active reinterpretation and reconstruction as well.

A second illustration of the power of the critical correlation of sources is the effort to uncover the response Christian theology and ethics should make to the contemporary feminist movement, particularly to the question of the equality of women and men. The need to reconstruct received traditions in order to retrieve their full meaning is particularly evident when the negative and even ethically oppressive elements within them are acknowledged. As Ogletree has pointed out, when we scrutinize the sources of ethical judgment, we not only encounter texts and events that disclose the normatively human but we also "confront meanings which distort and conceal rather than disclose."[46] From the perspective of the contemporary feminist movement, one of the most problematic aspects of the received theological and ethical memory of Christianity (and of most other ethical traditions as well) is its picture of the relative roles of men and women. The subordination of women to men that is present in much of Christian ethical and theological tradition has led theologians such as Mary Daly to reject this tradition altogether. Others, such as Rosemary Ruether, Phyllis Trible, and Elisabeth Schüssler Fiorenza have been led into a process of reinterpretation that is based on an acknowledgement of the polyvalent meaning of the tradition. In Ruether's words, "I believe we must recognize two things: (1) Practically all the inherited culture we have received from a male system of tradition has been biased. It tends either to ignore or directly sanction sexism; (2) All significant works of culture have depth and power to the extent that they are doing *something else* besides just sanctioning sexism."[47]

This something else, in Ruether's view, is the response that the texts of biblical faith provide to fear of death, estrangement, and oppression and their power as sources of hope for life, reconciliation, and liberation. In other words, the reason that the Christian tradition remains important and worth retrieving for Ruether and other Christian feminists is the same as the reason for their efforts to reconstruct it. The tradition's ability to provide ultimate meaning and guidance for fitting moral action is at the root of their desire *both* to retrieve *and* to reconstruct this tradition. Their goal is to make the central religious and moral meaning of the Christian story fully available to contemporary women— and to men in their relations with women as well. This task calls not only for retrieval but also for critical revision.

The argument here is analogous to the one David Kelsey has made about the meaning of the general theological claim that Scripture is the norm of Christian theology. He has observed that when a theologian affirms that Scripture is normative for theology, the affirmation is as much a declaration of the theologian's commitment to the Christian faith as it is a description of some property of the Bible. It is a self-involving statement that says something about the religious faith and experience of the speaker.[48] If the Bible did not provide religious meaning, vision, and guidance for persons in at least an incipient way, there would be no reason for them to declare that the Bible was normative for them. Therefore it is impossible to regard the Bible or the Christian tradition as a whole as the criterion for how to live in a way that excludes the insights that arise from contemporary understanding and experience.

Contemporary understanding and experience, of course, do not themselves generate Christian faith apart from retrieval of the Christian story from the Bible and tradition. But as Kelsey has observed, shaping one's life by this story depends on being able to give reasons why this story provides guidance in grappling with life's ultimate questions. The ethical content of this story must be open to rational assessment (which is different from rationalistic proof). It must also open up a "seriously imaginable" vision of the right way to live within the context of the wider culture in which the Christian lives.[49] Again, culture does not generate faith apart from retrieval of the tradition that tells the story of the God of Jesus Christ, and this story can challenge deeply held cultural convic-. tions in significant ways. However, if this challenge is finally perceived as an outright contradiction of one's most fundamental understanding and conviction it cannot be received as good news. Rather it will be experienced as a form of violence against the self.[50] Any claim, therefore, that the Christian story should form experience and guide moral reasoning in a way that leads to the violation of the equal dignity of women is neither rationally defensible nor seriously imaginable for many women and men today. This negative judgment serves as a critical principle for the retrieval of the Christian story. It will insist on reconstructing those ethical elements of the tradition that legitimate sexism, precisely in order to retrieve the good news of the God of Jesus Christ as a word addressed to men and women today.

Dialogue of the Sources and Christian Discipleship

The hermeneutic of critical correlation illustrated in these two examples is directly relevant to the debate about the distinctiveness of Christian ethics. The interplay between the sources that come from the past (Scripture and tradition) and those that we exercise in the present (reason and experience) suggests that the structure of this debate arises from a false way of posing the question. Those who stress the distinctive elements in Christian ethics focus on the contributions of Scripture and tradition and see them as giving Christian ethics a historical particularity not found in natural or rational ethics. Those who minimize the distinctive content of Christian moral norms stress reason and experience. They regard these sources as universally available to all human beings. The four sources of insight for Christian ethics, however, cannot be cleanly separated from each other this way. These sources are not independent variables in the theological or ethical equation; they mutually condition and mutually critique each other. This mutual and critical interplay of the sources of Christian ethics has become evident because of a deepened recognition that all of human existence is profoundly historical. All present understanding is shaped by some past, and all interpretations of the past are influenced by present personal, societal, and cultural circumstances. The mutual interaction of past and present constitutes the so-called "hermeneutical circle" that is an inescapable condition of all human understanding.

This means that the task of determining the right way for Christians to live in both their personal relations and social activity will never be finished so long as history lasts. The Scriptures and traditions of the church remain an ever-necessary source for Christian ethics. Without their constant retrieval in ethical discourse there will be no Christian ethic at all. At the same time there can be no question of formulating a script for the drama of Christian life in a way that sets it down on paper once and for all. New questions, new understandings, new forms of experience are constantly emerging. It is the permanent task of Christian ethics to retrieve the story of Jesus Christ in an ever fresh way so that this story might form lives in these new contexts. It is also the task of Christian ethics to reconstruct and develop the tradition in light of new insights that are critically judged to be true no matter what source they come from. The relation of Scripture, tradition, reason, and experience in the Christian moral life is one of continuing dialogue among them.

This dialogue must go on because Christian existence is essentially oriented to a God who transcends every interpersonal human relationship, every social arrangement, every cultural achievement. The life of a Christian in this world is never closed or finished but is always moving beyond what it has already become to the reality of the God whom Saint Augustine called both ever old and ever new. Christian faith is not yet the full vision of God, but it is the firm conviction that in Jesus Christ we have the guide to and promise of that vision. Christian life is always life "on the way." Therefore, as Avery Dulles has written,

> The Christian is defined as a person on the way to discovery, on the way to a revelation not yet given, or at least not yet given in final form. . . . The Christian trusts that, in following the crucified and risen Christ, he is on the route to the one disclosure that will fully satisfy the yearning of the human spirit. This confidence is sustained by a series of lesser disclosures which occur on the way, and are tokens or promises of the revelation yet to come.[51]

Since Christian ethics is the effort to understand how to live this life on the way, it too must also be always ready to welcome fresh discoveries of God's gifts of freedom and reconciliation. It will be able to recognize them as coming from the hand of the God of Jesus Christ only if it has been schooled in the story of that God. When it has been so schooled it will then be ready to recognize in new moral insights the lesser disclosures that anticipate the final and full gift that God intends to give us—God's own self. The hermeneutical task, in other words, is the intellectual counterpart in Christian ethics to the challenge of discipleship in Christian living. This insight, I believe, is the great contribution that fundamental theology can make to Christian ethics today.

Recommended Readings

Curran, Charles E., and Richard A. McCormick, eds. *Readings in Moral Theology No. 2: The Distinctiveness of Christian Ethics*. New York: Paulist, 1980. This anthology gathers together most of the important essays on the question of the distinctiveness of Christian ethics by scholars with quite different approaches.

Dulles, Avery. "Revelation and Discovery." In *Theology and Discovery: Essays in Honor of Karl Rahner*, edited by William J. Kelly. Milwaukee: Marquette University Press, 1980. Dulles relates questions of hermeneutics, the process of scientific discovery, and the shape of the Christian life of discipleship in a way that is most helpful for Christian ethics.

MacNamara, Vincent. *Faith and Ethics: Recent Roman Catholicism.* Washington, DC: Georgetown University Press, 1985. A helpful historical and systematic study of the way the question of the distinctiveness of Christian ethics has been treated in Roman Catholic theology, especially since the Second Vatican Council.

Ogletree, Thomas W. *Hospitality to the Stranger: Dimensions of Moral Understanding.* Philadelphia: Fortress, 1985. A hermeneutically informed discussion of the foundations of Christian ethics.

Russel, Letty M. ed. *Feminist Interpretation of the Bible.* Philadelphia: Westminster, 1985. The essays in this volume by Margaret Farley, Katharine Sakenfeld, Rosemary Ruether, Elisabeth Schüssler Fiorenza, Letty Russell, and Phyllis Trible present several ways that feminist hermeneutics is an important resource for Christian ethics.

Yoder, John Howard. *The Priestly Kingdom: Social Ethics as Gospel.* Notre Dame, IN: University of Notre Dame Press, 1984. A rigorous and methodologically sophisticated presentation of a radically "evangelical" understanding of the foundations of Christian ethics.

T W E L V E

Critical Witness: The Question of Method

Roger Haight

In his classic work, *Christ and Culture*, H. Richard Niebuhr uses historical data to construct five typical models of the way Christians conceive the relationship and significance of Christ for life in this world.[1] Niebuhr's editor asked him to add a conclusion to the work. The reader naturally expects that, since he has laid out the several options, Niebuhr will indicate which he thought was especially appropriate for the contemporaneous world. But he does not choose, at least not explicitly. Rather he explains to the possibly disappointed reader why the relativity and openendedness of our historical situation prohibit a final conclusion in a single answer.

A parallel may be drawn on the issue of the proper method for fundamental theology. From an empirical point of view, one could say that theology as a discipline is what theologians do, and they do not go about it in the same way. Thus no single method underlies this work of many authors, and one would be hard-pressed to collect more than the most general of principles that all would agree must be operative at all times. For some the pluralism of theologies and the methods underlying them may be cause for alarm; a natural desire for conclusive answers coincides with a deep insecurity in existence and a need for clarity in our complex history. But the relativity of our situation, as Niebuhr explains, does not necessarily lead to relativism and nihilism on the one hand nor the absolutization of one way of doing things on the other. It can also open out to reasonable discourse with others, both contemporary and from our past history, about the nature of our faith and what today's situation demands.

Because many methods are already reflected in these essays, I do not propose to add another by attempting to outline *the* method for fundamental theology. Rather I wish to raise the question of methodology, which may be considered the reflection on the principles that govern method itself. Instead of systematically developing a specific method, I will discuss a variety of issues and problems in fundamental theology today that need to be answered. These questions impose upon theology certain criteria for the adequacy of its method. Obviously, a

185

method of fundamental theology that begs fundamental questions will be inadequate. Although I shall not directly recommend any particular method for fundamental theology, I hope that these considerations will help one to judge the adequacy or inadequacy of any method. In the light of these remarks the reader may reflect back on the constructive content of this book from a new critical perspective. In many ways theology consists in asking and responding to questions over and over again in ever-new contexts.

The following discussion falls into four parts. To begin I discuss briefly what I mean by method in theology and why it is in itself an important and necessary consideration. I will then analyze some of the particular problems that underlie major areas of fundamental theology. This survey will review in one discussion the distinct areas treated in the whole book. In the third part I will analyze some tensions underlying theological thinking today, tensions which explain some of the diversity among theologies. I will also suggest ways in which these tensions might be held together. Finally, in the last section, I will simply underscore the practical character and intent of all theology by showing its relation to Christian life or spirituality.

The Importance of Method in Theology

Theologians today, like most people who participate in our intellectual culture, share two rather fundamental presuppositions that in large measure define modern consciousness. The first premise may be expressed in a variety of ways as the turn to the subject, or the existential quality of all knowing, or the idea that everything becomes known in its relation to us because of its action upon us and our reaction to it. As a result, knowing does not mean reproducing an exact representation of things as they are autonomously in themselves. We especially cannot completely capture subtle things like values and deeper meanings in self-evident quasi-mathematical formulas. If such were the case, we would not have the difficulty in communicating about profound matters that everyone experiences. When it comes to knowing about the transcendent mystery many human beings call God, it becomes evident that objective reasoning alone never decides the issue; one must take account of the differences between personal existential experiences.

Second, contemporary theologians for the most part also operate out of a historical consciousness. By that I mean the recognition that the experience of people always unfolds within the confines of a particular situation which, in some measure, limits their experience and shapes its contours. This is true of individuals within a community and whole societies within history, because all our knowledge unfolds in dialogue with the particular portion of the world that surrounds us and mediates to us the insights we gain as individuals or as communities. Most people today have experienced a cultural pluralism in which other groups or cultures have different sets of values and ideas about the world. These two principles account for the particularity and relatedness of all human knowing and discourse. Although this relativity should in no way be equated with a relativism that would rob knowledge of its validity (for all human beings share much in common), it accounts for the pluralism of religious thought generally and Christian theology as well. Moreover it explains the need and importance of theological method. In a homogeneous community or society in which pluralism did not exist because all shared the same suppositions, meanings, and values, one would not find a preoccupation with method.

Without giving a formal definition of method in theology, one may understand it descriptively as the way any theologian goes about affirming what he or she affirms. Method involves the premises and presuppositions of a theologian's position. Method concerns the starting point and the elementary data the theologian appeals to in taking a position. Method includes the logic, the kind of argument and its coherence, through which the theologian understands experience. In other words, a theologian's method generates the position he or she takes, so that beneath every position taken lies the method that generated the position. Sometimes the method of the theologian lies on the surface because he or she has explained it as part of the communication. At other times it remains implicit in what appears to be, but is not, a direct appeal to experience. By method, then, I am not referring merely to the organization of material, as in a table of contents, or to the procedural ordering of the elements of the subject matter, although these may indeed reflect an author's method. Method in a deeper sense refers to the processes of experience and logic of the mind that account for the very conclusions a theologian puts forward.

It should be clear that method alone does not determine a position in any absolute sense. Method in theology cannot exist without subject matter and the data upon which it works. Nor should method in theology, even as a formal process, be understood as some mechanical means that generates precise results. Two theologians who characterize their methods in similar ways may arrive at different conclusions. But this qualification should in no way minimize a concern for method in a quest for understanding, especially regarding a critical questioning of the presuppositions and deep structures of a theological imagination. For example, David Tracy has brought forward the implications of the difference between an analogical and a dialectical imagination in theology.[2] Another example may be seen in the way one's appreciation of liberation theology could ultimately depend on how one appreciated the notion of cooperative grace or on how one imaginatively portrayed eschatology.

The importance of method flows from the description of its function. If method generates the very meaning and truth of what a theologian affirms, then communication and understanding of the position held depends on some appreciation of the method involved. In other words, in the case of both the writer who affirms and the one who would grasp the theologian's position, *how* one comes to an appreciation and understanding of the subject matter has a bearing on the object itself, on *what* is understood. Of course one can read and know *that* a given theologian holds one position or another. But mere recitation of the conclusions to which a certain theology comes, without a critical or reflective appreciation of the way the conclusions were generated, yields knowledge about the theology or the theologian in question, but little real understanding of the subject matter.

Christian theology may be defined as the disciplined understanding of reality, of the self, the community and the race, of the world and our history in it, of God as its source and salvation, all through the lens of the tradition of the symbols of Christian faith. Whatever its definition, a common conception of theology regards it as a discipline which involves critical understanding. As such no theological understanding remains possible without some appreciation of method. By contrast, once one has grasped a theologian's method, many if not most of his or her positions fall into place.

Today we witness a pluralism of theologies and methods of theology. One could easily be tempted to say there are as many methods of theology as there theologians. Because of the many and extraordinary differences of method, and in the wake of the recognition of the experiential and historical character of the discipline itself, the question of method has rightly dominated the theological scene. Naturally many attempts are made to categorize and organize various groups of methods. Very broad types can be traced according to cultural shifts in the West since the beginning of the modern period.[3]

The variety of methods existing today can be grouped into families that share similar premises and modes of argument. Methods can be grouped according to the confessional constants of church traditions, according to continents that share a common language and cultural experience, according to major problem areas that we all face, according to the variety of other human sciences with which the theological imagination chooses to dialogue, according to the various subdisciplines into which theology can be divided. In other words, theology is so pluralistic and there are so many different ways of looking at this pluralism, that one could construct a typology of possible typologies of method.

In a tradition that descends from Max Weber, through Ernst Troeltsch and H. Richard Niebuhr, Avery Dulles has developed the construction of types or models into a theological art form. Since his development of models of the church in the early 1970s, the pattern of presenting types or families of positions on a particular topic has dominated his approach to issues.[4] This mode of presentation has many obvious advantages. It depicts some kind of order in theology. It enables a person with the vast erudition of Dulles to survey an enormous body of literature in a concise way. The presentation of types or models is pedagogically effective for it stimulates animated discussion. It is ecumenically sensitive; when the range of models roams all over history and across confessional lines, the technique relativizes positions in relation to each other and at the same time brings out the positive contributions of each. It thus enables communication and openness in dialogue.

It is important in a discussion of method in theology to realize that presentation of types is not a theological method but rather a procedural strategy of communication. Typologies involve an extremely subtle and complex epistemology. Types are generalizations constructed by a person; as such they do not exist literally as actual positions. Types are erected out of positions that theologians have held in various different historical situations. Each type, then, could be subdivided again and again until one reaches the real positions of the specific theologians organized within the type. Regularly, theologians who are typified do not find their positions adequately represented, because types systematically distort actual theologies which are always singularly related to history and usually betray nuances of detail. Types usually represent the conclusions of groups of theologians, and each typology is relative to the selected variables the designer chooses. Often the mere laying out of a typology may give the impression that the various options are equally viable.

In contrast to the procedure of laying out types, method in theology only begins when one begins to adjudicate between them. The real method of Dulles appears when he criticizes various models or constructs his own inclusive position and gives the reasons for it. This task always begins with the assumption by the theologian of his or her own presuppositions and method. In the end typologies are both valuable and deceptive. On the one hand they display a range of theological positions; on the other hand they may distract from the necessity of establishing the constructive bases and critical principles for establishing a position in the present situation.

Typology, then, cannot and does not really control the pluralism of theologies and methods in theology. One could, of course, overdramatize this pluralism. But two reflections kept in tension in relation to each other help to make sense of the situation. On the one hand, theology as it is actually practiced is hardly a science in the common North American sense of exact knowledge generated through a large commonly shared set of principles. It is genuinely pluralistic in the sense that one cannot reduce it to a single common method. As such it must appear to those entering it as a confusing morass. But on the other hand, theology need not be a Babel. Lines can be drawn between methods. The many different methods, at least in their constructive intent, do not necessarily exclude others. When theologians are clear about their method, others can understand them. Pluralism may not be overcome, but it can be negotiated by constant dialogue. In many respects theology unfolds as a collaborative and not a competitive discipline. Theologians seem more generally right in what they constructively affirm and more prone to error in what they deny. From this point of view theology should not be regarded as a confusing polemical debate. It makes more sense to regard it as some sort of complex unity of collective constructive effort held together by the common tradition of the Christian community as a whole.

Methodology responds to the problem latent in a pluralism of methods. I use the term methodology to refer to the study of method or methods; methodology consists in reflection on the logic of method itself. Essays in methodology can go a long way in clarifying what is going on in theology by constructing meta-methods or maps of the distinct operations that go into the fashioning of theological positions, or examining the processes by which the theological imagination relates to other kinds of knowledge, or distinguishing and interrelating the various subdisciplines that make up the whole field of theology.[5]

Fundamental theology as a discipline appears to be primordially methodological; one could almost say that fundamental theology is methodology.[6] It examines the first principles out of which one makes theological assertions; it attempts to establish common bases for communication across lines of diversity; it analyzes the method by which the theologian can or should proceed; it considers foundational issues and presuppositions upon which discussions of more specific problems are based. Theology as a discipline is in fact pluralistic, but this cannot mean that the theologian can legitimately say anything that he or she wishes. Human existence participates in a common inner drive toward truth and unity in wholeness. Some actual methods in theology, although they may seem sufficient to certain audiences and constituencies, may also be completely inadequate to what others know to be true about our world. Fundamental theology helps to build the grounds for adjudication.

Fundamental theology appears as "fundamental" in two different senses: it is fundamental insofar as it is methodological and insofar as it deals with those basic data and topical areas upon which Christian faith and theology rest. In the next part I shall consider some of these topics. As to the methodological consistency of fundamental theology it is important to appreciate the intrinsic tension and polarity of two dimensions that characterize it. Imagination in fundamental theology always alternates between the particular and the universal, between specifically Christian faith and transcendental human faith. Insofar as Christian faith understands itself not as a tribal religion but as containing the truth of human existence itself, it must be correlated against the horizon of precisely everything we know about the whole of reality.

This basic point deserves attention because it defines the critical and methodological nature of fundamental theology. Although fundamental theology is concerned with the concrete and specific origin, content, and meaning of Christian faith, it can never be satisfied with this. The truth of Christianity must also be measured by correlation against the field of a general anthropology, other religious faiths, what we know of the world through science, and so on. Christian faith is specifically unique in being mediated by Jesus, for example, but it must also be understood anthropologically in terms of the common faith of human beings as such. Christianity is a specific religion, but it must also share in the nature of religion as such and have something in common with all religions. To understand specifically Christian faith adequately, according to its own dynamic and claims, it must be conceived within the context of the whole of human wisdom. This tension cannot be escaped and it will be seen operating in each topic that fundamental theology considers.[7]

To sum up here, in this part of the discussion I have tried to explain the following propositions: (1) An inevitable pluralism reigns in theology. The distinctiveness of positions ultimately derives from differences in historical experience that become thematized by a variety of methods; (2) one must attend to method to understand any theology; (3) although the many methods are not reducible to one functionally comprehensive method, one can at least co-herently ground one's own assertions and at the same time communicate to others through the methodology of fundamental theology; (4) through methodology the pluralism of methods in dialogue positively expands theological wisdom; (5) the tension between the particular and the universal in theology requires that Christian self-understanding be measured within the context of a common understanding of human existence itself, so that it correlates with general human knowledge of the world. In the next section I wish to take up the various elements of fundamental theology in terms of the variety of bases for theology and some of the problems entailed in each one of them.

The Topics of Fundamental Theology

The point of departure for fundamental theology as a whole lies in the Christian community and its attachment to God who is mediated to it through Jesus. This community and its witness involve a way of life and a set of beliefs that express and explain the way of life. Fundamental theology deals with this phenomenon, as it were, as a whole; it finds its goal in a need to make the very foundations of the Christian community and its faith life intelligible and credi-ble. This effort can unfold on a very abstract level when it deals with the transcendental, that is, universal anthropological foundations for any kind of human faith. But since it must always also lay bare the bases for *Christian* faith and its theological assertions, fundamental theology must also become concrete and specific.

Thus the task of fundamental theology necessarily includes consideration of a series of elemental questions concerning the foundations of Christianity and their attendant topics. Some of the more important of these are faith, revela-tion, Scripture, Jesus Christ, church, world, ethics, and spirituality. Theolo-gians differ on how to understand these particular topics, but our contemporary culture and historical situation provide the context in which we must think about them. And this involves particular problems and questions that must be answered if we are to understand Christianity in a way that is adequate today. These issues, the preoccupations that arise from our own particular historical situation, and the way the theologian responds to them, normally provide the key that defines a particular method in theology.

In this section I want to review some of the central problems that underlie each of the major topics for fundamental theology. This will enable a review of the subject matter of the present book and a more specific consideration of fundamental theology. The point here is not to prescribe the specific method for dealing with these issues; in fact they may be dealt with in a variety of ways by different methodological suppositions, distinctions, and patterns of reasoning.

But in underlining some crucial questions with which fundamental theology must deal, this discussion enters into an implicit dialogue with the chapters of this book and suggests broad guidelines for method in a fundamental theology. Starting points and methods are adequate to the degree that they address the crucial questions of our day.

Faith and Revelation

Let me begin with the topics of faith and revelation, which may be considered as reciprocally related existential realities. By that I mean that wherever one has authentic faith one also has revelation, because faith, unlike knowledge, finds it object in. transcendent data.[8] To make Christian faith credible fundamental theology must show that faith, however one explains its nature, is a constitutive element of human existence itself. Faith should be so understood that it appears as "anthropological," that is, as integral to human being as such. In fact most fundamental theologies do explain the grounds of faith as part of the human condition so that in one form or another one finds it to be a universal phenomenon.

But this raises two crucial issues for a fundamental theology of revelation, one concerning its subjective dimension and the other its objective dimension. In stating these issues here I presume that revelation implies an action of God that comes from outside the human condition and *addresses* human beings. The universality of faith implies that we must also consider revelation to be a universal dimension of the human condition. Moreover we have no a priori grounds to consider all revelations other than Christian revelation as false and illusory. But this means that in a situation of a pluralism of revelations, each claiming to be true, the truth of the revelation cannot lie in its objective form, but must be located in a subjective or existential encounter with the transcendent God that lies embedded in external religious forms. To put this in Christian theological terms, if God wills the salvation of all, and if that salvation is conditional upon revelation to historical human existence, then revelation cannot be other than a subjective encounter that remains possible for every human being.

But this subjective dimension of revelation raises the problem of its historical mediation and objective form of expression from which existential encounter can never be separated. All human awareness and knowledge is mediated through sense data, and hence through the particular historical world in which any person or group lives. Today we witness a pluralism of revelations in history; the problem of revelation is not a scarcity of revelation, but a maelstrom of competing voices of God. The central issue for Christian fundamental theology concerning revelation today, therefore, is to develop a conception of the Christian medium and event of revelation that can relate it positively and appreciatively to other revelations which together make up our human condition.[9]

Jesus Christ

This leads naturally to the central topic of Christian fundamental theology, namely, Jesus Christ. I take it that distinctively Christian faith in God may be defined by its being focused and mediated by Jesus as the revealer of God. The task of fundamental theology focuses on the meaning and credibility of Jesus Christ as the basis of Christianity itself.

Without raising all the problems with which christology must deal, I wish simply to indicate the crucial issue in our cultural situation that challenges the foundation itself. That question, I think, may be stated in the following way: How can a particular revelation explain our universal human situation? Traditionally fundamental theology has focused on establishing the divinity of Jesus. The problem today does not undercut the importance of this issue, but is in a way prior to it. In concrete terms, how is the concrete life of this particular person, Jesus, so relevant to all human beings as to command their attention?

Given the pluralism of revelation, there arises a need for a definitive or finally clarifying initiative from God for our very self-understanding. But does this mean that God must act in history in an absolutely unique way at one time only? How should this "unique action of God in history" be understood so that it coheres with God's universal dealing with human beings? Could that event be understood inclusively, rather than exclusively, so that it underscored and did not undermine God's constant revelation to humankind from the beginning? In other words, how can God's acting uniquely in history in Jesus be made coherent with a universal anthropology? For our historical consciousness the problem for fundamental theology consists in so understanding the event of Jesus Christ that this particular and isolated event of history has an intelligible and credible significance that is universally relevant, bearing basic meaning to the concrete historical lives of all people.[10]

The Structure of Religious Awareness

The conjunction of faith and revelation on the one hand and their historical mediation through the event of Jesus on the other gives rise to another problem that may be considered basic for Christian theology. It concerns what one knows in and through revelation generally and Christian revelation in particular. One might call this the epistemological problem of faith and revelation. Faith cannot be considered knowledge in the ordinary sense of the kind of knowledge that we have of this world and things in it. Such an understanding would undermine the transcendence of the mystery toward which faith reaches. Nevertheless, faith does have a cognitive dimension; it intends a reality which has been given to it. This must be maintained lest faith and revelation be no more than a projected illusion. Thus one needs a tensive category for understanding the mediation of revelation, a kind of structure that preserves contact with faith's object without reducing that object to something of this world.

The category of symbol fills this need. From the point of view of other forms of human knowledge, symbolic kinds of knowing find acceptance in many fields of investigation including the study of psychology, art, sociology, anthropology, and language. Religious symbols are dialectical insofar as they both really mediate awareness of transcendence and make present something other than themselves, and yet are not to be taken literally because they are not themselves what they communicate. From the point of view of fidelity to the history of Christian thought, a strictly dialectical understanding of the symbol recapitulates the structure implicit in the traditional ideas of analogy or the dialectic between the *via positiva* and the *via negativa*. No understanding of God appears possible without some dialectical combination of the affirmation through negation that symbols and symbolic language provide. The epistemology of symbols also enables theology to be apologetically more sensitive to the many levels of human experience.[11]

Scripture and Theology

Methodology cannot ignore the question of the place and use of Scripture in theology. Scripture has generally been almost identified with revelation, so that theology has considered it the most fundamental source and authority. But new problems have arisen here that far transcend the doctrines of inspiration and inerrancy, and draw them into an entirely new context. Once one has accepted the existential nature of revelation itself, and once one begins to think in a historically conscious way, traditional doctrines must be examined in terms of a new pattern of thought. When the premise of all contemporary biblical exegesis (which determines what the author meant) is historicist, what can the assertion that God is the author mean? When we realize that all human ideas and values are historically conditioned, what can inerrancy mean? In an evolutionary and historically developing world, which contains a surplus of ever-new religious insight, what can it mean to say that we have a normative authority in the past or that revelation was complete in the past?

The very radicality of these questions, however, has opened up new ways of thinking about the nature and role of Scripture, and the symbolic structure of religious language helps a readjustment. Scripture cannot merely be dealt with as a set of words, propositions, or books. As a religious symbol itself, which contains a whole host of symbols, Scripture must find its center outside itself, even though mediated through itself, in the God revealed in and through Jesus. Any absolute qualities affirmed of Scripture do not belong to it of itself but derive from the God revealed in and through Jesus, that is, in the event to which it attests. In this sense authority, inspiration, and inerrancy are primarily predicates about Jesus. And looking forward from Jesus and Scripture, no appropriation of their religious meaning can escape constant reinterpretation. Change and adjustment of meaning must be written into our understanding of the normativity of our founding sources because we cannot escape the cultural horizon of our consciousness.

There are two commonly accepted criteria for Christian theology. What we affirm today theologically must be faithful to the original expression of that Christian faith in the sense of being radically identical; and it must at the same time be intelligible to people today in the sense of being coherent with what we actually know. Thus the task of fundamental theology insofar as it appeals to Scripture becomes explicitly hermeneutical, that is, it requires methods of interpretation. Moreover, interpretation of past meaning that claims fidelity to both past and present is inherently paradoxical or ambiguous: Karl Rahner both is and is not saying the same thing as Luke. To affirm what is essentially the same as the scriptural message in terms that are intelligible today inevitably means that it must also be different. Therefore one must find a deeper anthropological level at which the "sameness" subsists, one that abstracts from (is drawn out of) scriptural form. To affirm something which originated in a past revelatory event as intelligible today must inevitably be countercultural. Therefore one has to explain to our culture how scriptural language addresses today's deeper needs and experiences with religious authority. Christian theology cannot escape this tension of sameness and difference, and the subtlety involved in an interpretation that accommodates both of these two poles of the dialogue accounts for much of the division among theologians.[12]

The Development of Doctrine

Another set of problems that comes within the framework of fundamental theology involves the notion of received doctrine. While many of the issues here are implicitly addressed in the question of faith, revelation, the symbolic nature of religious language, and Scripture, doctrine is also a source of fundamental theology. The central doctrines of Christian faith were formulated after long and serious interpretative reflection on the sense of Scripture, so that they have come to be considered stable and unchanging. Thus theology considered development and reinterpretation of received doctrine as a problem, and it received a great deal of attention. But any serious reflection on the premises of our own historical consciousness at this point can only result in a landshift of our appreciation of the very nature of the problem. Our current perspective takes development for granted; it is simply evident that doctrine develops and cannot but change in people's consciousnesses. The problem does not lie in relativity and change; the problem lies in whether or not any human ideas and values can remain the same and in what sense. The task of fundamental theology at this point consists of establishing an anthropology, or at least "anthropological constants," in relation to which the deeper needs, values, and aspirations of humanity as such find consistent nourishment in the original Christian message. The deeper truths, rooted in repeated encounters with God mediated by Jesus, will appear constant even when they find different expressions in different historical situations. The many "doctrines" must be understood not as autonomous truths but as aspects of a single ongoing revealing action of God through Jesus.

Authority of the Church

Relative to the question of doctrine, fundamental theology, at least in the Roman Catholic Church, has put great emphasis on the authority of the church. As a discipline theology unfolds within the church as a reflection upon the faith of the church. The term *church* in its first meaning refers to the whole Christian movement, to all the organized traditions of those who witness to God revealed in Jesus Christ. The question of the authority of the church in its institutional form *over* theology constitutes less of a problem for theologians generally than it does for Catholic theologians because of the particular structure of authority in the Roman Church. Many of the problems to which Catholic theologians must respond can be handled practically with a distinction between disciplinary authority and religious authority. In other words, they are often not so much genuinely theological questions but issues of church discipline.

Below the political level, however, lurk deeper issues which must be addressed by all theologians. The problems concerning the objective authority of both Scripture and church are analogous. In an intellectual culture in which every notion of authority is suspect, what external and objective this-worldly authority can govern one's inner thoughts? What external historical authority can claim to speak with God's voice? The notion of any external power claiming divine authority has been so corrupted by historical events that the very conception of it must be almost abandoned. A central task of fundamental theology thus involves redefining religious authority as *religious*. Religious authority must be, like the faith and revelation it mediates, sui generis. As specifically Christian authority, it must share in the humility, compassion, and healing qualities of Jesus' authority. Although mediated externally, religious authority ceases to be either religious or authority when it fails to correspond to the interior existential realities of faith and revelation and to appeal to freedom and reason with values and wisdom that derive from Jesus.

Christianity and World Religions

Two final areas have become crucial for fundamental theology in our day. The first is the topic of dialogue with other religions which we have already touched upon in dealing with revelation and Jesus Christ. Along with historical consciousness has come a new respect for other religions. Christianity has always existed alongside other religions, but the open and positive attitude emerging among Christians toward the world religions today is profoundly new. Not only do the religions have a right to exist, they are recognized as positively willed by God. Pluralism appears as a value; one can learn from the revelation contained in other faiths. This appreciation cannot fail to elicit fundamental changes in Christian attitudes toward Jesus Christ and the church. The final and normative character of Jesus Christ and the nature and function of the church in history must be understood in a much more nuanced way than in the past.

Christianity, World, and Society

The other area that also provides a radically new context for fundamental theology arises from a new conscious imperative that the church play a positive role in the fashioning of public human history. What was taken for granted in the medieval period and denied by modern culture is being reasserted today in a new and extremely nuanced way. The church and the fundamental meaning of the Christianity of which it is a sign must be understood in relationship to the world. Considering the poverty, oppression, and suffering that characterize our historical existence today, one can hardly escape the threat of confusion and the existential terror of meaninglessness. Dehumanizing treatment of women is merely one example in a history of humanly inflicted suffering. The experience of needless human suffering on a massive social scale, more than any other human problem, calls Christianity to account for itself: What does the Christian message have to say to this issue?

A whole host of questions arises here with a direct bearing on the method by which one comes to a fundamental understanding of Christianity. For example, our elementary theory of knowledge must take account of the sociology of knowledge. An adequate anthropology and an understanding of the foundations of faith in relation to it must include a social dimension. The relationship between knowledge and action must be taken into account and made explicit. Public Christian life in the world must be recognized as having an intrinsic bearing on the truth itself of theological understanding. Awareness of the social dimension of our new context has shown us that all theology is practical theology in the sense that it must have a bearing not only on personal spirituality but also on our corporate and public responsibility as a church.

In surveying these common topics for fundamental theology my aim has been to show that new questions from our contemporary world situation make heavy demands on the method of fundamental theology. These questions are radical; they go to the roots of our understanding. But I do not mean to suggest that they are unanswerable. Many theologians and theologies have incorporated these questions into their methods and have generated positive, constructive positions in their regard. The essays of this volume witness to this. In a way many of these issues may be considered perennial, so that what has been analyzed here reflects simply the common historic task of fundamental theology in dialogue with our situation, which is both similar to and different from the past.

Perennial Tensions in Theological Method

The problems underlying the topics of fundamental theology help define theological method. The ability of a method to respond to fundamental questions is a measure of its adequacy. In this section I want to bring to the surface some constructive tensions underlying theological method and understanding. Often the poles of these tensions seem to militate against each other in an exclusive way, so that our situation appears to be marked by division and competing theologies. Some theologies appear polemically opposed to others, so that in the heat of the argument positive and constructive possibilities go unnoticed. In many cases, what appear as choices of alternatives may be matters of emphasis which, when combined in a tensive and creative way, allow one to move forward to new understanding. What follows, then, are descriptions of methodological presuppositions, points of view that shape the methods of theologians, which can be held together in a fruitful tension. In a way the terms in each set of these polarities reveal fundamental attitudes of the theologians who identify with them. The elements of the tensions thus provide categories for sorting out and evaluating the underlying assumptions of various theological methods and their adequacy.

A first tension can be seen in the relationships among anthropocentrism, christocentrism, and theocentrism. Does one have to choose one of these "centerings" of the imagination and exclude the others? And what does it mean if one does? How do they stand in relation to each other? These terms and the positions they vaguely represent are often used in different contexts to mean different things and need not be understood to exclude one another. For example, a theology "from below," which begins with and appeals to religious experience, often seems to be in conflict with a theology "from above," which begins with and appeals to sources of revelation. But if the terms are taken literally, it readily appears that theology *from* above is strictly speaking unimaginable. Revelation comes to us from God, but theology is nothing else than human reflection. All human thought necessarily begins with and draws upon actual contextualized experience from which it cannot escape even in transcending itself.

Theology, as a human discipline reflecting on God's revelation to us of our relation to God and God's to us, is inevitably anthropocentric. We cannot escape ourselves, our world, the questions of our existence and destiny. But at the same time, this same human experience can be drawn out of itself by God's action so that we can project God's point of view. Paradoxically, anthropocentism and theocentism can coexist.

The case is similar with theocentrism and christocentrism. When we think historically, that is, with a historical imagination that takes into account the whole history of humankind, it is difficult to think of God in relation to all humanity in any other than a theocentric context. Jesus is not historically available to the whole race. Theocentrism thus appears again as correlative to anthropocentrism, because historical consciousness forces us to see all of humankind standing before the same God. But at the same time the faith that the Christian has in God, the way God is conceived by Christian faith, cannot be other than christocentric. By definition Christian faith is the faith in God mediated historically by Jesus. Paradoxically, then, Christian faith, in imitation of Jesus' own faith, cannot be other than theocentric today, even while it remains christocentric and consists of a human experience of God that must be explained in anthropological terms.

Another tension appears between confessional and apologetic theology. I use these terms to characterize two fundamental sets of assumptions that may undergird theological reflection. Confessional theology rests on the conviction that Christian truth is one truth among many truths. Impressed by the pluralism and relativity of human experience and revelation, the theologian merely confesses and bears witness to Christian self-understanding. Christian theology is primarily directed to the Christian community. This theology does not regard Christian truth as absolute but as a finite, limited, and relative grasp of the only absolute—God.[13] The only mission of this theology beyond Christian culture consists of dialogue. It does not aim at conversion. By apologetic theology I mean a more aggressive kind of theology that rests on the conviction that Christian faith is absolute and that the whole world is meant to be Christian. While not necessarily attempting to demonstrate its truth, it seeks to explain Christian faith so as to make it intelligible as the truth of human existence as such.

One can understand the distinctive logics of both convictions, but need they be objectified into exclusive conceptions of reality and the status of Christian revelation? Cannot one theologian share the suppositions of both theologies without trying to dissolve the tension? By taking a stand on either side as an objective position one may be asserting more than we can know about absolute mystery. It seems to me, however, that a theologian can assume a confessional stance, like the rest of humankind who must live by a particular and therefore relative belief system, and at the same time strive to understand this particular faith as universally relevant and intelligible.

The tension between faith/revelation and knowledge of the world can also be appropriated in a positive and constructive way. This tension may be conceived as one between faith and reason whose extremes would be expressed in fideism and rationalism. Within the intervening spectrum everyone appears as both a fideist and a rationalist in relation to someone else. How then do faith and reason relate to each other positively and constructively? No one, it seems to me, has given a more adequate, short response to this issue than John Henry Newman, when he insisted that faith is a form or kind of reason.[14] By looking at the human person as a whole, and not dividing the person into faculties, Newman injects emotion, will, and freedom into the mind and reflectivity into the whole of human experience. Critical reflection can both destroy naive or childish beliefs and at the same time nourish faith's cognitive commitment. The pure option of faith is knowing, and the certitude of faith's knowledge is free. Faith should never be afraid of reason, and reason should have no fear of commitment to transcendent values. The tension here is practical and not theoretical.

The tension between the church and the world also divides theologians who adopt one of these poles as an exclusive point of view. Is theology done exclusively in the church, by the church, and for the church? Or is the horizon of theology precisely the world, God's action in the whole world, so that theology is missionary in its concern for the world and ecclesiocentrism is a temptation to sin? It seems clear that any exclusive concern with either side of this polarity would generate an unbalanced and therefore inadequate theology. It seems equally clear that the two dimensions of the polarity can be held in a genuinely creative tension. In the case of the individual person egoism is ultimately destructive whereas genuine concern for other people generates more self-possession. So too a kind of total dedication to the world by the church in mission can build up the community, whereas turning inward on itself can corrupt the very values it stands for. If the God revealed in Jesus has turned toward the world, can the church do less?

There must also be a tension in theology between a personal and a social understanding of human existence. As we said earlier, theology consists in large measure of correlating the meaning of Christian faith and revelation with the truth of human existence itself. In recent centuries theologians have almost exclusively stressed the personal and transcendent dimensions of human existence in constructing their religious anthropology. If the theologian understands Christian faith within the framework of a purely personalist anthropology in an individualistic way, the result is a privatized Christianity with which we are all too familiar. Of course the same error could be made on the other side. But once again the new imperative for a social anthropology and the need to explain why and how the church should be engaged in the world do not have to lessen concern for the personal dimension of human existence. The idea of competing dimensions of reality here is thoroughly misguided. The human person is no less a unique individual with personal responsibility and creativity for being at the same time an integral member of society, constituted by society, and shaped by his or her class and role in it. But when the social dimension of human existence is neglected, Christianity is understood in a distorted way.

Finally, all balanced theology will hold theory and action in tension. The failures here turn up in many different places. Some historical and systematic theologies try to explain the genesis of meaning without attending to the way in which all knowledge emerges out of action. Many theologies rest content with an interpretation of the meaning and truth of Christian belief without attending to the point of such an effort, namely, authentic human living that really gives praise to God. Theology often unfolds in complete separation from the questions of ethics, while Christian ethics unfolds as if it were a parallel discipline based on autonomous reasoning that begins once theology has finished. But theory and action completely interpenetrate each other. Each is inadequately distinct from the other, so that action influences thought as much as ideas direct action. These two dimensions of human existence cannot be separated from each other. Every theological position has a bearing on how one directs one's life and what the community as a body stands for, and every Christian ethical position, insofar as it is Christian, rests on theological assumptions and reasoning. This tension is such an important criterion for an adequate theological method that I shall return to it in the conclusion.

The limitation of this discussion to six such tensions is arbitrary. One could think of many more. But at the very least these particular tensions underlie what is actually going on in theology today. Method should strive to relate anthropo-centrism and theocentrism positively. Christology sets the paradoxical paradigm here, for in the human being Jesus, who is consubstantially and qualitatively one with us, we find the claim of God upon us. Theology must balance the posture of the confession of a particular faith with the desire to "explain" it in universal terms. Despite the distinction between faith and reason theology needs to appreciate the level at which they unite. The intermingling of church and world cannot fall out of view. The social and the personal dimensions of human existence demand integration. And most importantly the interaction of thought and action forms the context of all theology. These tensions, along with the questions that structure the topics of fundamental theology, form criteria for the methods of theology. A method will be adequate in proportion to its facility in handling these tensions.

Theology and Spirituality

In this methodological postscript to our essays in honor of Avery Dulles I have dealt with method abstractly, without proposing one method or another. I will conclude by proposing the most fundamental criterion for the choice of a method in theology.

Methods in theology correspond to the problematic character of the area being investigated. Like the methods of other disciplines, the method of the-ology should correspond to the objective data and the problem being investi-gated. But the methods theologians use also betray their own preoccupations in dealing with the subject matter and the fundamental convictions they have in relation to it. All theologians operate from fundamental biases or dispositions toward the issue. If they are at all systematic, they approach the subject matter from a wholistic, imaginative, and theological conception of the nature of Christianity.[15] The question of the most adequate method is frequently decided in a circular way. Theologians rarely choose a method and, following it to its conclusion, learn for the first time the position they hold. Rather the method is chosen from a fundamental conviction, attitude, insight, or position on the problem, and following the method through allows the more or less full rationale of the position to come forward. Systematic theologians always have a center of gravity, a centering concern, that brings all of their positions into some form of unity.

This a priori on the part of the theologian, then, shapes the relevance of the area under consideration. For example, why is this aspect of the problem considered more important than another? The precise nature of the problem and the importance of the data in relation to it arise within the subjectivity of the theologian. This can be put in terms of the hermeneutical strategy of question and answer. To interpret the subject matter contained in the data of the sources, the theologian must have some knowledge of and interest in the religious issues at stake. This interest shapes the questions that the theologian puts to the data of the community's witness and beliefs. But the questions in their turn determine in large measure the kind of answer that data will yield.[16] In other words, the interest and centering concern that the theologian brings to any given issue determines in turn the importance of the issue itself. In a way, the whole bearing of the subject matter on life today is largely decided by the subjectivity of the theologian. But this raises the question of the appropriateness of the questions. Do we possess any objective criteria for determining what questions and concerns are proper and adequate?

The tensive relation between theory and action discussed in the last section provides an entry into this issue. Human knowing in all its forms is for human living. Knowledge not only emerges out of life and action, but as reflective and critical awareness it is also oriented toward the exercise of human freedom.[17] Once one accepts a wholistic, existential, and historical anthropology, where theory and praxis are seen interacting and mutually influencing each other, the point of theology becomes clarified in a realistic and objective way. All methods of theology find their ultimate criterion in the Christian spirituality they spring from and generate. This assertion can be clarified by explaining what I mean by spirituality and by showing how it provides an objective criterion for the adequacy of theological method.

One is what one does. By action the human person constitutes himself or herself. From this it can be shown that fundamentally the term *spirituality* refers to the way a person leads his or her life. The term spirituality is properly Christian. But rather than view its reference as limited to Christians, one should realize that every human being has a spirituality. For all human beings lead their lives in a certain way. The concrete ways individuals and groups live make up their spirituality. This conception of things avoids from the outset every notion of spirituality that keeps it from having a larger life in the world.

This view of spirituality reaches more deeply than the question of "lifestyle." Since human existence is intentional and willed action, a spirituality reaches below the surface of this or that pattern of action to the fundamental option of a person. The multiple specific actions of a person fix and define the deepest commitment of that person's will, and ultimately of his or her being. One fashions the being of the self through action. To assign spirituality the profound significance it should have in the whole of life, there is no better way than to conceive it as embodied in human action itself.

The term spirituality can be understood on at least two distinct levels, one existential and the other reflective and explicitly conscious. On the first and deepest level of action, spirituality is constituted by the conscious decisions and actions that make the person be who he or she is; spirituality is the continuous line of action that fashions a person's identity. On the second, reflective level, spirituality refers to a theory or theoretical vision of human life in terms of the ideas, ideals, and ultimate values that should shape it. These two levels constantly interact in the thinking person. For example, in Christian spirituality one has a vision of God and reality mediated through the person of Jesus that supplies the ideas and values which in turn should shape a Christian's life. So too, various schools of spirituality within the Christian sphere—eremitical or Franciscan or Ignatian—supply variations and refinements of the Christian vision.

Looking at spirituality as action does not result in a limiting or exclusive definition. Indeed this approach intends the very opposite. Action includes and integrates dimensions of the spiritual life that frequently go overlooked. For example, all aspects of secular life in the world are drawn into the sphere of one's spiritual life. Moreover the category of action helps clarify the interrelationships of some elements of spirituality that are often dealt with separately. For example, faith and spirituality can be understood reductively to be synonymous. On the existential level of personal and subjective appropriation, faith and spirituality are identical because both refer to the fundamental option and commitment of a person that are actually lived out in his or her action. The more theoretical sense of faith, which appears when one addresses it objectively as "the faith," coincides with the understanding of the world and human life in it that in turn provides the vision for human action or underlies it. Spirituality, when recognized as grounded in human action, appears as nothing less than the living out of a vision of faith. Action is the actuality of the internalized vision.

The issue underlying spirituality, that which is at stake in it, is in every case union with God. This can be seen implicitly, even in the case of the atheist or the person not religiously inclined, through an analysis of the dynamics of human action. For just as the question of one's destiny cannot be escaped, neither can the correlative question of whether or not one's action and hence one's being in this world correspond to the ultimate reason of things. The question of whether or not one's action unfolds within the context of the all-encompassing truth of reality itself cannot logically be avoided. The dynamic of willing itself that underlies all human action is rooted in a love of being and an implicit demand for absolute being. In the Christian vision of things, this desire to be conformed to reality itself and thus affirmed in and by being itself, takes the form of union with the personal God whom Jesus called Father. Christian spirituality means living out this vision in action.[18]

When spirituality is thus conceived as human action, one has the basis for an objective consideration of the adequacy of the method of theology. Christian life and action unfold within the church in its mission to the world and within the world itself. The Christian is a responsible member of a church that exists in the world and has a relation to it, and like every other member of society the Christian also bears responsibilities for the world and for society. But this implies that the Christian must continually decide what that responsibility entails; what is the proper reaction to the world and action in society? This can only be answered by analyzing the world in which we live and the relationship of the church and the self to that world. Thus the inescapable imperative of action in the world, which is not just *any* world but the concrete world that surrounds and determines our actual existence, provides an objective standard for judging the adequacy of any method of theology.[19]

We have learned today from social and historical anthropology that individuals live in a world of objective social meanings and ideologies. One has to ask the objective social questions concerning whose interests theological positions support. Do the suppositions of a theologian's method adequately comprehend the social situation of our world? Where does this theological position lead socially? An objective, but not value-free, analysis of society enters intrinsically into theological method by shaping the fundamental interests and concerns of the theologian.

This criterion, of course, does not completely break the subjective circle of interpretation. There will be different analyses of the world in which we live and different responses regarding the meaning and truth of Christianity in relation to it. This is inevitable even with respect to the same situation in the same world. But the issue is never entirely subjective and must always remain in dialogue with the real historical and social conditions of the objective world. Theology provides itself with a reality principle by constantly asking the question, "What difference does this theology and its method make for responsible human life and action in the church in the world?" This binding of theology to life in history is demanded insofar as the very point of theology lies in the spirituality it engenders and nourishes. The most faithful witness is a critical witness in which the basis of criticism is the voice of suffering humanity in society and history.

Recommended Readings

Lindbeck, George A. *The Nature of Doctrine: Religion and Theology in a Postliberal Age*. Philadelphia: Westminster, 1984. A modest proposal for thinking about doctrine as purely regulative in a move to foster ecumenical dialogue.

Lonergan, Bernard. *Method in Theology*. New York: Herder and Herder, 1972. This influential volume on method presents theology as a set of interrelated functional specialties.

Ogden, Schubert M. *On Theology*. San Francisco: Harper and Row, 1986. A series of related essays covering the major issues in theological method with unusual clarity and precision.

Tillich, Paul. *Systematic Theology*. Vol. 1. Chicago: University of Chicago Press, 1951. This masterpiece is the point of reference for most subsequent discussions of theological method.

Tracy, David. *Blessed Rage for Order: The New Pluralism in Theology*. New York: Seabury, 1975.

———. *The Analogical Imagination: Christian Theology and the Culture of Pluralism*. New York: Crossroad 1981. These two volumes present the most thorough and sophisticated discussion of theological method in the current situation of pluralism.

Notes

One / Foundations for Theology: A Historical Sketch

1. Justin Martyr, *The First Apology*, in *The Ante-Nicene Fathers*, vol. 1, ed. A. Roberts and J. Donaldson (New York: Scribners, 1926), pp. 159–87.

2. Irenaeus, *Against Heresies*, in *The Ante-Nicene Fathers* 1:309–567.

3. Origen, *On First Principles*, trans. G. W. Butterworth (New York: Harper and Row, 1966).

4. Anselm of Canterbury, *Proslogion*, trans. M. J. Charlesworth (Oxford: Clarendon, 1965).

5. Anselm of Canterbury, *Cur Deus Homo?*, trans. J. G. Vose (Chicago: Open Court, 1926).

6. Thomas Aquinas, *Summa Theologiae*, Ia, q.1.

7. Immanuel Kant, e.g., in *The Critique of Practical Reason*, trans. L. W. Beck (Chicago: University of Chicago Press, 1949).

8. Friedrich Schleiermacher, *On Religion: Addresses to Its Cultured Critics*, trans. T. N. Tice (Richmond: John Knox, 1969).

9. G. W. F. Hegel, *The Philosophy of History*, trans. J. Sibree (New York: Willey Book Co., 1944). See also his *Lectures on the Philosophy of Religion*, trans. R. F. Brown et al. (Berkeley: University of California Press, 1984).

10. For an example, see John Brunsman and Arthur Preuss, *A Handbook of Fundamental Theology* (St. Louis: B. Herder, 1928).

11. Particularly F. A. Staudenmaier. For a secondary source, see Thomas F. O'Meara, *Romantic Idealism and Roman Catholicism* (Notre Dame, IN: University of Notre Dame Press, 1982), chap. 7.

12. For an introduction to the issues with which the Tübingen Cathoic theologians and those usually designated Modernists were concerned, see T. Mark Schoof, *A Survey of Catholic Theology 1800–1970* (New York: Paulist-Newman, 1970).

13. A major presentation of this is given by Rahner himself in *Foundations of Christian Faith* (New York: Seabury, 1978). For an introduction to his thought, see Leo J. O'Donovan, ed., *A World of Grace* (New York: Crossroad, 1980).

14. See Paul Tillich, *Systematic Theology*, vol. 1 (Chicago: University of Chicago Press, 1951), especially the Introduction.

15. See Bernard Lonergan, *Method in Theology* (New York: Herder and Herder, 1972).

16. Two sources in which these authors present their own case are: Jürgen Moltmann, *Theology of Hope* (New York: Harper and Row, 1967), and Wolfhart Pannenberg, *Theology and the Kingdom of God* (Philadelphia: Westminster, 1969). On the dimension of hope in Christian apologetics, see Avery Dulles, *The Survival of Dogma* (New York: Doubleday, 1971), chap. 4.

17. See J. B. Metz, *Faith in History and Society: Toward a Practical Fundamental Theology* (New York: Crossroad, 1980).

18. For issues particularly affecting fundamental theology, see especially Juan Luis Segundo, *The Liberation of Theology* (Maryknoll, NY: Orbis, 1976).

19. See the essays collected by Leonard Swidler, ed., *Toward a Universal Theology of Religion* (Maryknoll, NY: Orbis, 1987), and John Hick and Paul Knitter, eds., *The Myth of Christian Uniqueness* (Maryknoll, NY: Orbis, 1987).

Two / Defending Our Hope: On the Fundamental Tasks of Theology

1. See Bernard Lonergan, *Method in Theology* (New York: Herder and Herder, 1972), p. xi.

2. For the various changes in the conception of apologetics, see Avery Dulles, *A History of Apologetics* (New York: Corpus, 1971), and Giuseppe Ruggieri, "Per una storia dell'apologia nell'epoca moderna: Note bibliografiche et metodologiche," *Cristianesimo nella Storia* 4 (1983): 33–58.

3. Karl Rahner once bemoaned the lack of development in the manuals of theology between 1750 and 1950, despite the fact that "no one can deny that in the last two centuries cultural and spiritual transformations have taken place which, to say the very least, are comparable in depth and extent and power to mould men's lives with those which took place between the time of Augustine and that of the golden age of scholasticism" ("The Prospects for Dogmatic Theology," *Theological Investigations* 1 [Baltimore: Helicon, 1961], p. 2).

4. Hans Urs von Balthasar severely criticized the "consistent rejection (almost without exception) of all Catholic attempts to meet the modern intellectual world with empathy and dialogue. In an earlier time, the Inquisition prepared stakes for the burning of heretics; now it methodically burned that Catholic spirit which was attempting, in continuity with the Church Fathers and even with High Scholasticism (in its dialogue with Islam and Judaism), to make contact with the spirit of the new age" (*The Office of Peter and the Structure of the Church* [San Francisco: Ignatius, 1986], pp. 259–60).

5. "Instead of aiming at being a worldwide power, we are shrinking into ourselves, narrowing the lines of communion, trembling at freedom of thought, and using the language of dismay and despair at the prospect before us, instead of, with the high spirit of the warrior, going out conquering and to conquer" (*The Letters and Diaries of John Henry Newman*, ed. C. S. Dessain, vol. 22 [London: Nelson, 1972], pp. 314–15).

6. These two great historical paradigms of critical cultural engagement, however, differ in some important respects. One may advance the hypothesis that the choice of one or another as a model accounts for many of the tensions that first became apparent at the end of Vatican II and have become even more urgent since the council.

7. See, for example, Hans Urs von Balthasar, *Love Alone: The Way of Revelation* (London: Sheed and Ward, 1968), pp. 25–42; Joseph Ratzinger, *Principles of Catholic Theology: Building Stones for a Fundamental Theology* (San Francisco: Ignatius, 1987), pp. 161–71.

8. See Karl Rahner, *Foundations of Christian Faith: An Introduction to the Idea of Christianity* (New York: Seabury, 1978); Bernard Lonergan, *Method in Theology;* Edward Schillebeeckx, "Faith Functioning in Human Self-Understanding," in *The Word in History*, ed. T. Patrick Burke (New York: Sheed and Ward, 1966), pp. 41–59.

9. See Robert Schreiter, *Constructing Local Theologies* (Maryknoll, NY: Orbis, 1985).

10. Gustavo Guitérrez, *A Theology of Liberation: History, Politics and Salvation* (Maryknoll, NY: Orbis, 1973), pp. 135 and 149.

11. See Johann Baptist Metz, *Theology of the World* (New York: Herder and Herder, 1969), p. 111.

12. This is the "religious a priori" on which Schillebeeckx builds his articulation of the doctrine of salvation in *Christ: The Experience of Jesus as Lord* (New York: Seabury, 1980).

Three / "For the Salvation of All Who Believe": The Word of God as a Future for Humanity

1. Cf. *Dei Verbum* 2, 17. Quotations from the documents of Vatican II are taken from Walter M. Abbott's edition (New York: America, 1966). Wherever possible, I have retranslated the Latin text with a view to inclusive language.

2. *Gaudium et Spes* 53. More recently, this theme has been echoed in *Economic Justice for All: Pastoral Letter on Catholic Social Teaching and the U.S. Economy* (Washington, D.C.: National Conference of Catholic Bishops, 1986), on the final page of which the bishops state: "We have to move from our devotion to independence, through an understanding of interdependence, to a commitment to human solidarity."

3. In view of these guiding principles, Pope John Paul II, in his second encyclical, *Dives in Misericordia* 1, has called the council's theology indissolubly theocentric and anthropocentric. The pope returned to this theme in his talk on 2 September 1988 to a group of bishops from the western United States during their *ad limina* visits to Rome.

4. This may lead us to reflect further on the actual form our religious questions take when they do surface. Our questions about God and human life depend more on historical circumstances than we generally realize. Men and women living under great economic oppression may ask even more about the possibility of justice than about the meaning of life; their sense of God may come less from a desire for divine truth and more from a longing for liberation from their bondage. One set of questions need not exclude the other. Indeed, if humanity is called to be God's own family, the concerns of one people will imply the concerns of another. But if our searching for God is truly born and sustained by God's search for us, then concrete signs of the divine presence will already be present in evaluations of our culture and economy as well as in our personal hopes and fears.

5. For notes on the deist and rationalist critiques, see Avery Dulles, *Revelation Theology: A History* (New York: Herder and Herder, 1969), pp. 52–61.

6. H. Richard Niebuhr, *The Meaning of Revelation* (New York: Macmillan, 1941), p. 23.

7. Ibid., p. 69.

8. Avery Dulles, *Models of Revelation* (Garden City, NY: Doubleday, 1983). Among the most important essays anticipating this book, see Dulles's "The Meaning of Revelation," in *Theological Folia of Villanova University: Speculative Studies*, vol. 2, ed. Joseph Papin (Villanova: Villanova University Press, 1975), pp. 151–79, and "Revelation and Discovery," in *Theology and Discovery: Essays in Honor of Karl Rahner, S.J.*, ed. William J. Kelly (Milwaukee: Marquette University Press, 1980), pp. 1–29.

9. Evangelization, in other words, is a necessary consequence of revelation. The council continued to reflect this dynamic pattern as it drafted *Ad Gentes*, the Decree on the Church's Missionary Activity. Ten years later, Paul VI issued his eloquent encyclical on the subject, *Evangelii Nuntiandi*.

10. For the application of this distinction to the reality of faith, see the next chapter in this volume.

11. Mircea Eliade, *The Sacred and the Profane: The Nature of Religion* (New York:

Harcourt, Brace, 1959), p. 147. See also Eliade's own favorite introduction to his thought, *Cosmos and History: The Myth of the Eternal Return* (New York: Harper, 1959). His more comprehensive studies range from *Patterns in Comparative Religion* (New York: Sheed and Ward, 1958) to *A History of Religious Ideas*, 3 vols. (Chicago: University of Chicago Press, 1978, 1982, 1985).

12. A fuller discussion would of course examine the revelatory value of the Qur'an for Islam, the Upanishads for Hinduism, etc.

13. Paul Ricoeur, "Toward a Hermeneutic of the Idea of Revelation," in *Essays on Biblical Interpretation*, ed. with an introduction by Lewis S. Mudge (Philadelphia: Fortress, 1980), pp. 73–118, on p. 90.

14. Ibid., p. 94.

15. In the late eighteenth century, for example, J. G. Herder had advocated an aesthetic approach to the Bible which contributed in its own way to the advent of the "higher criticism"—studying the Bible as literature the way one would study any profane literary work. Early in the nineteenth century W. M. L. De Wette exercised great influence by promoting a historical critical method which was both literary and historical. Literary criticism established texts and determined their basic genres, while historical criticism sought to evaluate the sacred writings as historical documents. Later in the century Julius Wellhausen drew the strands of historical criticism together by developing his documentary theory of the four major sources in the first six books of the Bible. At the same time, the new discipline of the history of religions, resolutely eschewing prior philosophical or theological commitments, was conceiving all religions as products of human culture.

To the increasingly detached and analytical biblical studies of the late nineteenth century, Hermann Gunkel in the twentieth century responded by developing form criticism. First introduced in his commentary on Genesis and then refined over three decades of research, his form-critical method emphasized the oral tradition behind the conventional forms or genres with which Israel expressed its religious history. Form criticism distinguished units of tradition, sought to determine their vital context, and then traced their development and interaction with other forms.

Soon the form-critical method was applied also to the New Testament, with greatest effect in the writings of Martin Dibelius and Rudolf Bultmann. While study of the Old Testament had centered on the traditions of Israel, New Testament criticism was concerned above all with how the confession of the church had shaped its account of the life and death of Jesus. As in form criticism of the Old Testament, New Testament form criticism supposes a period before the written gospels when various stories and sayings of Jesus circulated among early Christians. According to the needs and interests of various communities, it was argued, these came to be recorded in the gospels and can be classified according to the literary forms, such as parables or sayings, miracle or appearance stories. The authors who edited the final version of each account should be understood not as offering a modern secular biography but rather as providing a confessional portrait of Jesus that was nevertheless grounded in the historical experience of his disciples. (On this latter point, see Avery Dulles, *Apologetics and the Biblical Christ* [Westminster, MD: Newman, 1963].)

16. While praising his predecessors' concern for biblical studies, from Leo XIII's encyclical *Providentissimus Deus* in 1893 to Pius XI's legislation on the academic degrees required for professors of Scripture, Pius XII also noted the advances that archeology, philology, the knowledge of ancient languages, and textual criticism had made possible.

17. *Divino Afflante Spiritu* 27.

18. Ibid., 35, 36, 37.

19. In subsequent years, the pope's basic positions were further clarified by an important response of the Pontifical Biblical Commission in 1948 to a question of Cardinal Suhard about the Book of Genesis, then by a further statement from the Commission on the teaching of Scripture in seminaries, and also by clarifications from its secretary and subsecretary in 1955 on the historically conditioned character of the Commission's decrees earlier in the century. See Thomas Aquinas Collins, O.P., and Raymond E. Brown, S.S., "Church Pronouncements," in *The Jerome Biblical Commentary*, ed. R. E. Brown, S.S., Joseph A. Fitzmyer, S.J., and Roland E. Murphy, O. Carm. (Englewood Cliffs, NJ: Prentice-Hall, 1968), 2:624–32.

20. On the sense of the faith which characterizes the People of God as a whole, see LG 12.

21. On the canon of Scripture and its inspiration, see Peter Schineller's chapter in this volume.

22. For Wright, the Bible offers above all a confession of the great saving acts by which God graciously directs human history; see his *God Who Acts: Biblical Theology as Recital* (London: SCM, 1952). For Cullmann, revelation includes not only the events through which God is effecting "salvation history" but also the prophet's inspired interpretation of the events and their interrelation. Distinguishing a series of redemptive epochs—Israel before Christ, the Christ event itself as the midpoint of time, the age of the church witnessing in the Spirit to Christ—Cullmann insisted that the "history of salvation" was not a construction of Lukan theology, as the more radical German critics alleged, but was rooted in the teaching of Jesus himself. He presented his position in *Christ in Time*, 3d ed. (Philadelphia: Westminster, 1964) and compared it with other theologians in *Salvation in History* (New York: Harper and Row, 1967).

23. With several theological colleagues, Pannenberg first presented his position programmatically in *Revelation as History* (New York: Macmillan, 1968). For an overview of his views, see Avery Dulles, "Pannenberg on Revelation and Faith," in *The Theology of Wolfhart Pannenberg: Twelve American Critiques, with an Autobiographical Essay and Response*, ed. Carl E. Braaten and Philip Clayton (Minneapolis: Augsburg, 1988), pp. 169–87, with Pannenberg's comments in response to Dulles, pp. 317–19.

24. Langdon Gilkey, "Events, Meanings, and the Current Tasks of Theology," in *Trajectories in the Study of Religion: Addresses at the Seventy-Fifth Anniversary of the American Academy of Religion*, ed. Ray L. Hart (Atlanta, Scholars, 1987), pp. 175–92, on p. 175.

25. The full text, with commentary, may be found in Joseph A. Fitzmyer, S.J., *A Christological Catechism: New Testament Answers* (New York: Paulist, 1982), pp. 97–140.

26. See Hebrews 1:1–4. It is a continuing task for systematic christology to consider how the divine and the human become personally united and remain indissolubly one, though unconfused, in Jesus Christ as God's incarnate Word. For this question, as Karl Rahner insisted, the Council of Chalcedon's doctrinal interpretation of the biblical witness is a sure beginning rather than a past conclusion.

27. For a fuller development of the symbolic character of both revelation and faith, see Justin Kelly's chapter in this book.

28. Ricoeur, "Toward a Hermeneutic of the Idea of Revelation," p. 73.

29. See John Langan's chapter in this book and also see Pope John Paul II's Apostolic Letter, "The Christian Meaning of Suffering" (*Origins* 13, no. 37, 23 February 1984, pp.

609–23) in which the pope states: "The second half of our century, in its turn, brings with it—as though in proportion to the mistakes and transgressions of our contemporary civilization—such a horrible threat of nuclear war that we cannot think of this period except in terms of an incomparable accumulation of sufferings, even to the possible self-destruction of humanity" (p. 612).

30. See L. J. O'Donovan, "Death as the Depth of Life: A Rereading of Eschatology in *Gaudium et Spes*," in *Vatican II: The Unfinished Agenda*, ed. Lucien Richard, O.M.I. (New York: Paulist, 1987), pp. 203–23.

31. For fuller treatment of the ethical dimension of theology's foundations, see David Hollenbach's chapter in this volume.

32. See Karl Rahner's "Reflections on the Unity of the Love of Neighbor and the Love of God," *Theological Investigations* 6 (Baltimore: Helicon, 1969), pp. 231–49, and also *The Love of Jesus and the Love of Neighbor* (New York: Crossroad, 1983). Also, L. J. O'Donovan, "The Word of the Cross," *Chicago Studies* 25 (1986): 95–110.

33. For an excellent systematic presentation of the liberation perspective, see Roger Haight, *An Alternative Vision: An Interpretation of Liberation Theology* (New York: Paulist, 1985).

34. On the relation of Christian faith to the experience of grace beyond it, see Thomas F. O'Meara's essay later in this volume.

35. See John 16:13; *Dei Verbum* 8.

Four / Faith in the God of Jesus Christ

1. See chapter 7 of the present volume.

2. On the relationship between faith and the church, see Hans Küng, *The Church* (New York: Sheed and Ward, 1967), pp. 30–34.

3. From the *Traditio Apostolica (Apostolic Tradition)* of Hippolytus of Rome (A.D. 215), cited in J. Neuner and J. Dupuis, eds., *The Christian Faith in the Doctrinal Documents of the Catholic Church*, rev. ed. (New York: Alba, 1982), p. 3.

4. On Jesus' relation to the reign of God, see, for example, Joachim Jeremias, *New Testament Theology* (New York: Scribners, 1971).

5. Karl Rahner, "The Death of Jesus and the Closure of Revelation," in *Theological Investigations* 18 (New York: Crossroad, 1983), pp. 132–42.

6. James D. G. Dunn, *Jesus and the Spirit: A Study of the Religious and Charismatic Experience of Jesus and the First Christians as Reflected in the New Testament* (Philadelphia: Westminster, 1975), pp. 11–67.

7. William James, *Varieties of Religious Experience: A Study in Human Nature* (New York: Collier, 1961), Lectures 4 and 5.

8. See, for example, the recent popular work by Rabbi Harold Kushner, *When Bad Things Happen to Good People* (New York: Schocken Books, 1981).

9. See Langdon Gilkey's discussion of secularity and God-talk in *Naming the Whirlwind: The Renewal of God-Language* (New York: Bobbs-Merrill, 1969). For an important exploration of the similarities between scientific reason in its creative aspects and religious faith viewed as discovery of hidden truth, see Michael Polanyi, *Personal Knowledge: Towards a Post-Critical Philosophy* (New York: Harper and Row, 1962).

10. Jon Sobrino insists that one only truly knows Jesus Christ through following him in the struggle for peace and justice. See his *Christology at the Crossroads: A Latin American Approach* (Maryknoll, NY: Orbis, 1978).

11. Ida Görres, "The Believer's Unbelief," *Cross Currents* 11 (1961): 51–59.

12. The Apostolic Exhortation of Pope Paul VI, *Evangelii Nuntiandi (On Evangelization in the Modern World)* (Washington, DC: United States Catholic Conference Publication Office, 1976); also, Kenneth Boyack, ed., *Catholic Evangelization Today: A New Pentecost for the United States* (New York: Paulist, 1987).

13. Walter E. Conn, *Christian Conversion: A Developmental Study of Autonomy and Surrender* (New York: Paulist, 1986).

14. Stephen Happel and James J. Walter, *Conversion and Discipleship: A Christian Foundation for Ethics and Doctrine* (Philadelphia: Fortress, 1986). See also Bernard Lonergan, *Method in Theology* (New York: Herder and Herder, 1972), and Donald Gelpi, "The Converting Jesuit," *Studies in the Spirituality of Jesuits* 18, no. 3 (St. Louis: Seminar on Jesuit Spirituality, 1987).

15. Avery Dulles, "Faith and Inquiry," in *The Survival of Dogma: Faith, Authority and Dogma in a Changing Church* (Garden City, NY: Doubleday, 1971), pp. 15–75. The First Vatican Council (1870), in its extensive treatment of the relationship between Christian faith and reason, was very careful to affirm both the need for evidence of credibility and the grace-character of faith (see Neuner and Dupuis, eds., *Christian Faith*, pp. 40–48).

16. James B. Dunning, "Dynamics of Evangelization in the Catechumenate," in Boyack, ed., *Catholic Evangelization Today*, pp. 111–20.

17. "Tradition" can refer to those things passed down through the ages or the dynamic process of transmission itself. See "Tradition" in Karl Rahner and Herbert Vorgrimler, *Dictionary of Theology*, 2d ed. (New York: Crossroad, 1981).

18. Avery Dulles, "Faith and Inquiry," pp. 15–30.

19. Karl Rahner, "Basic Theological Interpretation of the Second Vatican Council," *Theological Investigations* 20 (New York: Crossroad, 1981), pp. 77–89.

20. David Hollenbach, "A Prophetic Church and the Catholic Sacramental Imagination," in *The Faith That Does Justice: Examining the Christian Sources for Social Change*, ed. John C. Haughey (New York: Paulist, 1977), pp. 234–63. The following chapter in the present volume will treat extensively the symbolic dimensions of faith and revelation.

21. Thomas Aquinas, *Summa Theologiae*, Ia, q. 1, art. 4, ad 3; q. 2, art. 3, ad 2.

22. Karl Rahner, "Theology of Freedom," *Theological Investigations* 6 (Baltimore: Helicon, 1969), pp. 178–96.

23. Avery Dulles, "Faith and Inquiry," pp. 15–16.

24. Recent theology has pointed out that Christians not only believe in Jesus Christ but share as well in Jesus' faith in God. Faith here refers to Jesus' radical conviction, commitment, and trust vis-à-vis God whom he called "Abba." Unlike us, however, Jesus' unity with God was of an incomparable quality, and he knew no sin. See Jon Sobrino, "The Faith of Jesus," in *Christology at the Crossroads*, pp. 79–145.

25. Many people have found two books by the late Anthony de Mello to be very helpful in developing a relationship with Christ in prayer: *Sadhana: A Way to God* (Garden City, NY: Doubleday, 1984) and *Wellsprings: A Book of Spiritual Exercises* (Garden City, NY: Doubleday, 1986).

26. Jon Sobrino's previously mentioned work explores the relationship of prayer and praxis in Jesus' life. See pp. 146–78.

27. Karl Rahner, "The Concept of Mystery in Catholic Theology," *Theological Investigations* 4 (Baltimore: Helicon, 1966), pp. 36–73.

28. J. B. Metz, "Unbelief as a Theological Problem," *Concilium* 6 (New York: Paulist, 1965), pp. 59–77.

29. Karl Rahner, *On Heresy*, reprinted in *Inquiries* (New York: Herder and Herder, 1964), pp. 403–63.

30. Vatican Council I offers the classic, official Roman Catholic statement of these qualities of faith (see Neuner and Dupuis, eds., *Christian Faith*, loc. cit.).

31. On atheism in relation to religious experience see Michael J. Buckley, "Atheism and Contemplation," *Theological Studies* 40 (1979): 680–99.

Five / Knowing by Heart: The Symbolic Structure of Revelation and Faith

1. See Karl Rahner, "The Theology of the Symbol," *Theological Investigations* 4 (Baltimore: Helicon, 1966), p. 225.

2. Avery Dulles, *Models of Revelation* (Garden City, NY: Doubleday, 1983), pp. 131, 136–39.

3. I would like to stress the word "model." In my treatment of various biblical texts, what matters is not so much the historical truth (or exegetical accuracy) of the proposed readings, as the general validity of the patterns they describe, and their helpfulness in understanding what goes on in revelation.

4. Nevertheless, it "gives rise to thought" (Paul Ricoeur, quoted by Dulles, *Models*, p. 137), as Aquinas's notion of God as pure, subsistent *esse* amply demonstrates.

5. Mircea Eliade, *Patterns in Comparative Religion*, trans. Rosemary Sheed (New York: Sheed and Ward, 1958), p. 420.

6. William Shakespeare, *A Midsummer Night's Dream*, act 4, sc. 1, line 151.

7. Dulles, *Models*, p. 144.

8. *The Revelations of Divine Love of Juliana of Norwich*, trans. James Walsh (St. Meinrad, IN: Abbey Press, 1961), p. 53.

9. RSV translation, slightly modified.

10. Samuel Terrien, *The Elusive Presence* (San Francisco: Harper and Row, 1975), p. 320.

11. Dulles, *Models*, p. 133. Dulles's use of the notion of indwelling derives in part from the thought of philosopher Michael Polanyi.

12. Susanne K. Langer, *Philosophy in a New Key*, 2d ed. (New York: New American Library, 1951), especially chapters 8 and 9, pp. 178–224.

13. R. P. Blackmur, *The Lion and the Honeycomb* (New York: Harcourt, Brace, 1955), p. 224.

14. Dulles's fine essay, "Revelation and Discovery," shows that the apparent opposition of "acquired" and "revealed" knowledge is not as absolute as this facile dichotomy suggests. See *Theology and Discovery*, ed. William J. Kelly (Milwaukee: Marquette University Press, 1980), pp. 1–29.

15. Rudolf Otto, *The Idea of the Holy*, trans. John W. Harvey (London and New York: Oxford University Press, 1958), p.159.

16. Viktor Frankl, *Man's Search for Meaning* (New York: Washington Square, 1963), pp. 63–64.

17. See my article "Faith: the Human Dimension," *The Way* 11 (July 1971): 183–91.

18. Peter Berger, *A Rumor of Angels* (Garden City, NY: Doubleday, 1970), pp. 55–56.

19. F. Schleiermacher, cited by Otto, *The Idea of the Holy*, p. 160.

20. James D. G. Dunn, *Jesus and the Spirit* (Philadelphia: Westminster, 1975), p. 67.

21. Matthew 7:12 ("the holy spirit" in Lk 11:13).

22. This nonobjective awareness is Jesus' very self-consciousness, whereby he knows

himself as the beloved of God. In knowing God as Father, he knows himself as Son, and vice versa (Mt 11:27; Lk 10:22). See, regarding this, Karl Rahner, "Dogmatic Reflections on the Knowledge and Self-Conciousness of Christ," *Theological Investigations* 5 (Baltimore: Helicon, 1966), pp. 191–215 (especially p. 212), and also my "Prayer and the Incarnation," *The Way Supplement* 34 (Autumn 1978): 22.

23. Thus Hebrews 12:2 describes Jesus as our "pioneer" or leader *(archēgon)* in faith and also its "perfecter" *(teleiōtēn)*.

24. Thus Rahner observes that "the theology of the process of the act of faith and that of the revelation-occurrence are to a large extent identical." See K. Rahner, "Revelation," in Karl Rahner and Joseph Ratzinger, *Revelation and Tradition*, trans. W. J. O'Hara (New York: Herder and Herder, 1966), p. 19. Compare Otto, *The Idea of the Holy*, p. 177.

25. Karl Rahner, *Spiritual Exercises*, trans. Kenneth Baker, S.J. (New York: Herder and Herder, 1965), p. 241.

26. Leander Keck, *A Future for the Historical Jesus* (Nashville and New York: Abingdon, 1971), p. 235.

27. For an account of the psychology of this process, see my article "The Spirit Cries Out," *The Way* 19 (July 1979): 199–209.

28. Simone Weil, *Gravity and Grace*, trans. Arthur Wills (New York: Putnam, 1952), p. 141.

29. Dulles, *Models*, p. 219.

30. "Early Christian theology (as well as all subsequent theology) is the process of interpretative remembrance of Jesus, the Christ. . . . The Gospels, then, are paradigmatic remembrances" (Elisabeth Schüssler Fiorenza, *In Memory of Her: A Feminist Theological Reconstruction of Christian Origins* [New York: Crossroad, 1983], p. 102).

31. "On Christian grounds it may be held that the divine person who appears in Jesus is not exhausted by that historical appearance" (Dulles, *Models*, p. 190).

32. Dulles quotes the scholastic adage that "an article of faith is a perception of the divine truth toward which it tends" (*Models*, p. 226).

33. "The giving of the white stone with the new name is the communication of what God thinks about the man to the man. . . . The true name is one which expresses the character, the nature, the *meaning* of the person who bears it. It is the man's own symbol—his soul's picture, in a word—the sign which belongs to him and to no one else. Who can give a man this, his own name? God alone. For no one but God sees what the man is. . . . It is only when the man has become his name that God gives him the stone with the name upon it, for then first can he understand what his name signifies" (*George MacDonald Anthology*, ed. C. S. Lewis [London: Geoffrey Bles, 1946], pp. 27–28).

Six / The Wisdom That Leads to Salvation: Revelation and Scripture

1. Carlos Mesters, "The Use of the Bible in Christian Communities of the Common People," in *The Challenge of Basic Christian Communities*, ed. S. Torres and J. Eagleson (Maryknoll, NY: Orbis, 1981), p. 209. H. Richard Niebuhr makes the same point in his *Kingdom of God in America* (New York: Harper, 1959), when he writes: "Scripture without experience is empty, but experience without Scripture is blind" (p. 59).

2. See John Calvin, *Institutes of the Christian Religion* (Philadelphia: Westminster, 1960), bk. 1, chap. 6, pt. 1, and bk. 1, chap. 14, pt. 1, where he employs and develops this analogy.

3. Avery Dulles, *Models of Revelation* (New York: Doubleday, 1983), p. 117. Dulles's

chapter 12, "The Bible: Document of Revelation," presents some brief reflections on many of the issues I am treating now, such as canonicity, inspiration, and inerrancy. His further reflections on these topics from an ecumenical perspective can be found in "Scripture: Recent Protestant and Catholic Views," in *Theology Today* 37, no. 1 (April 1980): 7–26.

4. See Vatican II, *Dei Verbum* 10, where the Catholic position on the relation between Scripture and tradition is given. Both make up a single deposit which is entrusted to the church and in a special way to the magisterium or teaching office of the church. We will be referring to this key document of Vatican II on Divine Revelation in several places, since it is the most authoritative recent statement of the Roman Catholic Church on the meaning of revelation and Scripture.

5. *Dei Verbum* 19. Another official document emphasizing the creative process by which the gospels came to be written is the Biblical Commission's "Instruction Concerning the Historical Truth of the Gospels," found in *Theological Studies* 25 (1964): 402–8, with an excellent introduction and commentary by Joseph A. Fitzmyer, S.J. A 1973 declaration issued by the Congregation for the Doctrine of Faith, *Mysterium Ecclesiae*, addresses the question of the historical condition that affects the expression of revelation.

6. A number of books and essays have appeared recently on the meaning and significance of the canon. See especially the writings of James A. Sanders, most recently his *Canon and Community* (Philadelphia: Fortress, 1984). A brief treatment entitled "Canon of Scripture" is given by Daniel J. Harrington in *The New Dictionary of Theology*, ed. J. Komonchak, M. Collins, and D. Lane (Wilmington, DE: Michael Glazier, 1987), pp. 156–59. Longer development would be found in the *Jerome Biblical Commentary* and in the encyclopedias *Sacramentum Mundi* and *Sacramentum Verbi*.

7. This list is found in the decree *De Canonicis Scripturis*, DS 1501–1505 (Neuner-Dupuis, *The Christian Faith in the Doctrinal Developments of the Catholic Church*, pp. 73–75). The First Vatican Council repeats this canon; see DS 3006 (Neuner-Dupuis, pp. 75–76).

8. For a key essay of Rahner on this, see "The Death of Jesus and the Closure of Revelation," *Theological Investigations* 18 (New York: Crossroad, 1983), pp. 132–43. Dulles's *Models of Revelation*, chapter 10 treats this difficult topic, as does chapter 10 of this volume.

9. See chapter 10 of this volume, where Thomas O'Meara enters into the difficult question of the presence of grace outside Christianity.

10. A helpful recent treatment of inspiration is provided by Paul J. Achtemeier, *The Inspiration of Scripture* (Philadelphia: Westminster, 1980). Martin McNamara's essay "Inspiration" in *The New Dictionary of Theology*, and the entries in the *Jerome Biblical Commentary* and in *Sacramentum Mundi* are valuable. A classic presentation, very influential for both systematic and biblical scholars, is Rahner's *Inspiration in the Bible* (New York: Herder and Herder, 1964).

11. This idea forms the basis for Rahner's treatment in which he shows that in one sense the Christian community is prior to and the basis for the Scriptures. The next two chapters of this volume will further explore the relationships among Scripture, the church, and theology.

12. This process of examining the literary form is important in overcoming the fundamentalistic interpretation of Scripture. Vatican II (*Dei Verbum* 12) insists that this attention to literary forms is the only correct way to read and understand Scripture. See

also the references in note 5 above for further confirmation of this approach in biblical scholarship.

13. David Tracy, *The Analogical Imagination* (New York: Crossroad, 1981), p. 68. In chapters 3–7 of this important work Tracy first develops the notion of the classic in general, and then applies it to the Christian classic.

14. See, for example, Paul Ricoeur, "Towards a Hermeneutic of the Idea of Revelation," in *Essays on Biblical Interpretation* (Philadelphia: Fortress, 1980), p. 95.

15. In George Steiner's extended review of Robert Alter and Frank Kermode, *The Literary Guide to the Bible* (Cambridge: Harvard University Press, 1988), in *The New Yorker*, 11 January 1988, p. 97.

Seven / The Church: Context for Theology

1. Francis Schüssler Fiorenza, *Foundational Theology: Jesus and the Church* (New York: Crossroad, 1984), p. 171.

2. Alfred Loisy, *The Gospel and the Church* (Philadelphia: Fortress, 1976), p. 166.

3. Daniel J. Harrington, S.J., *God's People in Christ* (Philadelphia: Fortress, 1980), pp. 28–29 (emphasis mine).

4. Avery Dulles, S.J., *A Church to Believe In* (New York: Crossroad, 1982), p. 23.

5. Harrington, *God's People*, chap. 8.

6. Raymond Brown, *The Churches the Apostles Left Behind* (New York: Paulist, 1984).

7. Robert Schreiter, *Constructing Local Theologies* (Maryknoll, NY: Orbis, 1985).

8. See, for example, Yves M.-J. Congar, O.P., *A History of Theology* (Garden City, NY: Doubleday, 1968).

9. Avery Dulles, S.J., *Models of Revelation* (Garden City, NY: Doubleday, 1983), chap. 9.

10. *Unitas Redintegratio* 14; cf. *Lumen Gentium* 23.

11. Yves Congar, O.P., *Diversity and Communion* (Mystic, CT: Twenty-Third Publications, 1985), pp. 34–35.

12. For a recent discussion of the tensions between the local churches and the Church of Rome, see Patrick Granfield, *The Limits of the Papacy* (New York: Crossroad, 1987), chap. 5, pp. 107–33.

13. For the most sophisticated and influential attempt to deal with the culture of pluralism see the works of David Tracy, *Blessed Rage for Order: The New Pluralism in Theology* (New York: Seabury, 1975), *The Analogical Imagination: Christian Theology and the Culture of Pluralism* (New York: Crossroad, 1981), and *Plurality and Ambiguity: Hermeutics, Religion, Hope* (San Francisco: Harper and Row, 1987).

14. Dulles, *Models of Revelation*, p. 137.

15. Avery Dulles, *The Survival of Dogma* (New York: Doubleday, 1971) passim, but especially chap. 10.

16. For a recent review of this terminology, see Ladislas Orsy, S.J., *The Church: Learning and Teaching* (Wilmington, DE: Glazier, 1987). Also see Francis A. Sullivan, *Magisterium* (Mahwah, NJ: Paulist, 1983).

17. Congar, *Diversity and Communion*, p. 13.

18. Eric G. Jay, *The Church*, Vol. 1, *The First Seventeen Centuries* (London: SPCK, 1977), pp. 43–46.

19. Edward J. Kilmartin, "Reception in History: An Ecclesiological Phenomenon and Its Significance," *Journal of Ecumenical Studies* 21 (1984): 36–37.

20. For further discussion of reception and its ecumenical applicability, see Yves Congar, "Reception as an Ecclesiological Reality," in *Election and Consensus in the Church*, ed. Giuseppe Alberigo and Anton Weiler (*Concilium* 77, New York: Herder and Herder, 1972), pp. 43–68; and Thomas P. Rausch, S.J., "Reception Past and Present," *Theological Studies* 47 (1986): 497–508.

21. Yves Congar, O.P., "The Historical Development of Authority," in *Problems of Authority*, ed. John Murray Todd (Baltimore: Helicon, 1962), pp. 119–56.

22. Yves Congar, O.P., *Tradition and Traditions* (New York: Macmillan, 1967), pp. 182 ff., 336, passim.

23. Dulles, *A Church to Believe In*, chap. 9.

24. Dulles, *The Survival of Dogma*, p. 85. I have argued elsewhere that authority in the post–Vatican II church can best be understood as in the process, quite incomplete, of a paradigm shift from its form in the post-Tridentine and especially neoscholastic period. See T. Howland Sanks, *Authority in the Church: A Study in Changing Paradigms* (Missoula, MT: Scholars, 1974).

25. George A. Lindbeck, *The Nature of Doctrine: Religion and Theology in a Postliberal Age* (Philadelphia: Westminster, 1985), p. 34.

26. Ibid., p. 19.

27. Ibid., p. 33: "Turning now in more detail to the relation of religion and experience, it may be noted that this is not unilateral but dialectical. It is simplistic to say (as I earlier did) merely that religions produce experiences, for the casuality is reciprocal. Patterns of experience alien to a given religion can profoundly influence it."

28. Dulles, *Models of Revelation*, p. 226.

Eight / Scripture in Theology

1. D. Tracy (*Plurality and Ambiguity: Hermeneutics, Religion, Hope* [San Francisco: Harper and Row, 1987], pp. 48–61) suggests that both positivism and romanticism permitted the illusion that the human ego is master of its world.

2. F. Nietzsche (*On the Advantage and Disadvantge of History for Life*, trans. P. Preuss [Indianapolis: Hackett, 1980], p. 39) commented: "A religion . . . which . . . is to be transformed into historical knowledge, a religion which is to be thoroughly known in a scientific way, will at the end of its path also be annihilated."

3. Reprinted in *The Hermeneutics Reader: Texts of the German Tradition from the Enlightenment to the Present*, ed. Kurt Mueller-Vollmer (New York: Crossroad, 1985), pp. 241–55.

4. See the discussion of Bultmann and Gadamer in L. M. Poland, *Literary Criticism and Biblical Hermeneutics* (AAR Academy Ser. 48; Chico: Scholars, 1985), pp. 5–39, 165–67.

5. See the discussion of this issue in relationship to the hermeneutics of Paul Ricoeur by F. Schüssler Fiorenza, *Foundational Theology: Jesus and the Church* (New York: Crossroad, 1984), pp. 29–31.

6. Werner Kelber attempted to point out the exegetical consequences of this transformation in *The Oral and the Written Gospel* (Philadelphia: Fortress, 1983). His discussion of the change in the sayings tradition "Q" when it became part of a gospel narrative indicates the significance of the shift to textuality: "By pressing the sayings into the

service of their written gospels, the authors of Matthew and Luke deprived Q of the very trait constitutive of its oral hermeneutic: the prophetically living voice of Jesus became the unalterable words of Jesus' past authority" (p. 203).

7. See D. H. Kelsey, *The Uses of Scripture in Recent Theology* (Philadelphia: Fortress, 1975), p. 15.

8. See H. Koester, "The History-of-Religions School, Gnosis and the Gospel of John," *Studia theologica* 40 (1986): 119–21.

9. See J. Painter, *Theology as Hermeneutics: Rudolf Bultmann's Interpretation of the History of Jesus* (Scheffield: Almond, 1987), pp. 90–91, 162.

10. See the analysis by L. Chouinard, "Gospel Christology: A Study of Methodology," *Journal for the Study of the New Testament* 30 (1987): 22–24.

11. Koester, "History-of-Religions School," pp. 122–27.

12. Painter, *Theology as Hermeneutics*, pp. 1–9, 24–25.

13. See Kelsey, *Uses of Scripture*, pp. 74–77.

14. E.g., J. L. Segundo,*The Humanist Christology of Paul* (Maryknoll, NY: Orbis, 1986), pp. 7–18.

15. P. J. Cahill ("Bultmann: Reminiscence and Legacy," *Theological Studies* 47 [1986]: 486–93) has even proposed that Bultmann's approach should be expanded into the debate about religion and public policy. A public policy which took into consideration the human longing for the absolute would (a) acknowledge that a common transcendent good must form the basis for the unity of all peoples; (b) that public policy is to be human policy; (c) that knowledge and concern born of the motives of religious love transcend the boundaries of ideologies.

16. Kelsey, *Uses of Scripture*, pp. 90–91.

17. Kelsey, *Uses of Scripture*, pp. 123–24; Poland (*Literary Criticism*, pp. 112–60) criticizes the excessive formalism of some contemporary approaches to parables such as D. Crossan's claim that the formal structure of parables represents a radical reversal of values such that we can only speak of them as representing "permanent eschatology."

18. Tracy, *The Analogical Imagination: Christian Theology and the Culture of Pluralism* (New York: Crossroad, 1981), pp. 68, 102–103, 193–94; *Plurality and Ambiguity*, pp. 12–20.

19. Tracy, *Analogical Imagination*, pp. 260–64.

20. Kelsey, *Uses of Scripture*, pp. 37–43.

21. Chouinard, "Gospel Christology," pp. 25–32.

22. S. R. Sutherland, *God, Jesus and Belief* (New York: Oxford, 1984), pp. 145–47, 165–67; R. E. Creel (*Divine Impassibility: An Essay in Philosophical Theology* [Cambridge: Cambridge University, 1986], pp. 149–57) grounds a "moral obligation" to believe in theism in the claim that Jesus' death shows that innocent suffering is not final or senseless but can have meaning, since evil will be defeated.

23. E. Schillebeeckx, *Jesus* (New York: Crossroad, 1979), pp. 86, 104.

24. Ibid., pp. 484, 586.

25. See the discussion of this challenge in Tracy, *Analogical Imagination*, pp. 73–75, 137 n. 16.

26. For a discussion of these issues from the feminist perspective, see E. Schüssler Fiorenza, *In Memory of Her: A Feminist Theological Reconstruction of Christian Origins* (New York: Crossroad, 1983).

27. S. McFague, *Models of God* (Philadelphia: Fortress, 1987).

28. Tracy, *Analogical Imagination*, pp. 76–78, 86 n. 34.

29. Ibid., p. 208.

30. Ibid., pp. 311–19. One can view the gospel message as "disorienting" to our established human patterns in very different contexts so that the various christologies which claim to be built on the New Testament look very different (p. 334, n. 15).

31. See the discussion of this problem in J. Elliott, "Social-Scientific Criticism of the New Testament," *Semeia* 35 (1986): 10–24.

32. Concern for such correlation between Jesus' religious language and "this world" is fundamental to liberation theology; see R. Haight, *An Alternative Vision: An Interpretation of Liberation Theology* (Mahwah, NJ: Paulist, 1985), pp. 7–10.

33. R. A. Horsley, *Jesus and the Spiral of Violence: Popular Jewish Resistance in Roman Palestine* (San Francisco: Harper and Row, 1987), pp. 157–208.

34. See W. Meeks, *The First Urban Christians: The Social World of St. Paul* (New Haven: Yale University Press, 1983), pp. 9–25, 51–110.

35. So P. Schrodt, *The Problem of the Beginning of Dogma in Recent Theology* (Frankfurt: Peter Lang, 1978), pp. 233–39.

36. R. Brown, *Biblical Exegesis and Church Doctrine* (Mahwah, NJ: Paulist, 1985), pp. 28–29. See the discussion of theology and emerging Christian self-understanding in chapter 7 of this volume.

37. Brown, *Exegesis and Doctrine*, p. 72.

38. B. Hebblethwaite, *The Incarnation: Collected Essays in Christology* (Cambridge: Cambridge University Press, 1987), pp. 14–19.

39. C. F. D. Moule, "The Borderlands of Ontology in the New Testament," in *The Philosophical Frontiers of Christian Theology: Essays Presented to D. M. Mackinnon*, ed. B. Hebblethwaite and S. Sutherland (Cambridge: Cambridge University Press, 1982), pp. 2–8.

40. H. Fries, *Fundamentaltheologie* (Graz: Styria, 1985), p. 180.

41. See A. J. Hultgren, *Christ and His Benefits: Christology and Redemption in the New Testament* (Philadelphia: Fortress, 1987), pp. 193–99.

42. See the discussion of this problem from the perspective of foundational theology in F. Schüssler Fiorenza, *Foundational Theology*, pp. 60–72, 93–97, 157–59, 172.

43. The beginnings of such a "patriarchal" transformation of Christianity are already evident in the Pauline churches. See Elisabeth Schüssler Fiorenza, "Rhetorical Situation and Historical Reconstruction in 1 Corinthians," *New Testament Studies* 33 (1987): 386–403.

44. See J. Sanders, *Canon and Community: A Guide to Canonical Criticism* (Philadelphia: Fortress, 1984), pp. 46–60.

45. W. Meeks, *The Moral World of the First Christians* (Philadelphia: Westminster, 1986), p. 120.

46. So R. Lafontaine, "Pour une Nouvelle Évangélisation," *Nouvelle revue théologique* 108 (1986): 643–47, 663–64.

47. See R. Brown, *Biblical Exeqesis*, pp. 114–34; R. Collins, "Glimpses into Some Local Churches of New Testament Times," *Laval théologique et philosophique* 42 (1986): 291–314.

48. P. Achtemeier, *The Quest for Unity in the New Testament Church* (Philadelphia: Fortress, 1987), pp. 36–66, 78.

49. A. Dulles, *The Survival of Dogma* (New York: Crossroad, 1971, 1982), pp. 80–94.

50. Dulles (*Survival*, p. 93) raises the question whether our ethical traditions are too bound up with the moral conventions of the first-century western Mediterranean world.

Galatians 5:13–6:10 is a clear example of such ethical material being incorporated into New Testament Christianity.

51. So E. Schlink, *Ökumenische Dogmatike Grundzüge* (Göttingen: Vandenhoeck & Ruprecht, 1985), pp. 3–4.

52. A. Dulles, "Paths to Doctrinal Agreement: Ten Theses," *Theological Studies* 47 (1986): 32–47.

53. H. Fries and K. Rahner, *Unity of the Churches: An Actual Possibility* (Philadelphia: Fortress/Mahwah, NJ: Paulist, 1985), pp. 13–15.

54. These criteria are the starting points proposed by Dulles in "Doctrinal Agreement," pp. 35–36.

55. Dulles ("Doctrinal Agreement," pp. 37–38) has rightly questioned the Fries/Rahner proposal on this point. Since doctrine may well determine the reading of ambiguous passages of Scripture and its development introduces concepts that are not explicitly part of Scripture at all, different communions may even find that others are "in error" in the implications they draw from Scripture.

56. Dulles, "Doctrinal Agreement," p. 46.

57. See N. A. Beck, *Mature Christianity: The Recognition and Repudiation of the Anti-Jewish Polemic of the New Testament* (Cranbury, NJ: Associated University Presses, 1985).

58. See P. von der Osten-Sacken, *Christian-Jewish Dialogue: Theological Foundations* (Philadelphia: Fortress, 1986), pp. 2–4, 72–75, 93, 129.

59. See Osten-Sacken, *Christian-Jewish Dialogue*, pp. 47–59.

60. Osten-Sacken, *Christian-Jewish Dialogue*, p. 130.

61. The typology is Hultgren's in *Christ and His Benefits*, pp. 42–43, 137.

62. See Osten-Sacken, *Christian-Jewish Dialogue*, pp. 82–83.

Nine / Christian Doctrine in a Historically Conscious World

1. The reckoning of years from the birth of Christ was first carried out by Dionysius Exiguus, a monk and canonist who died in Rome in the first half of the sixth century. See L. E. Bayle, "Chronology," in *New Catholic Encyclopedia* (New York: McGraw-Hill, 1967), 3:674.

2. See P. Kyle McCarter, "Plots, True or False: The Succession Narrative as Court Apologetic," *Interpretation* 35 (1981): 355–67, for a recent treatment of this material which emphasizes its function in legitimating the ascent of Solomon to the throne of Israel. See also Gerhard von Rad, "The Beginnings of Historical Writing in Ancient Israel," in *The Problem of the Hexateuch*, trans. Trueman Dicken (New York: McGraw-Hill, 1966), pp. 166–204.

3. John Finley, *Thucydides* (Cambridge, MA: Harvard University Press, 1947), chap. 8.

4. See, for instance, *Federalist*, 18, which deals with ancient confederacies.

5. See Joseph A. Fitzmyer, *The Gospel According to Luke I–IX* (Garden City, NY: Doubleday, 1981), pp. 171–79 and 287–302.

6. Eusebius, *The History of the Church from Christ to Constantine*, trans. G. A. Williamson (Harmondsworth, Middlesex: Penguin, 1965) is a recent translation. Eusebius was born about 260 and died around 340. His work was continued in the fifth century in the works of Socrates and Sozomen. See Johannes Quasten, *Patrology*, vol. 3 (Westminster, MD: Newman, 1960).

7. Aristotle, *Poetics* 9.1451b. 5–7, trans. Ingram Bywater (Oxford: Clarendon Press, 1924).

8. René Descartes, *Discourse on Method*, Part One, *The Philosophical Works of Descartes*, trans. Elizabeth S. Haldane and G. R. T. Ross (Cambridge: Cambridge University Press, 1931).

9. Gotthold Ephraim Lessing, *Die Erziehung des Menschengeschlechts*, ed. Louis Ferdinand Helbig (Bern: Lang, 1980).

10. Paul Hazard, *The European Mind 1680–1715*, trans. J. Lewis May (London: Hollis and Carter, 1953), pp. 140–46, 180–97.

11. Ibid., pp. 99–115.

12. Gottfried Wilhelm Leibniz, *Discourse on Metaphysics*, VIII–IX, trans. R. N. D. Martin and Stuart Brown (New York: St. Martin's, 1988).

13. Giambattista Vico, *The New Science*, trans. Thomas Goddard Bergin and Max Harold Fisch (Ithaca, NY: Cornell University Press, 1948), p. 382, par. 1108.

14. See the treatment of the different assessments of the virtues by Aristotle and Aquinas in Henry Jaffa, *Thomism and Aristotelianism* (Chicago: University of Chicago Press, 1952).

15. Rudolf Bultmann, "New Testament and Mythology," in *Kerygma and Myth: A Theological Debate*, ed. Hans Werner Bartsch; trans. Reginald H. Fuller (London: SPCK, 1953), p. 5.

16. The interpretation of evolutionary theory offered in the writings of Pierre Teilhard de Chardin is a good example of an effort to preserve a distinctive destiny for human persons in an evolutionary cosmos.

17. An ambitious comparative account of this period has been given by Robert R. Palmer, *The Age of the Democratic Revolution: A Political History of Europe and America, 1760–1800*, 2 vols. (Princeton, NJ: Princeton University Press, 1959–1964).

18. Alexis de Tocqueville gave this line of interpretation a classic form in *The Old Regime and the French Revolution*, trans. Stuart Gilbert (Garden City, NY: Doubleday, 1955).

19. A brief presentation of the calendar and of the spirit animating its adoption can be found in *A Documentary Survey of the French Revolution*, ed. John Hall Stewart (New York: Macmillan, 1951), pp. 508–13.

20. Georg Wilhelm Friedrich Hegel, *The Philosophy of History*, trans. J. Sibree (New York: Dover, 1956), pp.438–52.

21. See A. J. Ayer, *Language, Truth, and Logic* (London: Gollancz, 1935), chap. 6.

22. Karl Raimund Popper, *The Open Society and Its Enemies*, Vol. 2; *The High Tide of Prophecy: Hegel, Marx, and the Aftermath* (Princeton, NJ: Princeton University Press, 1962), chap. 12, pp. 27–80, is a particularly vehement example.

23. Wilhelm Dilthey, *Pattern and Meaning in History: Thoughts on History and Society*, ed. H. P. Rickman (New York: Harper and Row, 1962), pp. 116–32.

24. Richard Rorty, *Philosophy and the Mirror of Nature* (Princeton, NJ: Princeton University Press, 1979).

25. Alasdair MacIntyre, *After Virtue: A Study in Moral Theory* (Notre Dame, IN: University of Notre Dame Press, 1981).

26. Avery Dulles, S.J., *Apologetics and the Biblical Christ* (Westminster, MD: Newman, 1963), p. 33.

27. Ibid., p. 14.

28. Ibid., p. 39.

29. Jacob Burckhardt, *The Civilization of the Renaissance in Italy*, trans. S. G. C. Middlemore, 4th ed. rev. (New York: Phaidon, 1951), pp. 81–87.

30. Avery Dulles, *The Survival of Dogma* (Garden City, NY: Doubleday, 1971), p. 117.

31. Ibid.

32. Ibid., p. 194.

33. Hegel, *The Philosophy of History*, p. 21.

34. Ernst Troeltsch, *The Absoluteness of Christianity and the History of Religions*, trans. David Reid (Richmond, VA: John Knox, 1971), p. 63.

Ten / Expanding Horizons: A World of Religions and Jesus Christ

1. For the theologies of Justin Martyr, Irenaeus, and Clement, see Chrys Saldanha, *Divine Pedagogy* (Rome: Liberia Ateneo Salesiano, 1984); Paul Knitter, *No Other Name? A Critical Survey of Christian Attitudes Towards the World Religions* (Maryknoll, NY: Orbis, 1985), pp. 120ff.

2. Augustine, *Retractiones* 1.13.3; *Epistola* 102.2; Clement, *Stromata* 1.13; 5.87.

3. *Nostra Aetate* (Declaration on the Relationship of the Church to the Non-Christian Religions) 2. Quotations from the documents of Vatican II are taken from Austin Flannery's edition (Grand Rapids: Eerdmans, 1975) and have occasionally been modified with a view to inclusive language.

4. Ibid.

5. *Lumen Gentium* 17.

6. Karl Rahner, "Christianity and the Non-Christian Religions," in *Theological Investigations* 5 (Baltimore: Helicon, 1966), pp. 115–34.

7. Karl Rahner, *Foundations of Christian Faith* (New York: Crossroad, 1978), pp. 164, 167.

8. "Revelation," in Karl Rahner, *Theological Dictionary* (New York: Herder and Herder, 1965), p. 267.

9. Hans Küng, *On Being a Christian* (New York: Doubleday, 1976), pp. 97f.

10. Rahner, "Christianity and the Non-Christian Religions," p. 143.

11. Avery Dulles, "The Emerging World Church: a Theological Reflection," *Proceedings, Catholic Theological Society of America* 39 (1984), pp. 3, 10, 11.

12. Rahner, *Foundations*, p. 138.

13. Thomas Merton, *Seeds of Contemplation* (New York: New Directions, 1949); these ideas were removed in the revised text which was published in 1961.

14. Thomas Merton, *The Seven Storey Mountain* (New York: Harcourt, Brace, 1948), p. 198.

15. Thomas Merton, *The Ascent to Truth* (New York: Harcourt, Brace, 1951), p. 26.

16. Thomas Merton, *Zen and the Birds of Appetite* (New York: New Directions, 1968), p. 4.

17. Thomas Merton, *Mystics and Zen Masters* (New York: Delta, 1961), p. 205.

18. Thomas Merton, *The Asian Journal of Thomas Merton* (New York: New Directions, 1973), p. 118.

19. Ibid., p. 143.

20. Ibid., p. 143.

Eleven / Fundamental Theology and the Christian Moral Life

1. Vatican Council II, *Optatam Totius* (Decree on Priestly Formation) 16. Quotations

from the documents of Vatican II are taken from Walter M. Abbott's edition (New York: America, 1966).

2. *Gaudium et Spes* (Pastoral Constitution on the Church in the Modern World) 4.

3. Ibid. 22. In some of the quotations from Vatican II, such as this one, the texts have been retranslated in this essay in a way that reflects the fact that in the original Latin words such as *homo* denote both man and woman, not simply the male of the species.

4. Ibid. 12.

5. In the council's words, "If by the autonomy of earthly affairs we mean that created things and societies themselves enjoy their own laws and values which must be gradually deciphered, put to use, and regulated by men and women, then it is entirely right to demand that autonomy. Such is not merely required by modern men and women, but harmonizes also with the will of the Creator. For by the very circumstance of their having been created, all things are endowed with their own stability, truth, goodness, proper laws, and order" (ibid. 36).

6. *Dignitatis Humanae* 2.

7. As John Courtney Murray commented, "The objective foundation of the right to religious freedom is presented in terms that should be intelligible and acceptable to all men, including nonbelievers. The simple essence of the matter is that man, being intelligent and free, is to be a responsible agent. Inherent in his very nature, therefore, is an exigency for freedom from coercion, especially in matters religious" (commentary on *Dignitatis Humanae* contained in the footnotes of the Abbott-Gallagher edition of *The Documents of Vatican II*, p. 680, n. 7).

8. See *Dignitatis Humanae* 10 and 11.

9. Avery Dulles, *The Catholicity of the Church* (Oxford: Clarendon, 1985), p. 66.

10. Much of the writing on this topic has been very usefully collected in *Readings in Moral Theology No. 2: The Distinctiveness of Christian Ethics*, ed. Charles E. Curran and Richard A. McCormick (New York: Paulist, 1980). For a helpful study of this literature, see Vincent MacNamara, *Faith and Ethics: Recent Roman Catholicism* (Dublin: Gill and Macmillan/Washington, DC: Georgetown University Press, 1985), pp. 14–66.

11. Dulles, "The Meaning of Faith Considered in Relationship to Justice," in *The Faith that Does Justice*, ed. John Haughey (New York: Paulist, 1977), pp. 10–46, and "The Gospel, the Church and Politics," *Origins* 16 (19 February 1987): 637–46.

12. Hans Urs von Balthasar, "Nine Theses in Christian Ethics," in *Readings in Moral Theology No. 2*, ed. Curran and McCormick, p. 191.

13. See James M. Gustafson, *Can Ethics Be Christian?* (Chicago: University of Chicago Press, 1975), pp. 81–86.

14. Richard A. McCormick, *Health and Medicine in the Catholic Tradition: Tradition in Transition* (New York: Crossroad, 1984), pp. 59–60.

15. Ibid., p. 59.

16. Ibid.

17. Joseph Fuchs, "Is There a Specifically Christian Morality?" in *Readings in Moral Theology, No. 2*, ed. Curran and McCormick, p. 6.

18. See David Hollenbach, "Modern Catholic Teachings Concerning Justice," in *The Faith that Does Justice*, ed. John Haughey, pp. 207–31.

19. For an example of such a libertarian theory of justice, see Robert Nozick, *Anarchy, State, and Utopia* (New York: Basic Books, 1974), chap. 7.

20. See, for example, Max L. Stackhouse, *Public Theology and Political Economy: Christian Stewardship in Modern Society* (Grand Rapids, MI: Eerdmans, 1987), pp. 4–15;

Lisa Sowle Cahill, *Between the Sexes: Foundations for a Christian Ethic of Sexuality* (Philadelphia: Fortress/New York: Paulist, 1985), pp. 1–13 and passim.

21. George Lindbeck, *The Nature of Doctrine: Religion and Theology in a Postliberal Age* (Philadelphia: Westminster, 1984), pp. 16, 31–32, and passim.

22. David Tracy, *Plurality and Ambiguity: Hermeneutics, Religion, Hope* (San Francisco: Harper and Row, 1987), p. 49.

23. McCormick, *Health and Medicine in the Catholic Tradition*, p. 60. See also his "Does Religious Faith Add to Ethical Perception?" in *Readings in Moral Theology No. 2*, ed. Curran and McCormick, p. 162. In both of these discussions McCormick relies explicitly on James Bresnahan's interpretation of the theology of Karl Rahner, citing Bresnahan's article "Rahner's Christian Ethics," *America* 123 (1970): 351–54. Though I will disagree with McCormick's and Bresnahan's views, I think Rahner's approach is more complex than either they or George Lindbeck have made it out to be. For an interpretation that sees Rahner's thought as more radically historical than McCormick, Bresnahan, or Lindbeck maintain it is, see Leo J. O'Donovan, "A Journey into Time: The Legacy of Karl Rahner's Last Years," *Theological Studies* 46 (1985): 621–46.

24. Lindbeck, *The Nature of Doctrine*, p. 33.

25. As Francis Schüssler Fiorenza has put it, "Experience takes place within the context of memory, the memory of previous examples and similar cases. Moreover, experience is embedded within a cultural tradition and a network of social interaction and mutual interpretation. Memory, tradition, and interpretation are as much a part of experience and as determinative of experience as are the acts of consciousness, sensation, or feeling" (*Foundational Theology: Jesus and the Church* [New York: Crossroad, 1985], p. 296).

26. In the words of David Tracy, "we do not first experience or understand some reality and then find words to name that reality. We understand in and through the languages available to us" (*Plurality and Ambiguity*, p. 48).

27. Tracy, *Plurality and Ambiguity*, p. 15.

28. Francis Schüssler Fiorenza, *Foundational Theology*, pp. 287–88.

29. See the formative, but not unchallenged, discussion of this point in Thomas Kuhn, *The Structure of Scientific Revolutions*, 2d ed. (Chicago: University of Chicago Press, 1970).

30. See Richard McKeon, "The Philosophic Bases and Material Circumstances of the Rights of Man," in *Human Rights: Comments and Interpretations*, ed. UNESCO (New York: Columbia University Press, 1949), p. 35.

31. See David Hollenbach, "Human Rights and Religious Faith in the Middle East: Reflections of a Christian Theologian," *Human Rights Quarterly* 4 (1982): 94–109.

32. Lindbeck, *The Nature of Doctrine*, p. 129.

33. Ibid., p. 114.

34. Ibid., p. 40.

35. Ibid., p. 84.

36. Ibid., p. 118.

37. Ibid., p. 128.

38. Ibid., p. 127.

39. David Tracy, "Lindbeck's New Program for Theology: A Reflection," *Thomist* 49 (1985): 461.

40. Avery Dulles, "Revelation and Discovery," in *Theology and Discovery: Essays in Honor of Karl Rahner*, ed. William J. Kelly (Milwaukee: Marquette University Press,

1980), p. 10. See also *Gaudium et Spes* 10 and 11; Tracy, *Plurality and Ambiguity*, pp. 86–87.

41. Tracy, "Lindbeck's New Program for Theology," p. 464.

42. Lindbeck, *The Nature of Doctrine*, p. 85.

43. John Howard Yoder, *The Priestly Kingdom: Social Ethics as Gospel* (Notre Dame, IN: University of Notre Dame Press, 1984), p. 75.

44. Paul Ramsey, *War and the Christian Conscience: How Shall Modern War Be Conducted Justly?* (Durham, NC: Duke University Press, 1961), chap. 3.

45. Thomas Ogletree, *Hospitality to the Stranger: Dimensions of Moral Understanding* (Philadelphia: Fortress, 1985), p. 119. The entire chapter in Ogletree's book entitled "The Activity of Interpreting in Moral Judgment" makes a valuable contribution to the matters treated here.

46. Ibid., p. 114.

47. Rosemary Radford Ruether, "A Religion for Women: Sources and Strategies," *Christianity and Crisis* (10 December 1979): 309.

48. David H. Kelsey, *The Uses of Scripture in Recent Theology* (Philadelphia: Fortress, 1975), pp. 89, 109.

49. Ibid., pp. 170–75.

50. Margaret A. Farley, "Feminist Consciousness and the Interpretation of Scripture," in *Feminist Interpretation of the Bible*, ed. Letty M. Russell (Philadelphia: Westminster, 1985), pp. 41–51.

51. Dulles, "Revelation and Discovery," p. 27.

Twelve / Critical Witness: The Question of Method

1. H. Richard Niebuhr, in "A 'Concluding Unscientific Postscript,'" *Christ and Culture* (New York: Harper and Row, 1951), pp. 230–56.

2. David Tracy, *The Analogical Imagination: Christian Theology and the Culture of Pluralism* (New York: Crossroad, 1981).

3. See David Tracy, *Blessed Rage for Order: The New Pluralism in Theology* (New York: Seabury, 1975), pp. 22–42.

4. See especially Avery Dulles, *Models of the Church* (New York: Doubleday, 1974) and *Models of Revelation* (New York: Doubleday, 1983). These two books illustrate a consciously patterned procedure in theological exposition that has governed Dulles's writing for the last fifteen years.

5. Perhaps the leading North American example of a comprehensive methodological position is in Bernard Lonergan's *Method in Theology* (New York: Herder and Herder, 1972). This work is very influential among a segment of Roman Catholic theologians.

6. Schubert M. Ogden, *On Theology* (San Francisco: Harper and Row, 1986), p. 16. For myself I would qualify this statement in the following way: Fundamental theology attends especially to questions of method. But no method exists without subject matter, and methodology, as critical reflection on method, even in its most abstract form, always implies reference to content. Because of the pluralism of both the content and method of theology, a fundamental theology that is not primarily methodological risks becoming in the same measure fideistic. The tension between rationalism and fideism will be discussed further on in this chapter.

7. This tension is a constant and important theme running through the whole of Ogden's *On Theology*, although he expresses it in much stronger terms than I have here.

I am not in a position in which I can clearly differentiate fundamental theology from systematic theology. On the one hand, David Tracy in his *Analogical Imagination* has helped considerably by distinguishing the disciplines of foundations, systematics, and practical theology in terms of their respective audiences of academy, church, and society. This initially extrinsic differentiation reflects back on thought processes to fashion intrinsic differentiations in the methods of mediation. But, on the other hand, Tracy is also clear that these three subdisciplines cannot be separated, so that, in the end, the distinction he proposes is not an adequate one. Because, for example, the world is *within* the church, it often happens that the churchgoer may be an academic interested in the way Christian values and action affect society. I believe that I am interpreting Tracy correctly, then, in saying that fundamental, systematic, and practical theology cannot be adequately distinguished, and that the tasks of each of the three subdisciplines are all mutually implied in any one of them. As for the audience of this essay, I am responding in almost every instance to questions that arise from the reflection of students in the Toronto School of Theology.

8. Juan Luis Segundo, *Faith and Ideologies*, trans. John Drury (Maryknoll, NY: Orbis, 1984), pp. 72–74. In the logic of Paul Tillich, if faith is an existentially ultimate concern, then it must have for its object something truly ultimate, that is, transcendent, infinite, absolute, God (Paul Tillich, *Dynamics of Faith* [New York: Harper and Row, 1957], p. 96). Karl Rahner, by linking revelation to the universal offer of God's self-communication in grace, explains in what sense revelation too is universal (Karl Rahner, "Christianity and Non-Christian Religions," *Theological Investigations* 5 [Baltimore: Helicon Press, 1966], p. 131).

9. This problem finds one of its best expressions in Immanuel Kant's *Religion within the Limits of Reason Alone*. Kant reasoned that in our historical situation, if God were to deal with all human beings equally for their salvation, God *had* to deal with each through a subjective principle in which they all shared equally. Thus he conceived natural religion or the religion of pure reason as that vehicle. But while Kant was successful in establishing the necessity of a subjective core of revelation, he did not perceive as clearly as we today the historicity of reason itself, being as it is tied to the concrete data of the world. Historicism established that there is no pure or natural religion; all revelation is particular. The genius of Karl Rahner, however, with his distinction (but not separation) between the categorical and transcendental dimensions of human awareness, lies in the way he preserves both the historical nature of all revelation and the universal subjective dimension of Kant through a transcendental anthropology that goes beyond the categories of "pure reason."

10. For a treatment of this tension see Paul F. Knitter, *No Other Name? A Critical Survey of Christian Attitudes Toward the World Religions* (Maryknoll, NY: Orbis, 1985).

11. Avery Dulles has presented his own theory of the symbolic structure of revelation in his article "The Symbolic Structure of Revelation," *Theological Studies* 41 (1980): 51–73. A slightly revised version of this important article appears as "Symbolic Mediation," in his *Models of Revelation*, pp. 131–54.

12. For a good example of the inexorable tension between sameness and difference in a current understanding of a biblical text and its past historically situated meaning, see Juan Luis Segundo's interpretation of Paul's "Letter to the Romans" in J. L. Segundo, *The Humanist Christology of Paul*, trans. John Drury (Maryknoll, NY: Orbis, 1986).

13. H. Richard Niebuhr, *The Meaning of Revelation* (New York: Macmillan, 1960), pp. 18–19, 38–42.

14. John Henry Newman, *Newman's University Sermons: Fifteen Sermons Preached before the University of Oxford, 1826–43*, Introductory Essays by D. M. MacKinnon and J. D. Holmes (London: SPCK, 1970), Sermon 11, "The Nature of Faith in Relation to Reason," p. 203 and passim. A more recent example of this approach is William Lynch's *Images of Faith: An Exploration of the Ironic Imagination* (Notre Dame: University of Notre Dame Press, 1973).

15. Cf. David H. Kelsey, *The Uses of Scripture in Recent Theology* (Philadelphia: Fortress, 1975), pp. 158–81 and passim, and James M. Gustafson, *Protestant and Roman Catholic Ethics: Prospects for Rapprochement* (Chicago: University of Chicago Press, 1978), p. 141, for analogous analyses.

16. As was said earlier, the theologian, like every other individual, is shaped by society, class, and his or her position in it. Interests and dominant concerns are also determined by society and the groups with which one identifies. The point at issue here, however, is not the individuality of the theologian but the subjectivity of person or group, a subjectivity that appears arbitrarily to control the variety of different methods of theology.

17. Maurice Blondel, *Action: Essay on a Critique of Life and a Science of Practice*, trans. Oliva Blanchette (1893; Notre Dame, IN: University of Notre Dame Press, 1984), p. 434.

18. I cannot at this point develop the role of the Spirit of God in a fuller theological account of spirituality. See Roger Haight, *Foundational Issues in Jesuit Spirituality: Studies in the Spirituality of Jesuits* 19, no. 4 (St. Louis: Seminar on Jesuit Spirituality, 1987).

19. In his fundamental theology Schubert Ogden shows that all Christian theology today should be liberation theology. Liberation theology alone is *appropriate* to the Pauline doctrine that the only faith that justifies is the faith that works through love; that theology alone is also *credible* to our situation (*On Theology*, pp. 134–50). The argument presented here complements Ogden's from a fundamental philosophical anthropology; it follows the Blondelian pragmatist tradition that understands all knowledge as in service of human life. The idea that spirituality is an objective criterion for all theology becomes itself a criterion of fundamental theology insofar as it reflects a universal anthropological condition.

Contributors

Roger Haight, S.J., Professor of Systematic Theology at Regis College in Toronto, is the author of *An Alternative Vision: An Interpretation of Liberation Theology.*

Monika K. Hellwig, Professor of Theology at Georgetown University, is the author of *Gladness Their Escort,* among other books.

David Hollenbach, S.J., Professor of Moral Theology and Social Ethics at Weston School of Theology, Cambridge, Massachusetts, is the author of *Justice, Peace, and Human Rights: American Catholic Social Ethics in a Pluralistic Context.*

Justin J. Kelly, S.J., Assistant Professor of Religious Studies at the University of Detroit, writes frequently for *The Way.*

Joseph A. Komonchak, Professor of Theology at the Catholic University of America, is the chief editor of *The New Dictionary of Theology.*

John Langan, S.J., Rose Kennedy Professor of Christian Ethics in the Kennedy Institute of Ethics and Senior Fellow of the Woodstock Theological Center, is the editor of *The Nuclear Dilemma and the Just War Tradition.*

Brian O. McDermott, S.J., Professor of Systematic Theology at Weston School of Theology, Cambridge, Massachusetts, is the author of *What Are They Saying About the Grace of Christ?*

Leo J. O'Donovan, S.J., President of Georgetown University, is the editor of *A World of Grace: An Introduction to the Themes and Foundations of Karl Rahner's Theology.*

Thomas F. O'Meara, O.P., Professor of Systematic Theology at the University of Notre Dame, is the author of *Theology of Ministry.*

Pheme Perkins, Professor of New Testament at Boston College, is the author of *Reading the New Testament: An Introduction,* among other books.

T. Howland Sanks, S.J., Associate Professor of Historical/Systematic Theology at the Jesuit School of Theology at Berkeley, is the author of *Authority in the Church: A Study in Changing Paradigms.*

Peter Schineller, S.J., formerly Associate Professor of Systematic Theology at Weston School of Theology, Cambridge, Massachusetts, and now Superior of the Nigeria-Ghana Jesuit Mission, will soon publish his "Handbook on Inculturation."

Index